# IN SEARCH OF THE
# PROMISED
# LAND

FOR AMY, AOIFE AND JACK

# IN SEARCH OF THE
# PROMISED LAND

## THE POLITICS OF POST-WAR IRELAND

## GARY MURPHY

MERCIER PRESS
IRISH PUBLISHER – IRISH STORY

MERCIER PRESS

Cork

www.mercierpress.ie


Trade enquiries to CMD BookSource,
55a Spruce Avenue, Stillorgan Industrial Park,
Blackrock, County Dublin

ISBN: 978 1 85635 638 1


10 9 8 7 6 5 4 3 2 1


A CIP record for this title is available from the British Library

Typeset by Dominic Carroll, Co. Cork

Printed and bound in the EU.

# CONTENTS

# Glossary of Abbreviations

| | |
|---|---|
| CAP* | Common Agricultural Policy |
| CII | Confederation of Irish Industry |
| CIO | Committee on Industrial Organisation |
| CIU | Congress of Irish Unions |
| ECA | Economic Co-operation Administration |
| EEC | European Economic Community |
| EFTA* | European Free Trade Association |
| ERP | European Recovery Programme |
| EU | European Union |
| FII | Federation of Irish Industries |
| FIM | Federation of Irish Manufacturers |
| FUE | Federated Union of Employers |
| GATT* | General Agreement on Tariffs and Trade |
| IBEC | Irish Business and Employers' Confederation |
| ICMSA | Irish Creamery Milk Suppliers' Association |
| ICTU* | Irish Congress of Trade Unions |
| IDA | Industrial Development Authority |
| IFA | Irish Farmers' Association |
| ITGWU | Irish Transport and General Workers' Union |
| ITUC | Irish Trade Union Congress |
| NATO* | North Atlantic Treaty Organisation |
| NFA | National Farmers' Association |
| NIEC | National Industrial and Economic Council |
| OECD | Organisation for Economic Co-operation and Development |
| OEEC | Organisation for European Economic Co-operation |
| PPF | *Programme for Prosperity and Fairness* |
| PUTUO | Provisional United Trade Union Organisation |
| UCD | University College, Dublin |
| UN | United Nations |
| WTO | World Trade Organisation |
| WUI | Workers' Union of Ireland |

*acronym

# GOVERNMENTS OF IRELAND, 1923–2009

| Election | Government | Head of Government |
|---|---|---|
| 27 Aug. 1923 | Cumann na nGaedheal | William T. Cosgrave |
| 9 June 1927 | Cumann na nGaedheal | William T. Cosgrave |
| 15 Sept. 1927 | Cumann na nGaedheal | William T. Cosgrave |
| 16 Feb. 1932 | Fianna Fáil | Eamon de Valera |
| 24 Jan. 1933 | Fianna Fáil | Eamon de Valera |
| 1 July 1937 | Fianna Fáil | Eamon de Valera |
| 17 June 1938 | Fianna Fáil | Eamon de Valera |
| 23 June 1943 | Fianna Fáil | Eamon de Valera |
| 30 May 1944 | Fianna Fáil | Eamon de Valera |
| 4 Feb. 1948 | Inter Party | John A. Costello |
| 30 May 1951 | Fianna Fáil | Eamon de Valera |
| 18 May 1954 | Inter Party | John A. Costello |
| 5 Mar. 1957 | Fianna Fáil | Eamon de Valera to 1959<br>Seán Lemass from 1959 |
| 4 Oct. 1961 | Fianna Fáil | Seán Lemass |
| 7 April 1965 | Fianna Fáil | Seán Lemass to 1966<br>Jack Lynch from 1966 |
| 18 June 1969 | Fianna Fáil | Jack Lynch |
| 28 Feb. 1973 | Fine Gael/Labour | Liam Cosgrave |
| 16 June 1977 | Fianna Fáil | Jack Lynch to 1979<br>Charles J. Haughey from 1979 |
| 11 June 1981 | Fine Gael/Labour | Garret FitzGerald |
| 18 Feb. 1982 | Fianna Fáil | Charles J. Haughey |
| 24 Nov. 1982 | Fine Gael/Labour | Garret FitzGerald |
| 17 Feb. 1987 | Fianna Fáil | Charles J. Haughey |

| | | |
|---|---|---|
| 15 June 1989 | Fianna Fáil/<br>Progressive Democrats | Charles J. Haughey to 1992<br>Albert Reynolds from 1992 |
| 25 Nov. 1992 | Fianna Fáil/Labour/<br>Fine Gael/Labour/<br>Democratic Left | Albert Reynolds to 14 Dec. 1994<br>John Bruton from 15 Dec. 1994 |
| 6 June 1997 | Fianna Fáil/<br>Progressive Democrats | Bertie Ahern |
| 17 May 2002 | Fianna Fáil/<br>Progressive Democrats | Bertie Ahern |
| 24 May 2007 | Fianna Fáil/Progressive<br>Democrats/Green Party | Bertie Ahern to 6 May 2008<br>Brian Cowen from 7 May 2008 |

*Change of Government without an election*

# ACKNOWLEDGEMENTS

I have been researching and thinking about post-war Ireland for some time, and have accrued significant intellectual and personal debts.

For advice and guidance at various times, I thank Frank Barry, Raj Chari, Robert Elgie, Tom Feeney, Tom Garvin, Tom Hachey, John Hogan, David Jacobson, Michael Kennedy, Dermot Keogh, Tim Meagher, Andrew McCarthy, Deirdre McMahon, Mark O'Brien, Emmet O'Connor, Seán O'Connor, Tim O'Neill, Kevin Rafter, Rob Savage, Joe Skelly, Mary Shine Thompson, Damian Thomas, Tony Varley and Bernadette Whelan. I am particularly grateful to Niamh Puirséil for bringing a number of documents to my attention, and for valuable and insightful comments on a variety of issues.

The imprint of three close friends is apparent throughout this book. Though they might not agree with all that is in it, I am very grateful to Brian Girvin, John Horgan and Eunan O'Halpin, who have all, in their various ways, supported me over the years. They have been generous both with their own research and time, and I owe all three a tremendous debt.

Over the years, I have had the privilege of interviewing some of the leading luminaries of Ireland's post-war economic development;

I am grateful to them all. Some are now sadly deceased. A particular memory is of a cold April afternoon when I met with the late Paddy Lynch in his house in Wellington Road. It was one of the most memorable experiences of my academic life, which began with him quizzing me on my knowledge of Keynes and what it was like to have been educated at UCC, and ended with me helping to move furniture around his vast house. In between, he gave me two hours of his time, and it was clear to me that the Irish state was lucky indeed to have had this intellectual titan serve it.

I am grateful to the various archives and libraries that I have used. In particular, I thank the staff of Dublin City University (DCU) Library, National Archives of Ireland, National Library of Ireland, University College Dublin Archives, Irish Labour History Society and the National Archives and Records Administration, College Park, Maryland. I also thank Colm Gallagher of the Department of Finance and Philip Hannon – then of Fianna Fáil – for granting me early access to papers that were not in the public domain.

I thank the team at Mercier Press, particularly Wendy Logue, for being enthusiastic supporters of this project and for seeing it through to publication so professionally. I thank Declan Ryan and Anne Kearney of the *Irish Examiner* for use of the *Examiner*'s photo archive and Susan Kennedy of Lensmen for the use of its archive. I thank the publication assistance fund at DCU for supporting this work.

I owe a particular thanks to the staff of the Office of the Vice President of Research at DCU, who have had to put up with me since my secondment there as director of graduate research in 2007. I thank Eugene Kennedy, Declan Raftery, Tanya Keogh, Jonny Hobson, Fiona Killard, Fiona Brennan, Michelle Meehan, Ana Terres, Mark Rushforth, Mary Colgan, Niamh O'Dowd and Deirdre Donnelly for their support, professionalism and good humour.

Away from my desk, I have been lucky to have some close friends who have helped me keep my mind off the promised land. I thank Colm O'Callaghan, Michael Moynihan, Dave Hannigan, Denis Walsh, Donagh McGrath, Aengus Nolan, Michael O'Brien, Joe O'Hara and Colm O'Reilly. My Cork-born friends were particularly supportive during the dark days of the Cork hurling strike! Thanks also to Jack, Peg, Liam, Gina, Eric and Jacqui for being there.

Finally, I would like to thank my wife Mandy and children Amy, Aoife and Jack. Their presence in my life has made the writing of this book possible, and I could not have completed it without them.

Gary Murphy
*Dublin, July 2009*

# INTRODUCTION

# THE PROMISED LAND?

In December 2008 the Fianna Fáil (FF)/Green Party/Progressive Democrats coalition Government presented to the public its blueprint for dealing with the increasingly grim economic crisis. The *Plan for Economic Renewal* was the Government's response to six months of catastrophic economic news after more than a decade of boom, during which the twin processes of social partnership and European Union (EU) membership were seen as pillars of the country's economic success. Amongst a number of initiatives, the plan called for heavy investment in research and development so as to incentivise multinational companies to locate more capacity in Ireland, thus ensuring the commercialisation and retention of ideas that flowed from that investment. Two months earlier Minister for Finance Brian Lenihan had issued the budget for 2009, which he described as nothing less than a patriotic call to action in the face of a deterioration in the state's fiscal position. The budget, Lenihan said, was introduced during one of the most 'difficult and uncertain times in living memory', where the global credit crunch had created turmoil in the world's financial markets, and after steep increases in commodity prices had placed enormous pressures on economies across the globe, including Ireland's.[1]

The financial position in 2009 was completely different to that which any Irish Government had faced in a generation. The dark days of the 1980s had been replaced by a period of economic boom which had pretty much lasted through the two terms of the Fianna Fáil/Progressive Democrats Government from 1997 to 2007. There were significant decreases in both personal and corporation tax rates, and substantial increases in the numbers of people at work, with the creation of 600,000 jobs in that ten-year period, leading to over two million people at work. Moreover, by the late 1990s the Government was in the 'black' for the first time in thirty years, with the exchequer able to meet day-to-day spending without recourse to borrowing.

The attraction of foreign direct investment, together with social partnership and EU membership, was central to the boom in economic development in modern Ireland. The Irish Government was able to advertise itself to investors as an ideal location due to its low corporation-tax rates, membership of the EU, a stable partnership process and a young, educated workforce. In recent surveys, Ireland was considered to have one of the most open economies in the world. The A.T. Kearney/Foreign Policy Globalisation Index – an annual empirical measure of globalisation and its impact – ranked Ireland first in 2002, 2003 and 2004, and second in 2005.[2] Moreover, the 2006 Index of Economic Freedom – compiled jointly by the *Wall Street Journal* and the Heritage Foundation – found Ireland's was the world's third-freest economy, and the freest in Europe. In 2008 Ireland was ranked third in the Heritage Foundation's index of economic freedom and was fourth in 2009.[3]

Yet by the end of 2008 both EU membership and social partnership were in troubled waters. The rejection of the Lisbon Treaty in June 2008

– the second such Government defeat in seven years in referendums concerning Europe – reopened the debate about Ireland's role within the EU. The 83 per cent 'yes' vote from a turnout of over 70 per cent in 1972 for entry into the European Economic Community (EEC), seems but a distant memory now, as the Irish electorate grows increasingly sceptical about European treaties, tending to view them as threats to Irish interests. It was noticeable that the two major opponents of the Lisbon Treaty – Sinn Féin and Libertas – both campaigned specifically on the basis that it was bad for Irish interests, whether of a capital or social nature. The EEC – seen as the panacea to Ireland's economic ills during the 1972 referendum – had by 2008 become a victim of its own success, at least where the Irish electorate was concerned. The rejection in 2001 of the Nice Treaty (subsequently approved in a second referendum on the subject) and the Lisbon Treaty in 2008 suggests that the Irish electorate no longer views European treaties as entities to which it must sign up. The public needs to be convinced of the merits of a project much more so than in the past, and the days when 'yes' campaigners believed that approval of European treaties could be achieved by faith alone are well and truly gone.

Involving the main interest groups in the policy-making process has been a central element of the Irish economic success story. Yet the centrality of the social partners in economic policy-making has differed over time. The relationships established between the social partners in the early and late 1970s had been based largely on terms defined by the Government, and then brusquely terminated when a new economic strategy of fiscal restraint in the early 1980s required it. Thus, policy-making in the economic sphere remained both flexible and adjustable. The process of social partnership put in place by the Fianna Fáil minority Government in 1987 differed markedly from the pay agreements of the 1970s. Upon its return to office in 1987, Fianna Fáil faced a grave fiscal crisis, and sought an agreed strategy with the social partners to overcome Ireland's economic difficulties. Interested actors such as farmers' organisations, trade unions and business groups were invited to negotiate with the Government in what might be called a process of economic governance – something that continues to the current day. It has evolved into a system that aims to keep the major interest groups reasonably happy by giving them a role in defining the broad economic approach of the state, thereby perpetuating a national economic and social coalition of sorts. Social partnership binds these 'social partners' to a coherent and consistent policy framework. This consensual approach mirrors that of northern European social democracies such as Sweden, Norway and Denmark; indeed, since the mid-1990s Ireland has experienced the kind of economic success that was previously associated with such countries.

The social partnership in place since 1987 has been somewhat flexible and adjustable but in a significantly different manner to that of the 1970s. It has on occasion been reworked, most notably in December 2000 when the 2000–03 *Programme for Prosperity and Fairness* (PPF) was renegotiated in response to a sharp rise in inflation and increasing strains on the terms of the pay agreement in some sectors. This resulted in the unions securing an upward revision of the pay terms of the PPF.

The most significant aspect of social partnership is that it has given both the Government and the social partners a remarkable twenty years of continuity in economic macro-management, and certainly helped in abating the dire economic crisis of the mid-1980s. As the then Taoiseach, Bertie Ahern, pointed out in June 2006 in his introduction to the *Towards 2016* agreement:

> Social partnership has helped to maintain a strategic focus on key national priorities, and has created and sustained the conditions for remarkable employment growth, fiscal stability, restructuring of the economy to

respond to new challenges and opportunities, a dramatic improvement in living standards, through both lower taxation and lower inflation, and a culture of dialogue, which has served the social partners, but more importantly, the people of this country, very well.[4]

Nevertheless, it is important to note that this type of partnership agreement has the tendency to be only as good as its last deal; significantly, each successive agreement has been increasingly difficult to negotiate. For instance, the linked-pay deal of September 2008 was only agreed after mammoth negotiations that were described as the toughest in the twenty years of pay talks since social partnership began. By the time the Government published the *Plan for Economic Renewal*, the voices demanding a reworking of the deal had reached a pitch unheard of since the first agreement in 1987. The very semblance of a threat from any of the social partners to withdraw from an agreement usually precipitated intense discussions to ensure that the demands of the aggrieved sector were met without jeopardising the remit of the agreement as a whole.

Social partnership, for all its success, was showing significant signs of wear and tear as the economy went into its downward spiral in late 2008. Nevertheless, in the *Plan for Economic Renewal*, the Taoiseach, Brian Cowen, renewed his Government's commitment to social partnership, noting that it was the Government's intention to work with the social partners on the development and implementation of the plan using the well-established mechanisms of the social-partnership process, which was consistent with the principles and vision underpinning *Towards 2016*.[5]


## BACK TO THE FUTURE?

Social partnership, foreign direct investment and membership of the EU have their origins in post-war Ireland. The aim of this book is to show how Irish isolationism in the late 1940s and 1950s has been overstated and misunderstood, and how the factors that have shaped the success of modern Ireland can be traced back to the period between the end of the Second World War and the beginning of the 1960s. This period saw Ireland first tentatively and then wholeheartedly explore the option of joining a European trading bloc. It is also the period when Governments began to contemplate the inclusion of economic interests in the charmed circle of power. Both changes in policy can be attributed primarily to economic considerations.

The dismal economic conditions of the post-war period brought with it significant political uncertainty. The fluidity of politics during this period saw successive changes of Government in the four elections between 1948 and 1957. Momentous shifts in thinking at both Governmental and non-Governmental level led to the adoption of an interdependent approach to economic policy-making – symbolised by the most famous economic plan in Ireland's history, T.K. Whitaker's *Economic Development* of 1958, published a full fifty years before the *Plan for Economic Renewal*. On the fiftieth anniversary of *Economic Development*, the Minister for Finance, Brian Lenihan, spoke of how it remained highly relevant as a vision for Ireland's future. More significantly, he noted that it was the political class that took the decision to implement *Economic Development*.[6] While some policy-makers were reluctant to accept any form of multilateral trading arrangements that would alter protected industry and the country's privileged access to British markets, the severe economic crisis that affected Ireland throughout the 1950s led to the development of fresh economic thinking both within and beyond the civil service. Such thinking led in 1961 to the Government seeking entry into the EEC, and to eventual membership twelve years later. In that context, the Irish policy-making community was much more acutely aware of events in Western Europe and how they would impact on Ireland than previously thought.

It has long been assumed that the culture of isolationism in foreign affairs fostered by Fianna Fáil since 1932 was continued by successive Governments up to the time when Seán Lemass' minority Fianna Fáil Government applied for entry into the EEC in July 1961. This assumption is manifested in the belief that the years between 1945 and 1961 saw a strong sense of public complacency, while elite opinion maintained that the depression, war and post-war recovery justified the continuation of isolationist policies that had been in place since 1932. Ireland's refusal to join GATT (General Agreement on Tariffs and Trade) in 1948 and NATO (North Atlantic Treaty Organisation) in 1949 is seen as a further reflection of isolationism and the conviction that national solutions were the most appropriate in Ireland's case. This is also perceived in domestic politics, where the reliance on protectionism since Fianna Fáil first took power in 1932 is taken as evidence that the Irish state was most comfortable with conservative, insular policies that would provide an acceptable living standard for at least most of the population. Yet all political parties in this period were acutely aware that Ireland did not exist in a vacuum – either political or economic – where events in Western Europe could be ignored and where the better standards of living on offer in Britain and the United States would not entice Irish people. This awareness was spawned by the realisation that without an improvement in the state's economic fortunes, there could be no certainty as to the intention of voters at the ballot box.

Thus, the post-war period up to the early 1960s can be classified as a search for the promised land of economic fulfilment. The promised land did not appear as soon as the Fianna Fáil Government of Seán Lemass decided in 1961 to apply for membership of the EEC, after it had persuaded the economic interest groups to support the application. Nor did it become a reality when the Government actually entered the EEC in 1973 after the overwhelming 'yes' vote of 1972. Indeed, by the mid-1980s – when Ireland was the EU's worst performing economy and emigration rates began to mirror those of the 1950s – the EEC as a gateway to the promised land looked very much like a mirage. Yet few policy decisions have had such a profound impact on life in Ireland as the decision to apply for entry into the EEC, and then entry itself.

A second instrumental policy development in Ireland's economic success was the decision in 1987 to underwrite pay agreements through social partnership. The process of social partnership implemented in 1987, coupled with the support of EU structural funds and the wider market that the EU gave Irish and multinational companies access to, laid the foundations for the 'Celtic Tiger' of the late 1990s and 2000s. This could not have happened without the developments in both domestic and foreign policy that began in the post-war period.

Whilst the recession of 2008–09, amidst a global economic downturn, has again raised fears about Ireland's economic future, it is well to remember that the search for the promised land of economic success in Ireland is ongoing. It may be an unattainable utopia, but it is one that can only be brought closer by active economic engagement between Governments and social partners.

Opening the annual European Construction Industry Federation Congress in June 2008, Brian Lenihan noted that he had the misfortune to become Minister for Finance as the building boom was coming to a shuddering end, the effects of which had been exacerbated by the international credit crunch.[7] In many ways, this might also be seen as a bad time to be writing a book about economic development. Yet it is a very good time, because what the post-war period in Ireland shows is that political will is necessary to lead the Irish state through lean times, and political decision-making is what counts. In *Preventing the Future: Why was Ireland so Poor for so Long* – one of the celebrated works of Irish history of recent years – Tom Garvin comments that Ireland, 'faced with the conditions and circumstances that pertained in the changed world of 1945, made a series of "non-decisions" that in the short to medium term were disastrous to the country's development prospects'.[8] The current book, however, argues that it was Irish politicians, and not the nebulous concept of Ireland itself, who actually did take significant decisions to move the country out of the economic morass that it found itself in. Politicians must make decisions, and policy-making cannot be left to the dismal science of economics nor the invisible hand of the market. Such political decision-making is the lesson of post-war Ireland that current politicians and policy-makers need to be aware of.

# 1

# THE WAR WAS OVER,
# BUT THE EMERGENCY WAS NOT

During the war years, maintaining supplies was of one of the greatest problems facing the Government. The promotion of industry and commerce was secondary to making sure that the people had food to eat and that there was sufficient fuel to keep at least some services in operation. Eamon de Valera's decision to move his most capable lieutenant, Seán Lemass, into the new Department of Supplies was proof of its importance. Under the stewardship of 'half-ounce' Lemass (so-called after the weekly tea ration), the standard of living in Ireland was 'relatively high', although it was an especially hard time for the poorer sections of Irish society.[1] Between 1940 and 1944, the official cost of living increased by 50 per cent (the cost of goods on the black market was significantly higher), but the introduction in 1941 of the Wages Standstill Order meant that those lucky enough to be in employment saw their purchasing power all but collapse as their wages failed to rise in conjunction with rising prices. A survey conducted in Cork city in 1944, for instance, found that 45 per cent of households were living in poverty.[2]

One apparently positive economic development during the war was the fall in the live register, from 15 per cent to 10 per cent, although this was due largely to the 'significant increase in Irish migration to Britain together with the expansion in the total number employed in the Irish defence forces'.[3] With conscription in Britain creating demand for emigrant labour in its factories, 'taking the boat' became increasingly popular during the war years: between September 1939 and March 1944 (when travel restrictions were introduced prior to D-Day), 188,254 travel permits for employment outside the state were issued. Even if not all of those issued with permits actually travelled to the UK,[4] the figure was colossal nonetheless, with Delaney estimating that at least 100,000 people left Ireland for civilian employment in Britain during the war.[5]

## SAFETY-VALVE AGAINST REVOLUTION

While acknowledging that an exodus on such a massive scale could have serious implications for national morale, the benefits of emigration were all too obvious to policy-makers: significant reductions in Government expenditure on unemployment benefits, together with revenue from emigrants' remittances (estimated at between £100,000 and £150,000 per week). Perhaps even more importantly, emigration was regarded in some quarters – including at the highest level in the Department of Finance – as 'a safety-valve against revolution'.[6] With would-be malcontents (that is, the unemployed) kept busy in another country, the chances of social upheaval at home were diminished, for the time being, anyway. It was only towards the end of the war that these same bureaucrats began to wonder what fate would befall the country when these men and women returned from their sojourn in godless England, having imbibed the teachings of welfarism while there. However, most of these emigrants did not return home.

23

Foremost of the Government's priorities during the Emergency was the maintenance of the country's neutrality and its safety, followed by the provision of supplies. Clearly, changes to economic policy at this time were neither advisable nor feasible, but as the fortunes of the Allies turned for the better, attention began to focus on post-war economic reconstruction, and specifically the question of national economic planning. The need for planning had been one of the key policy planks of the labour movement since the mid-1930s at least, with the Irish Trade Union Congress (ITUC) producing a document entitled *Planning for the Crisis* at the beginning of the war. Beyond the labour movement, however, the attitude towards planning – with its Stalinist connotations – remained hostile. Nevertheless, over time there had been something of a shift in some quarters regarding state intervention, in large part due to the increase in state activity during the war. Although individuals such as George O'Brien, the Victorian-minded professor of economics in University College, Dublin (UCD), remained avowedly opposed to 'welfarism', their reflexive opposition to state intervention in the economy was no more. Writing in the Jesuit journal *Studies* in 1942, O'Brien argued that laissez-faire was a thing of the past, and that in common with other small nations, Ireland would have to develop a planned economy.[7]

The publication in Britain of Beveridge's *Full Employment in a Free Society* (1944) proved a great influence on Seán Lemass, whose interventionist views on the economy and planning had reached a zenith between 1942 and 1945 that was never to be surpassed.[8] In April 1945 Patrick Lynch and T.K. Whitaker, both young officials in the Department of Finance at the time, addressed a meeting of the Statistical and Social Inquiry Society on the 'problem of full employment';[9] the meeting was held against a backdrop of the British White Paper on employment policy (1944) and Beveridge's response, *Full Employment*. During his contribution, Lynch made a similar point to that of George O'Brien in *Studies*:

It is clear that a proper direction of the Irish economy will imply increased state intervention. We have had state intervention in this country, as in other countries, for a great many years. What will be needed to develop a policy of full employment is controlled and planned state intervention. Unless intervention is co-ordinated in a unified pattern no lasting result can be achieved.[10]

The extent of the shift towards Keynesianism and planning ought not be exaggerated, however. The speaker following Lynch that evening was J.P. Colbert, former chairman of the state-controlled Agricultural Credit Corporation, and at that time chairman of the state's Industrial Credit Corporation; he was adamant that the terms 'full employment' and 'free society' were mutually exclusive.[11] Furthermore, while tyros such as Lynch and – to a lesser extent – Whitaker were advocating a new approach to national economic management, their bosses in the Department of Finance were very much wedded to the old school of thought. Still, among the contributions to the debate – as the chairman, George O'Brien, noted during his summing up – there were a number of commonalities: one was the acceptance that the differences in the Irish and British economies (not least, the dominance of agriculture here) meant that the suggestions outlined in both the White Paper and Beveridge's *Full Employment* could be applied in Ireland. Another was the dearth of usable statistics, thus making planning near impossible. However, O'Brien noted, of all the solutions for creating full employment, one that had not been put forward by any of the speakers was that being pursued at the present time:

There is a further thing we could do, and have been doing for the last 100 years, and that is just to let them go. That solution has not been mentioned in this evening's discussion. We have solved our unemployment problem for the last 100 years in the most expensive and most defeatist manner. We have exported the unemployed. Are we going to continue to accept that solution? If a country is prepared to let everyone who cannot find work at home to go away without protest, that would be one way of solving its unemployment problem. Just put them on a boat and let them sail away. The question is, can we find another solution.[12]

In December 1945, a book entitled *Full Employment in Ireland* was published. Written by the headmaster of Drogheda Grammar School, Arnold Marsh, and others, its arguments were similar to those of Beveridge (although the authors were at pains to point out that they had written their draft before Beveridge's *Full Employment* had been published).[13] Marsh and his colleagues saw the solution to Ireland's unemployment problem as lying with increased capital investment. Somewhat bizarrely, they ignored the impact that protectionism might have on Ireland's ability to trade. As Bew and Patterson and (separately) Horgan have observed, the war years had seen Lemass become increasingly disenchanted with the use of tariffs, but he had not yet reached the stage when he could abandon them.[14] The idea remained unthinkable in his Department of Industry and Commerce, and as far as Irish commerce was concerned, things would have to get much better before the protectionist safety net could be eliminated. The debate on employment was ultimately inward looking, and sought solutions in planning and capitalisation rather than changing the terms of trade through liberalisation. However, as the new economic order began to emerge in the post-war period, it was increasingly obvious that Ireland would have to broaden its horizons a great deal if it was to prosper.

Economically, Ireland emerged from the war relatively unscathed. As the cultural historian Clair Wills has pointed out, the rhetoric of surviving the Emergency turned not only on patriotism but also on the need for self-sufficiency. While the poor experienced severe hardship, the experiences of shortages did not lead to intolerable suffering among the masses, and, indeed, the 'apparatus of rationing lent neutrality a much-needed epic tone'.[15] More fundamentally, Eunan O'Halpin has noted that, apart from isolated German bombings and an occasional explosion caused by drifting mines, the independent Irish state suffered not at all, and unlike continental neutrals, the Irish 'were largely shielded from any sight or sound of the catastrophe that had befallen most of Europe. The intervening bulk of the United Kingdom ensured that there had been no streams of importunate refugees at border crossings or seaports pleading for their lives'.[16] The extraordinary trading conditions engendered by the war meant that Ireland was exporting more than it imported, so that by the time the conflict had ended, the country had built up large reserves of sterling. Judged by its external assets and on the basis of population, Ireland was one of the wealthiest countries in the world;[17] judged by less theoretical measures, Ireland's wealth was a chimera. At a very basic level, judging wealth per head of population in a country with mass emigration was a poor gauge of national wealth. Moreover, the external reserves belied the structural problems in the economy. Irish agriculture was overly reliant on the British market; the cattle sector had failed to recover from the self-inflicted wound of the Economic War in the 1930s, while production in tillage was hindered by a lack of fertilisers. Even if output had increased somewhat during the war, the numbers employed on the land had, in fact, fallen. Industrial production had also decreased as a result of shortages of manufacturing materials, while securing spare parts for machinery was often difficult as they could only be bought from the United States and for dollars.[18] This remained a significant problem when the war ended, since external reserves were largely held in sterling. During the 'dollar crisis' of 1947, which saw the suspension of sterling-dollar convertibility in August of that year, this problem became all the more acute.

Once the war was over the Government was faced with a number of economic problems. In the short term, unemployment was not one of them, however, since the rate of emigration to Britain increased after the war. Between road and house building and the Attlee Government's new National Health Service, Britain had become a magnet for Irish men and women, many of whom had low-paid, low-status and irregular employment at home. Though it was widely accepted in the post-war world that the solution to emigration lay in improving economic and social environments, things were different in Ireland. While the principle might have been accepted, the view that the Government could do anything about it was not commonplace. As the Department of External Affairs noted in December 1947:

> If it is agreed that the solution of the emigration problem lies primarily in the constant creation of new employment outlets in industry, commerce and other fields of non-agricultural economic activity, what has been and is being done is as much – particularly having regard to the circumstances of the wars – as anyone could hope to do … Emigration could only have been prevented, therefore, if the Government had succeeded not only in maintaining industrial and commercial employment at its pre-war level throughout the war years, but in increasing it over the period by creating 150,000 new employment outlets. To blame the Government for not having been able to do that during a period in which, as everybody knows, raw materials and equipment were virtually unprocurable, is, of course, ridiculous.[19]

For those who did remain, it was not employment but rising prices that caused greatest resentment, together with the ever-increasing regulation of Irish society as more areas of life came under the control of Government. The cost of food, in particular, was rocketing, and with the Wages Standstill Order coming to an end in 1946, the Government faced the prospect of large-scale industrial action across the economy. The Government's primary concern, then, was keeping the cost of living stable and making sure that wage claims were kept under control. With regard to the latter, the Labour Court was established by Seán Lemass in 1947, while the Government attempted to alleviate the cost of living through food subsidies. Even then, bread rationing had to be introduced when a terrible winter across Ireland and Britain in 1946–47 led to severe wheat shortages. In the Department of Industry and Commerce, Lemass was effectively alone in Government in wanting to push economic policy in a more expansionist direction. His policy initiatives included developing the areas of electricity, turf, aviation and tourism, but progress was slow and he was resisted on each occasion by the Department of Finance. Ultimately, by focusing on *urgent* tasks to the detriment of *important* tasks, the Fianna Fáil Government failed to address the fundamental backwardness of both the industrial and agricultural sectors.

## 'PUT THEM OUT'

A general election in February 1948 resulted in Fianna Fáil being 'put out' (in response to Clann na Poblachta's slogan, 'Put them out'), having been in Government for sixteen years. Many factors led to its losing power, but unhappiness at the cost of living was perhaps the most important. A supplementary budget in October 1947 – which had increased income tax and taxes on items such as cinema seats – proved fatal for Fianna Fáil, even though much of the income derived from these taxes was spent on food subsidies, thus robbing Peter to pay Paul. The Fianna Fáil estimates had included an increase of expenditure of £6 million, of which most was spent on food subsidies, rural electrification and the treatment of tuberculosis.[20] Nevertheless, as Joe Lee put it, 'many people could not, or would not, understand why the hardship should continue'.[21]

Consequently, when the first Inter-Party Government took office, it endeavoured to do too much too soon. According to Patrick Lynch:

> If dissatisfaction about the cost of living appeared to be the cause of the defeat of the Fianna Fáil Government in 1948, the fate of its successor, the Inter-Party Government, in 1951, was also to be associated with problems of rising prices resulting from inflation. No doubt, Mr de Valera might have made the distinction, with which I would agree, that in 1951 the Inter-Party Government was to be the victim of its own inflation, whereas the inflation between 1946 and 1948 had been imported at a time when the Fianna Fáil Government had little choice in the matter.[22]

Or, as the first Inter-Party Government's Minister for Finance, Patrick McGilligan, noted in 1956:

> Most of the difficulties of the recent past are due to Governments in 1948–51 and since 1954 trying to do too quickly what could and should have been done leisurely and safely over a 20 year stretch.[23]

The Inter-Party Government was comprised of elements with sharply diverse views, ranging from the more interventionist, left-wing perspective of Labour, National Labour and Clann na Poblachta, to the rural emphasis of Clann na Talmhan, and the economic liberalist and middle-class outlook of James Dillon and Fine Gael. Taoiseach John A. Costello appointed Patrick McGilligan as Minister for Finance – a man famous for his 1924 remark in the Dáil that: 'There are certain limited funds at our disposal. People may have to die in this country and may have to die through starvation'.[24]

McGilligan had to deal with an economy with major deficiencies in its social and infrastructural facilities. Savings, which had been relatively high during the war because of the shortage of consumer goods, had declined considerably; in 1947 total savings amounted to only 4.5 per cent of gross national product (GNP), and personal savings in the same year were virtually zero. Manufacturing industry accounted for less than 20 per cent of total employment, and much of this owed its existence to the protectionist policies of the 1930s. Furthermore, most industry had not yet sought export opportunities.[25] Adding to this problem was the fact that there was comparatively little overt tradition of entrepreneurship, and that prospective capitalists faced considerable difficulties in raising capital. A businessman who began his career in the 1940s sums up the situation:

> There just were not many businessmen with the entrepreneurial drive who were willing to take a chance. Capital was difficult enough to raise, but people just did not think of going into industry to make a big profit. Protectionism was so complete, with no danger from outside, that if you had a market, you had it tied up completely. Yet there just were not many big businessmen with the get-up-and-go mentality. By the 1950s industry was still being promoted on the basis of the old Sinn Féin policy that we had to be independent and we could only be independent if we had our own industries, and it was more that than any thought of being able to develop large companies that we have now. This applied to politicians as well as businessmen.[26]

In essence, very few of the firms created since independence could survive without the protectionism that had brought them into existence. They were relatively small, unsophisticated and based on local markets. Within this protected sphere, 'profitability and wages were high, inefficiencies endemic'.[27] Ireland did, however, have important assets from a developmental viewpoint, most notably a large supply of labour and a sizable accumulation of external reserves that had been built up during the war. In these circumstances, there was a case for an expansionary fiscal policy and a direct state contribution to raising the investment rate. This was not how the mandarins in the Department of Finance saw the situation. A week before John A. Costello was appointed Taoiseach, J.J. McElligott, the imposing secretary of the Department of Finance, wrote to the outgoing Minister for Finance, Frank Aiken, outlining the bleak economic situation:

> The position regarding state debt and capital outlay gives ground for anxiety. The state debt already large and for the greater part non-productive is undergoing rapid increase. The heavy new commitments which are being constantly added will necessitate a further rise in taxation which has already reached an intolerable height. The resultant budgetary difficulties are accentuated by the charging of an unduly low rate of interest to such capital works as are productive. Our serious balance of payments position is bound to be worsened as a result of heavy imports for state capital projects which do nothing to raise our alarmingly low export capacity.[28]

For the Department of Finance, this capital expenditure entailed not only an immediate but also a continuing outlay on hard-currency imports. Capital commitments were being undertaken at a rate greatly in excess of the current savings of the community, and were thus a strong reinforcement of inflationary pressures. McElligott argued that through their effect on domestic purchasing power, these commitments aggravated Ireland's tendency as a nation to spend beyond its means, and that the situation would be a lot worse but for the existence of sterling assets upon which the country was drawing to meet its excessive expenditure on imports of consumer goods. Domestic production – which in the view of the Department of Finance was the ultimate measure of the country's capacity to consume and to undertake capital investment – was below its 1939 level both in agriculture and industry as a whole, including building, and the prospects for improvement were not encouraging.

Yet the new Inter-Party Government did not quite see the financial position in the same light. Lord Glenavy, governor of the Bank of Ireland and a member of the board of the Central Bank, and James Dillon, Minister for Agriculture, communicated regularly throughout the first Inter-Party Government's period in office, and their correspondence regarding the state of the economy is illuminating. Although Dillon was something of a maverick within the Government, he had a definite view on the way economic policy should be shaped, and argued his case trenchantly both within the Cabinet and beyond. A letter from Dillon regarding the Central Bank report of 1948 shows how the Government viewed the situation; the bank, according to Dillon, had implied that the Government was both 'ignorant and incompetent', but he felt the 'boot was on the other foot':

> The net surplus of external assets cannot be much less than twice as great as they were in 1939. Our national debt is trivial compared with that of any other nation in the world. We are almost alone outside of the United States in meeting our requirements from our own purse. We have virtually no damage to capital assets to restore. In fact we are in a state of disgusting affluence and our principal danger is that instead of spending wisely we may either squander our resources or scrooge-like gather our seedy rags around us and count our wretched chattels as deflationary poverty gradually settles in gloom around us.[29]

Dillon disliked both options, and claimed that the Government would adopt neither. Nevertheless, he stated that if he had to choose between the two, he would prefer to 'go down with my flags flying and the band playing rather than to sink in dismal dereliction so dear to the hearts of the Central Bank'.[30] In response, Glenavy argued that to believe that the Second World War had brought the country affluence was delusional. Net sterling assets were nominally twice as great as in 1939, but since prices had doubled, 'they are worth no more than in 1939, a time when representations were being made to the Government that they had fallen to an undesirably low level'. Monetary authorities, he insisted, 'are bound to indicate pitfalls, the primrose path needs no pilot'.[31]

## STERLING: ASSET OR HINDRANCE?

The question of sterling assets was a particularly thorny one. Patrick Lynch, who was appointed personal advisor on economic issues to Costello on the recommendation of McElligott, was a critic of the Central Bank's policy on the issue:

> Here we were building up a great quantity of sterling assets, a much bigger quantity than the banks needed at a time when the value of sterling was progressively decreasing. There was a very strong case therefore for the repatriation of sterling assets to counteract the chronic under-investment in Ireland. There was immense scope for very useful investment and I was using Keynesian arguments to support my own arguments for investment in the Irish economy which had been so under-developed because of the conditions left by the war.[32]

Naturally, Clann na Poblachta – whose economic policy included a demand for the repatriation of external assets – was also severely critical. Its acerbic leader, Seán MacBride – who had a very keen interest in economic policy – was most outspoken. At a meeting of the Cork city branch of Clann na Poblachta in September 1949, he declared that:

If even a fraction of the money which had been poured down the drain of sterling assets and thus irretrievably lost had been utilised at home, the economic life of this country could have been transformed. The fundamental problem of the Irish economy is one of under-development and under-employment due to chronic under-investment at home. We are the only country in the world that exports both people and money to create wealth somewhere else.[33]

In essence, MacBride wanted to break the link with sterling and move away from the fixed-parity relationship. The Central Bank and the Department of Finance took the view that, notwithstanding the fact that the British economy and sterling were facing great dangers and uncertainties, parity between the Irish currency and sterling should be maintained, and the country should stick to the practice of keeping the bulk of its external assets in Britain. Disagreement between the Central Bank and the Department of Finance on the one hand and some members of the Government on the other became more pronounced when the Government was forced to follow the British line and devalue against the dollar by 30.5 per cent in September 1949, thus enabling the Irish pound to continue to be exchangeable with the pound sterling.[34]

For MacBride, the inextricable link with sterling was the ultimate cause of the morass the country and the economy found itself in. In March 1950 he declared that:

In national economics we have behaved like misers who have kept their money in the bank instead of utilising it to develop our own business. Every available statistic establishes that the country suffers from gross chronic under-investment, while at the same time we boast of having 400 million in sterling assets. More fantastic still, over 50 million of the sterling assets are held by the Central Bank and bring in an income of slightly over one per cent.[35]

The Department of Finance's attitude towards devaluation can be seen in a memorandum penned after the Inter-Party Government had lost power, where it countered MacBride's views by claiming that if parity was abandoned, there were three alternatives to be considered: the Irish pound would remain at par, which entailed no change; it would appreciate, for which there was no prospect as increasing deficits in the balance of payments and the higher wage structure in Ireland indicated that the pound was already overvalued in relation to sterling, and any enlargement of the programme of public works would weaken it further; or it would devalue, which in the circumstances was the only real alternative:

> It would be a grave error to look upon this as a solution to our economic and financial problems. Leaving aside the practical and political objections to abandoning the parity relationship and the repercussions in public confidence in our currency, a depreciation which nobody would be convinced was final would have serious effects on the cost of living particularly at a time when import prices were still rising. Nothing less than a 25 per cent reduction in the external value of our currency would have even the appearance of finality and seeing that imports enter so largely into domestic consumption, the effect of raising import prices by 33⅓ per cent would obviously be very great.[36]

For the Department of Finance, the temporary stimulus to exports normally associated with depreciation would misfire in this case because Ireland's export surplus derived from a stagnant agricultural output and was therefore incapable of immediate expansion. Finance further argued that nothing more than a short-term curtailment of imports could be expected because of the pressure for increased money incomes 'to compensate for the rise in the cost of living that would be exerted by the trade unions and all classes of the working population. Depreciation of the currency is evidently an evil to be shunned'.[37]

The thrust of financial thinking as pursued by the Central Bank and the Department of Finance has been defended by Seán Cromien, a former secretary of the department, who worked in the economic forecasting branch between 1952 and 1960. Cromien has argued that, to some extent, the conservative policies pursued were justified as the institutions were creatures of their times. Keynesianism had not yet taken a grip on Irish financial thinking, and it is questionable as to what success it might have had, had it been implemented:

> We had to watch very carefully what we were doing. We were part of the sterling area and no substantial foreign exchange was earned other than sterling. We had to use that to gain foreign dollars from the dollar pool through the British sterling area. That limited our freedom very much to do things. We had to show the British that we were keeping our economy under control, that we were not extravagant spenders … Thus the effort was on maintaining external reserves. There was a feeling that you did not get involved with foreign borrowing, a feeling that you were quite constrained by what people were prepared to save at home. You watched what they were saving, watched their level of consumption and watched the level of foreign reserves. So in a sense while it was very conservative, it probably was understandable in the conditions of the time.[38]

This policy undoubtedly had some success, as by 1949 personal savings had risen to 7.1 per cent of personal disposable income from virtually zero in 1947. Furthermore, the balance-of-payments deficit fell from £30 million in 1947 to £9.7 million in 1949, and unemployment was down to 8.3 per cent by the end of 1949, compared to 9.6 per cent in the first quarter of 1947.[39]

## MASTERMIND PLANNERS

Ultimately, it was economic ideology that determined the various solutions proposed for solving Ireland's economic problems. In the late 1940s two distinct coalitions had emerged from within the Irish bureaucracy. One – as we have seen – centred on the mandarins of the Department of Finance and the Central Bank, and promulgated conservative action – the standard answer to any economic problem. This faction feared both inflation and the establishment of bureaucratic bodies that would lie beyond their control. The ideological underpinning of this faction was based on the contention that the country's problems could only be solved by reducing the role of Government spending in favour of monetary or credit instruments. The second group consisted of a number of influential politicians and outside interests, but also contained an administrative base within the Department of Industry and Commerce. In essence, they wanted to encourage export-oriented investments and state direction of industry in order to make it more efficient.[40] This was not achieved. The conservatives opposed both options: the first would have inflationary consequences, while the second would unjustly extend Government control over private enterprise. Virtually all policy-makers, politicians and other interest groups believed that private enterprise was the bedrock upon which the Irish economy was based.[41]

Nevertheless, some politicians began to identify protected Irish capital as a major problem in the post-war economy. Seán Lemass made many proposals for the overhaul of the Irish economy, and in 1945 put forward elaborate and ambitious plans to generate full employment after the war. The Industrial Relations Act of 1946, which established the Labour Court, was a further attempt to co-ordinate the economy and its various interest groups.[42] Moreover, Lemass also proposed a drastic shake-up of trade policy, a change that would have increased state involvement in the exporting sector of the economy. A final measure – undoubtedly the most radical – was the introduction of the Control of Prices and Promotion of

Industrial Efficiency Bill of 1947, which, if passed, would have given the Government unprecedented control over the running of the economy. This was an attempt by Lemass – the progenitor of protectionism in the 1930s – to create an industrial-efficiency bureau that would combat excess profit-making and restrictive trade practices in protected industries, thereby bringing a semblance of competitive practices to these sectors. It was an early illustration of his belief that the country would be better served by the Government playing a more active role within the economy – not to perpetuate protectionism but to lay the foundations for a more competitive economy that would include free trade.

Lemass was defeated by the more conservative forces in society. The industrial-efficiency proposals, in particular, drew a hostile reaction. Lemass' envisaged bureau was to have unprecedented powers to ensure reasonable standards of efficiency that, according to the Department of Industry and Commerce, were lacking in 'those industries which enjoy the benefits of tariff or quota instruments on imports'.[43] At first, the bureau was to be a 'friendly advisor' with some price-control powers. But for those companies that did not respond adequately, a court of inquiry would be set up to subpoena documents on quality, price, methods of management, labour recruitment and training, materials used, marketing, overhead charges, capital structure and other such matters. If such businesses did not then comply with the bureau's directives, the state would be empowered to stop the distribution of profits, fix prices, fix maximum profit limits, confiscate excess profits, and – for some, most seriously of all – remove protection.[44] Tadhg Ó Cearbhaill – who at this time was private secretary to Lemass – said that the bill had two aims:

> ... one for consumers, to keep the price of goods to the consumer down, but also to keep control of industrial raw materials, to keep costs to industry down. That was the proposal. It didn't develop as it was

strongly opposed politically, both within Fianna Fáil and the opposition and also by Irish manufacturers. The Federation of Irish Manufacturers were very hostile to it.[45]

McElligott responded to the proposal by arguing trenchantly that the public interest did not require such a drastic degree of supervision and control of industry.[46] Even more significantly, Irish industry was atypically united in its opposition. A conference called by the Federation of Irish Manufacturers (FIM) was attended by fifty-seven industrial associations, and concluded rather dramatically that 'until this country has declared for a Communist form of Government, the Bill should be withdrawn'.[47] The federation also demanded a meeting with the new Taoiseach to discuss what it considered to be the general belief among ministers – as well as the general public – that manufacturers made excess profits at the expense of the consumer. One such industrialist in the textile business recalled:

> … [the] horror with which businessmen viewed this rather draconian bill. What was the point in setting up in business and trying to foster an enterprise culture if at the slightest sign of bother the Government was going to come in and practically seize your company?[48]

Given the conservative nature of Irish society, Lemass' innovative plans were not implemented by the first Inter-Party Government, despite Labour having supported the Control of Prices and Promotion of Industrial Efficiency Bill while in opposition (indeed, some of the earliest proposals from the expansionary coalition *did* involve direct administrative control of industry). It is questionable, however, if Fianna Fáil would have implemented these measures had it been returned to power, such was the opposition of interest groups, including the trade unions.

## THE WORKERS DIVIDED

The position of the trade union movement was complicated by a split in January 1945, which had seen the Congress of Irish Unions (CIU) break from the Irish Trade Union Congress (ITUC). The split was the culmination of several years of division on tactics, and deeply felt animosity between William O'Brien, leader of the Irish Transport and General Workers' Union (ITGWU), and James Larkin of the Workers' Union of Ireland (WUI). From the mid-1920s there had been a growth in the number of trade unions operating in Ireland, leading to inter-union rivalry. As Emmet O'Connor has noted, 'sometimes unions fought over their respective merits, sometimes over the advantages of craft or industrial unionism, sometimes over the principles behind Irish or British based unionism; always they fought over members'.[49] The proliferation of unions ran contrary to the ideal of 'One Big Union' championed by the country's largest union, the ITGWU, which was involved in the inter-union disputes more often than not. Moreover, the ITGWU was an Irish union with a strong nationalist ethos, and resented the presence of British-based unions in the state. The number of unions and their propensity to fight not only employers but each other had left Seán Lemass increasingly exasperated. Convinced that consolidation of the movement was necessary, in 1936 he advised the ITUC that if the unions did not resolve its problems, the Government would intervene and do it for them. William O'Brien was happy to oblige, but the ITUC as a whole was not. Unhappy with the rejection of his proposal, in May 1939 O'Brien established the Council of Irish Unions as a faction within the ITUC for the pursuit of Irish national objectives. This mirrored a split of a year earlier when a majority of Labour Party TDs who were also members of the ITGWU had left to set up the National Labour Party.[50]

As a result of the unions' failure to reorganise, the Government stepped in with its 1941 Trade Union Act, which was intended to ensure that only a small number of large Irish-based unions would be allowed to operate in Ireland. The act owed much to O'Brien's thinking (he had advised the Government on its drafting), but was wholly unacceptable to most other unions, with Larkin's WUI and the British-based amalgamated unions to the forefront of the opposition. The ITGWU and some others eventually split from the ITUC in January 1945 to form the rival CIU. Although the ITUC membership outnumbered the CIU's by almost two to one (the CIU represented 77,500 workers, the ITUC 146,000),[51] the Government appeared to favour the smaller congress; in 1945, for instance, the Government nominated two CIU officials as Ireland's delegates to the International Labour Organisation conference.[52] The ITUC received a boost in July 1946, however, when an appeal by the National Union of Railwaymen against the constitutionality of part III of the Trade Union Act (which had been rejected by the High Court in 1945) was upheld by the Supreme Court on the grounds that it contravened the right of the citizen to free association.[53] Furthermore, it seems that the Fianna Fáil Government, and Lemass in particular, was becoming suspicious of the CIU, which it felt was running a dirty operation.[54] By 1948 relations between the two had cooled to the point of freezing following the CIU's failure to ensure that its National Labour Party deputies voted to keep a Fianna Fáil Government in office.[55]

It may have seemed that the unconstitutionality of banning British-based unions together with the CIU's falling out with its erstwhile ally, Lemass, would bode well for the reunification of the movement, not least when two of its key rivals, William O'Brien and James Larkin, had left the stage,[56] and when both Labour and National Labour were together in Cabinet as members of the Inter-Party Government. The fissure between the two groups was not easily mended, however, and although the two labour parties reunited in 1950, the two congresses failed to follow suit for several years.

Despite the weaknesses wrought by division, the creation of the Labour Court under the 1946 Industrial Relations Act strengthened the unions by bringing them into the mainstream and establishing them as a part of the 'social furniture'.[57] There was also a sense of achievement at the setting up of the court, with the writer and WUI official, James Plunkett Kelly, speaking of it as a symbol of:

> ... the victory of trade unionism in its fight for a respected and influential place in the social and economic life of modern Ireland. Here was the beginning of a new stage in labour relations, with its machinery for direct negotiations and conciliation representing new privileges for trade unionism, but also putting on its shoulders new responsibilities.[58]

Yet while it had these new responsibilities, the greatest problem for the union movement was the existence of two congresses. Both employers and Government met with both congresses together, and – as Donal Nevin points out – 'were not slow to play one off another to the detriment of workers. Lemass was not too bothered by two congresses as it kept the Labour Party and the labour movement as a whole weak'.[59] While this may indeed have been the case, Lemass was to suffer politically during the Fianna Fáil Government of 1951–54 when he found himself sidelined by Seán MacEntee's performance as Minister for Finance. As Brian Girvin points out, in a political environment where Lemass was clearly the architect of the Government's industrial strategy, his failure to co-opt and integrate into his support base a unified congress weakened him within Fianna Fáil.[60] Alternative industrial and economic strategies would have received a better hearing if the workers' movement had been united, especially since a boosted Lemass would have exerted more influence within Government. He had been able to defeat the conservative elements within the party on the issue of co-operation with the Labour Party after the 1943 general election, but following the 1948 election was unable to counter the conservative economics dominant in Fianna Fáil, and was effectively marginalised by MacEntee.[61]

At a time when Irish politics in general was moving in a conservative direction, the trade union movement was unable to present a united common front to the state or the employers. The consequences of this were grave. Despite the ascension to power in 1948 of the expansionist Inter-Party Government, conservative economic policy prevailed. Wage levels remained depressed for a considerable time, while unemployment and emigration rose sharply.

## THE POWER AND THE GLORY

The creation of the Industrial Development Authority (IDA) in 1949 – combined with a package of industrial incentives – amounted to a significant increase in Government control of industry. The IDA had the support of important sectors of the business community. According to the original proposal, it was to have two functions: primarily, it was to initiate schemes to establish new industries and to investigate the necessity of revising tariffs, quotas and other protective measures; it also had powers to subpoena witnesses and documents relating to Irish industry. The original content was, however, modified to exclude provisions for IDA control of industry. Lemass was critical of the setting up of the IDA, fearing that it would usurp the traditional role of the Department of Industry and Commerce. Some of Lemass' objections sprang from the fact that the new agency consisted of former officials of Industry and Commerce doing the same tasks for the IDA as they had done for the department.[62] Bew and Patterson speculate that Lemass' opposition to the formation of the IDA was 'bowing both to party and industrialists' pressure'.[63] While this may, to an extent, be true, it seems more likely that he thought that the IDA would supersede Industry and Commerce in attempting to develop the country's industrial sector. Tadhg Ó Cearbhaill also maintains that Lemass' great fear was that the Department of Industry and Commerce would have been downgraded by the time Lemass returned to office.[64] He had, however, recognised that increasing exports alone could be an effective stimulus for the economy. The IDA echoed his view, and maintained that an increase of manufacturing exports should be the clear focus of any export policy. Recognising the difficulties facing exporters, it proposed that an organisation to promote and co-ordinate exports be established:

> We hold the definite view that there is no likelihood of any appreciable increase in industrial exports on the basis of the individual efforts of manufacturers. Our manufacturers as a whole have very limited knowledge or experience of export trade and apart from their reluctance to enter into an unknown and highly competitive field, the share of any particular manufacturer in export trade would be relatively so small that it could not bear the expense of an adequately staffed and operated export department.[65]

Industrial exports, the IDA added, would not be generated unless financial inducements were forthcoming. Finance, however, was dismayed at the prospect of public finance or tax concessions being made available to exporters. There was, it claimed:

> An air of unreality about this interim report of the IDA. It does not seem to come to grips with the problem at all. If, however, the Government agree to the proposals, there is not the slightest doubt that the manufacturers will receive the IDA with open arms. Why shouldn't they? The state will be doing for them something which they should do themselves.[66]

The Department of Finance was worried about the creation of the IDA on two accounts: primarily, that industrial incentives would be inflationary, and, secondly, that the creation of a new bureaucratic agency with resources to attract capital was 'a dangerous machine for the exercise of corruption'.[67] Minister for Finance Patrick McGilligan also had doubts about the scheme:

> The Board should not be envisaged as a board of mastermind planners – to divert and plan the industrial development of the country – but rather as a Board of fact finders and advisors to the community and to the Government on the activities of private enterprise. They are there to search out possibilities of industrial development, to collect facts and statistics and to bring them to the notice of entrepreneurs in some fair and suitable manner. It should definitely not be within their scope or function to themselves run or plan industry or any branch thereof.[68]

Colm Barnes maintains that large sections of Irish capital joined the Department of Finance in its opposition to the investigative powers of the IDA, but not to the creation of the board itself. He agreed with McGilligan's views that the board should not be made up of a gang of 'crack-pot socialist planners', 'but as long as manufacturing men were involved, we thought it would be all right'.[69] The complaints had a marked effect on the final make-up and powers of the IDA. Its first board of directors included representatives of the FIM and the Federated Union of Employers (FUE), as well as prominent company directors; all these, however, were expansionist in viewpoint.[70] The president of the FIM publicly welcomed the formation of the IDA, and expressed pleasure at the level of consultation between the FIM and Government ministers and departments.[71] Schemes to promote exports had been proposed since 1946, but met with indifference from protected capital and the outright opposition of the Department of

Finance. Lemass had attempted to introduce a bill to assist industries engaged in foreign trade, and a new Foreign Trade Corporation was to oversee an exporters' insurance scheme and to provide grants to exporters for factory premises and training. The scheme was eventually withdrawn because of opposition from Finance on the predictable grounds of cost. One other initiative was the establishment of the Dollar Export Advisory Committee in 1950, which was an attempt to devise policy initiatives to achieve meaningful growth in manufacturing enterprise and to stimulate exports to the United States of America. This, however, was as much a response to the general economic turmoil that resulted from a shortage of dollars in Europe, as a major policy commitment to use government money to increase economic growth.[72]

The development of Córas Tráchtála Teoranta as a promotional agency for Irish exports did not meet the recommendations of the IDA, as it was basically an advisory body and did not have the finance or the power to induce industrialists to export.[73] Yet without Government intervention, it was unlikely that many manufacturers would develop an export trade. Many of those involved in industry at the time have commented on a perception within industry generally that it would not survive free trade; thus, they were satisfied to produce for the home market only. According to a number of industrialists active at the time, there was great security in Irish manufacturing industry because it had a captive market and high tariff walls that kept out imports; consequently, most Irish industries were not geared towards international competition.[74] The success of import substitution and the continuing expansion of the protected sector in the late 1940s and early 1950s indicated that further possibilities for internal growth remained available. Daniel Morrissey, Minister for Industry and Commerce in the first Inter-Party Government, drew attention in the Dáil to the high level of imports in 1950, estimating that

£60 million of such imports could be replaced by Irish products, and with it the creation of 45,000 new jobs. He also claimed that there was still considerable scope for further industrial development within the protected economy.[75] There is no real evidence that such possibilities for industrial expansion did indeed exist. Industrialists did not view their businesses in such a manner. While they accepted the need for a strong industrial arm for what was essentially an agricultural country, the main aim of industrialists, it seems, was to provide employment and make a reasonable profit. Most businessmen of the time did not even know how to go about attempting to export. Few companies had staff able to communicate in a foreign language. The idea that Irish industry could compete with foreign companies was not entertained, and there was little sense of entrepreneurship. It is reasonable to assume that if industrialists could make an ample profit without providing employment, they would do so, but what is striking is that earning a profit was not considered the harbinger of industrial success.

Lemass had pinpointed the problems of industrialists. In a letter to a Cork industrialist, William Dwyer – who had stood previously as an unsuccessful Dáil candidate for Cumann na nGaedheal, and with whom Lemass carried on an intermittent exchange – he berated the lack of entrepreneurial drive:

The extent to which industrial development is to be brought, must be decided by national policy and not by the interests of individual industrialists. It has always been a handicap to our industrial progress that the best of our industrial leaders show a tendency to exhaust their initial impetus and to slow down and stop when they have reached a stage of development which gives them maximum security with the minimum of additional effort ... The function of Government as I see it is to keep on pushing development to the limits of practicability whether individual industrialists like it or not.[76]

While Lemass may have felt that the Inter-Party Government failed to push industrial developments to the limit – as suggested by one of his biographers, Michael O'Sullivan – he cannot escape the charge that most of his post-1948 industrial ideas were opposed by Irish industrialists. Lemass did make strenuous efforts to give Irish industry a fundamentally strong basis; for instance, he had Joseph McCullough – in his capacity as a member of the National Economic Advisory Group of Cumann na n-Innealtoiri (the engineers' association) – carry out a confidential report for him on the idea of overseas contracting. As McCullough later pointed out to me, 'Irish people had been contracting all over the world since after the First World War, so I set out to examine could we do that here [in Ireland]'.[77] The IDA, however, clearly had some way to go if it hoped to persuade Irish industry to develop an export-led approach to business. One of the IDA's main problems was that it lacked any power to grant incentives for the attraction of foreign industries to the country; thus, its establishment should be seen not as a complete break with previous industrial policy in that it was not an alternative approach but a method of supplementing the framework already in existence.[78]

There was, to an extent, a consensual approach to the validity of protection. Tadhg Ó Cearbhaill has commented on how there was a scaling down of the number of new tariffs after the war, with no new quotas introduced, and how this was an agreed political objective:

> Yet while both Governments were trying to use protection only as a last resort, industrial policy was originally designed to replace imports. A local development group that went into Industry and Commerce were handed the import statistics and prepared reports on what we could make here. The view was taken that a secure home base, protected if necessary, was the best basis for developing exports. If the Government were expecting an industry to develop exports, that industry was entitled

to have its own market secure. Teams from Industry and Commerce, employers and unions went off to the United States to study methods there. This was to encourage industry to become more efficient, not by compulsion, but it was visualised that protection had to be scaled down.[79]

This led to some innovative IDA schemes being put into operation. A 1951 grants scheme for new industrial investments in underdeveloped areas provided infrastructural development by the state, land and buildings to new industry, grants for the full cost of new factories, fifty-per-cent grants for the cost of new machinery and equipment, training grants, exemptions from local charges, and reduced electricity rates. The scheme was managed by a new grants authority, An Foras Tionscal, which was loosely tied to the Department of Industry and Commerce but was semi-independent, like the IDA.[80] The conservative faction in the public-policy arena were again very much opposed to such a scheme. Finance argued that 'in view of the present and prospective condition of the Irish exchequer, it is merely common sense to refrain from taking on new commitments either of a capital or a current nature'.[81] As a response to the thousands leaving the country every year, this was hardly inspiring stuff.

## A HELPING HAND?

The Marshall Plan was one such potential commitment, and brought with it opposing views within the political and administrative Irish elite. It is commonly accepted in much historical analysis of this period that Ireland was a reluctant participant in the European Recovery Programme (ERP).[82] The predominant view supports T.K. Whitaker's oft-quoted words:

No one who took part in preparing the Recovery Programme (and that includes myself) ever looked on it as a development programme, but rather as an exercise that had to be undertaken to persuade the Americans to give us Marshall Aid.[83]

Whitaker – at that stage moving up to the top echelons of the Irish civil service – has consistently argued this point ever since, and has been supported by others who were involved at the time.[84] Charles Murray, who succeeded Whitaker as secretary of the Department of Finance, substantiated this interpretation, claiming that:

Some maintain that preparation of documents to validate our claim for Marshall Aid represented Ireland's first steps in economic planning. I never felt that myself and I think it was very much a paper effort. I'm not decrying it in that sense but certainly it fell far short of the inter-departmental involvement in *Economic Development*.[85]

Yet the Department of Finance's view was not the only one within Irish administration circles in this period. Tom Murray of the Department of Industry and Commerce reckoned that 'it was the first effort to forecast the economic future', while Frederick Boland of the Department of External Affairs noted that 'it did lay Ireland open to planning'.[86]

Evidence exists that the first Inter-Party Government had a certain commitment to Europe and European integration, and that – ultimately – Ireland's application to join the EEC in 1961 has its genesis in the response of the Department of External Affairs to the Marshall Plan. At the original Marshall Aid discussions – held from July to September 1947 under the auspices of the Committee for European Economic Co-operation (the precursor to the Organisation for European Economic Co-operation) – Ireland's representative, the secretary of External Affairs, Frederick Boland, made an important speech in which he said Ireland would sign the Plan no matter what the Government was able to negotiate for itself.[87] As Boland later commented, 'we didn't look to get anything free out of the thing but our interest was that Europe should be prosperous, because without a prosperous Europe, we couldn't be prosperous ourselves'.[88] Seán MacBride – who succeeded Eamon de Valera as Minister for External Affairs – also considered himself to be something of a Europhile, which contrasted greatly with his Anglophobia, and he took a keen personal interest in the course of European integration, and welcomed to Dublin various groups supporting that particular aim. He sent a delegation to the Congress on European Union, held in The Hague in May 1948, and was very supportive of the setting up of the Council of Europe in 1949.[89]

Before the 1948 general election, de Valera had already appointed the Department of External Affairs as the controller of Ireland's participation in the European Recovery Programme, and in May 1948 the Inter-Party Government confirmed that decision. De Valera's Fianna Fáil Government was originally hesitant about the exact meaning of the Marshall Plan. As Minister for External Affairs, de Valera did not attend the conference in July 1947, but instead sent Seán Lemass, the Minister for Industry and Commerce, and Paddy Smith, the Minister for Agriculture. It may be that as the US Congress insisted that Marshall Aid be contingent on the liberalisation of European trade, de Valera sent the political representatives of those departments that would be most affected by such a move. De Valera also sent Boland to Paris; one of the most able civil servants in the history of the Irish state, he was to play a key role.

In the first official comment on the Marshall Plan, Lemass welcomed it, maintaining that Ireland 'could not insulate herself from the effects of economic decline in other states, that question was true of all countries, but particularly of small ones'.[90] He also used the occasion to assert that Ireland's economic development was hindered by the lack of political development, which was of course hampered by the 'division of the national territory'. It was common for Fianna Fáil ministers to raise the partition issue on their travels, no matter what the circumstances, and by raising it here, Lemass was saying nothing unusual for an Irish minister. Indeed, when Fianna Fáil lost office in 1948, de Valera's first action was to take himself off on an anti-partition tour of the US, Australia, New Zealand and India. Lemass' final remarks stressed, however, that the Irish Government would do all in its power to help the conference succeed, and he welcomed the 'growth of economic interdependence', asserting that Ireland 'is not in this conference to work against any nation or group of nations. We are here for our own good and for that of Europe'.[91]

Whatever about Lemass' rather anodyne remarks, the importance of this conference for Europe is reflected in a report sent by Boland from Paris to Dublin in August 1947. It painted a pretty bleak picture of the Western European economic and political landscape:

Without outside aid of a magnitude that only something like the Marshall Plan can supply, Europe is headed for economic collapse and social revolution within the next two or three years. Even if this outside aid is forthcoming it is more than doubtful whether Western Europe can stand on its own legs after 1952 without reductions in living standards which Governments, already faced with dangerous internal communist drives, can only contemplate with the utmost dismay. It would be difficult to exaggerate the extent to which this realisation of the general position of Western Europe is conditioning the work of this conference.[92]

The drafting of the report outlining a joint European Recovery Programme was adopted on 22 September 1947. De Valera represented the Government, and outlined its thinking in relation to Marshall Aid:

> To seek from another what one could supply by one's efforts is always unworthy. It is doubly so when the assistance is requested from a friend who has proved himself generous repeatedly. I am happy to sign this report on behalf of Ireland because I believe it is an honest report. In it self-help is recognised as a primary duty, and no more aid is sought than is absolutely necessary if the damage of the war years is to be repaired within a reasonable period of time and the nations of Western Europe restored to a position in which they can provide for their own needs and preserve their traditional civilisation.[93]

While de Valera in this speech repeated his well-worn views on the need for economic self-sufficiency, the reality was that by the time Ireland signed the Convention for European Economic Co-operation in Paris on 16 April 1948, it was the first Inter-Party Government that would have the chance to utilise Marshall Aid.

Boland, to some extent, stuck to de Valera's position when he outlined his view of what Marshall Aid and the Paris conference signified. In a letter to the secretaries of Agriculture, Industry and Commerce and Finance early in March 1948, he said:

> The Marshall Plan is not a cure for the economic problems of Western Europe. If use is not made of the respite to tackle the problem, we shall all be in as bad a position at the end of the four year period as we are now. All this was clearly realised by the Paris conference.[94]

For the Inter-Party Government, however – and MacBride in particular – Marshall Aid seemed to hold out the prospect of enabling the implementation of an ambitious programme of development.

For Fianna Fáil, being in opposition for the first time since 1932 was not easy. A meeting of the parliamentary party in June 1948 discussed the signing of the Convention for European Economic Co-operation by the Inter-Party Government the previous April. Lemass pointed out that visits to Paris by himself, Paddy Smith and de Valera during 1947 were preliminary steps to the drawing up of the convention, and he was therefore seeking approval from the Fianna Fáil parliamentary party 'not to oppose it' when it came before the Dáil on 1 July 1948. He explained that the 'Bilateral Economic Co-operation agreement between Ireland and the USA which was signed in Dublin on 28 June 1948 was a necessary step to be taken by each of the 14 participating European nations as a preliminary to the receipt of Marshall Aid'.[95] Lemass' insistence that Fianna Fáil support the implementation of the Marshall Plan in Ireland is more than likely an indication of his belief that the Inter-Party Government would fall on its own sword before very long, at which time he would be in a position to oversee the spending of the Marshall largesse.

## GRANTS, NOT LOANS

The Inter-Party Government was to prove more stable than Lemass imagined. In its consideration of the plan, a number of problems presented themselves: of primary concern was whether US aid would be granted in the shape of grants or loans. This led to a clash between the Government – specifically, MacBride – and the Central Bank and the Department of Finance. MacBride had made clear to the US State Department as early as May 1948 that Ireland needed a grant as it would not be able to repay a loan. A document written by T.K. Whitaker the following month graphically illustrated the need for a grant. While it was, in essence, an analysis of the weaknesses of the Irish economy, Whitaker called attention to the role that Ireland could play in the agricultural sphere in furtherance of the European Recovery Programme:

> We can most effectively strengthen our own economic structure and contribute to the economic recovery of Europe by an increase in food production. The resultant expansion of Irish exports of meat, eggs and dairy produce, the high protein value which Ireland is particularly suited to produce, will meet an urgent European demand and reduce Europe's present dependence on dollar sources of supply. Ireland depends on this recovery in food exports from their present depressed level for the increase in earnings necessary to restore equilibrium in her overall balance of payments. US aid is essential if these twin objectives are to be attained because the requisite improvement in agricultural output cannot be secured without imports of grains, feeding stuffs, machinery, and other commodities from the Western Hemisphere, for which Ireland, whose available dollar resources are meagre and uncertain is not in a position to pay.[96]

To assert that Ireland would not be in a position to pay put down the Government's marker in no uncertain terms: a grant would be required. Ireland's dollar expenditure was normally met by the conversion of sterling earnings through the London exchange. However, the reserves of the sterling area had sunk so low that Ireland could no longer look to such reserves as a source of dollars. As its external investments were confined almost solely to Britain, with earnings predominantly in sterling, Ireland wanted a restoration of the free convertibility of sterling. Until this was achieved, however, the conservation and strengthening of the gold and dollar reserves of the sterling-area pool were paramount. Given such considerations, the Government entered into a formal agreement with the British wherein it would not rely on the sterling-area pool for dollar requirements during the ERP. For Whitaker, then:

The reserves of the pool being unavailable, Ireland's dollar resources in the absence of aid under the European Recovery Programme would be entirely inadequate to defray the cost of essential imports from the dollar area. It is sufficient indication of the inadequacy of our resources that in 1947 current earnings of US dollars amounted to $28 million while dollar expenditure was approximately $120 million and is expected to remain of this order. Ireland's dollar earnings, which consist for the most part of emigrants' remittances, legacies and tourist receipts are not capable of material expansion; indeed, of their nature, they are uncertain and liable to contract.[97]

A similar, though more explicit, memorandum regarding Ireland's case for a grant – entitled 'General considerations on Ireland's position in relation to ERP' – began by proclaiming that:

Ireland is anxious to contribute to the maximum of her ability in the economic recovery of Western Europe. Her desire to do so is based on her desire to assist in the creation of economic conditions that will enable the survival and the regeneration of free institutions and Christian civilisation. Ireland's approach to political and economic problems is not based on materialism; basically Ireland is moved more by a genuine desire to serve the ideals in which she believes. These ideals are the democratic way of life, Christian social and economic principles, human liberty, the right to national self-determination and family life. Rightly or wrongly Ireland believes in a policy based on idealism rather than on materialism.[98]

The language here is remarkably similar to that used when Ireland first applied to join the EEC. The application document carefully placed Ireland's Christian heritage and its commitment to Christian values in a European context, and mentioned that:

[For] some centuries after the break up of the Roman Empire, Ireland was a haven of spiritual and intellectual life in which the essence of the European tradition was preserved and from which it was brought back again to many continental lands.[99]

The Marshall Aid document went on to place Ireland's Christian beliefs in the context of the regeneration of Western Europe, maintaining that Ireland appreciated the urgency of co-operative action in rendering material aid:

Indeed Ireland was among the first nations to send large shipments of completely free gifts of food to European countries since the war ended. Likewise the Irish people voluntarily collected and sent very substantial assistance to the Italian Christian parties during the recent elections. There was no reward motive for these acts; the motive was based on idealism. These matters are not stated out of any sense of self-righteousness or boastfulness but merely to emphasise the earnestness of our desire to do everything we can to co-operate fully with the United States in the splendid work it is doing in this sphere and to indicate our psychological approach to these problems.[100]

Having outlined Ireland's idealistic nature, and having all but said that Ireland was not a neutral spectator with regard to the West-versus-East conflict by virtue of having supported the Italian Christian parties, the document then referred to the US desire that Ireland continue to produce food for export to Western Europe. Reports by Willard Thorp, US Assistant Secretary of State, that Ireland needed only a loan as it had not sustained any real damage in the war were, the memorandum stated, 'entirely erroneous':

Ireland's small farmsteads are in effect her factories. There are 382,710 of them. During the war years and since, in order to feed herself and Britain, each one of these exhausted its soil fertility and livestock owing to the absence of feeding stuffs and fertilisers. It is just as if 382,710 small factories ran their machines without lubricant until it [*sic*] became worn out.[101]

The premise was clear. Without a grant, Ireland had no chance of making any worthwhile contribution to the ERP:

On the one hand, Ireland's interest in the European Recovery Programme and her desire to do her utmost to contribute to its success, and, on the other hand, the problems which the task of Irish recovery presents and our concern that participation in the programme should not entail the contracting of a heavy and irrepayable [*sic*] external debt.[102]

Such arguments fell on deaf ears in Washington, as the Americans quickly announced that Ireland's initial amount would be a $2.5-million-dollar loan to cover the period April to June. Both the method of payment and the amount came as a shock to Seán MacBride.[103]

MacBride had assiduously courted George Garrett, the US minister (ambassador) in Dublin, since July 1947 in an attempt to persuade the Americans that aid should be given to Ireland in grant form. By the end of April 1948 it appeared to the Irish ambassador in Washington, Seán Nunan, that MacBride's efforts might bear fruit. He reported to Boland that Paul Hoffman, the head of the Economic Co-operation Administration (ECA) – the organisation charged with administering Marshall Aid – had told him that:

He was at the University of Chicago with George Garrett, the American Minister and is a member of the same college fraternity. He said he had heard from Mr Garrett who spoke very highly of the attitude of our Government towards the European Recovery Programme and indicated that ours is not a 'hat in hand' attitude … I do think that Mr Garrett's favourable report on our Government's attitude towards the plan will do us no harm when the question of the terms on which aid will be given will be decided.[104]

The loan-versus-grant question was beginning to fray the nerves of Irish officials. When Ireland's case came up at a meeting of the Foreign Relations Committee of the US House of Representatives, Willard Thorp asserted that Ireland should receive a loan as this was the best way for the country to rehabilitate itself. This was too much for Boland, who wrote to J.J. McElligott, secretary of the Department of Finance, in scathing terms about what he regarded as a particularly sorry episode:

> A more deplorable performance it would be hard to imagine! How well founded were the apprehensions that the State Department had not got the men of the calibre necessary to pilot the European Recovery Project through the Congressional committees … Marshall passed the buck to Thorp who proceeded to make a fair 'haymes' of the issue … Thorp gravely misled the committee about Ireland.[105]

The misleading, however, was not all on the US side. A speech by the Irish vice-consul in New York, Frank Coffey, to the Jersey City Lions Club on 16 March 1948 caused pandemonium back in Dublin. While defending Irish neutrality in the Second World War, Coffey asserted that:

> … under the scheme which is at present before Congress, Ireland would receive only a dollar loan. No aid on a grant basis would be given …

I should like to impress upon you that in giving us a loan you will not be taking very much of a risk. Ireland is one of the few countries today which is not in debt. On the contrary Britain, as a result of our exports during the war owes us approximately two billion dollars. There is thus nothing at all unreasonable about lending money to Ireland.[106]

Coffey went on to place Ireland at the heart of Western Europe, stressing how important a role a united Ireland could play in the revitalisation of Western Europe. He ended his speech in ringing terms, proclaiming that:

The revitalisation of Irish agriculture is part of the great effort to save Western Europe from economic and political ruin ... An Ireland free and united from shore to shore may still prove to be a decisive influence in the destiny of Western Europe. Ireland has had a long and troubled night, the dawn at last is here, she has risen to the sunlight of a glorious day.[107]

Two days after Coffey's speech, the Department of External Affairs cabled Washington:

Press report Coffey as saying in speech, New Jersey, answering criticism of Ireland in relation to ERP that we do not want grants but loans. As this is the reverse of the real position please cable whether he has been correctly reported.[108]

Washington replied that Coffey had indeed been quoted correctly, and a copy of his speech was sent to Dublin.[109] There is no more correspondence in the file relating to this issue until two weeks later, when Washington again wrote to Dublin; the communication maintained that 'no doubt he was misled by the statement made on the same lines by Thorp of the State Department'.[110] The embassy in Washington was also worried about another aspect of Coffey's speech, which had wider foreign-policy implications than his stated position on the Marshall Plan: in his speech, Coffey had made reference to Russia's veto of Irish membership of the United Nations (UN) in 1946:

> We are rather proud of Russia's opposition in this instance for we feel it is indicative of a realisation that the Irish delegates to the United Nations would ever be on the side of liberty, justice and international morality and that our membership would be yet another voice contributing to the condemnation of totalitarianism and aggression.[111]

The embassy stated to Boland that Coffey's statement 'about Russia's objecting to our admission to the United Nations is rather strong for a vice-consul'.[112] Coming some fourteen years prior to Michael Moran's celebrated speech, when the then Minister for Lands argued that 'neutrality [between communism and freedom] is not a policy to which we would even wish to appear committed', Coffey's words seem remarkable for a relatively junior External Affairs official.[113] Although he was speaking in the US on the day before St Patrick's day, his words nevertheless offer an indication that there were those within External Affairs who placed the Marshall Plan in the wider perspective of West-versus-East, and who had little doubt as to where Ireland should stand. It is also significant – as Diarmaid Ferriter points out – that George Garrett erroneously believed that the Irish state was as vulnerable as any other country to communist infiltration owing to the economic depression, despite its seemingly impeccable anti-communist credentials.[114]

Early June saw frantic activity on the question of a loan. At a meeting on 1 June of Government officials dealing with the European

Recovery Programme, J.J. McElligott, secretary of the Department of Finance:

> … thought that with the future course of the ERP uncertain because of the interaction of American politics there were grounds for bagging all we could now. It would not be essential to take the whole of the $10 million offered and he had in mind we might take a lesser sum. He admitted that possibly some tactical advantage might be lost by taking a loan in face of our very recent protestations of our inability to repay and our moral rectitude in financial matters. The point was also made that to take a loan might prejudice the possibility of a reasonable grant allocation in future quarters. Not to take a loan would, however, be inconsistent with our stand against drawing on the sterling area pool.[115]

The following day, the *Irish Press* reported that the position on Marshall Aid was that under Fianna Fáil, whatever aid Ireland received under the ERP would be by way of grant, 'but that something happened … which altered the picture and resulted in the decision that the $10 million earmarked for Ireland for the current quarter should be granted by way of loan'.[116] This sent the Department of External Affairs into something approaching apoplexy: 'the suggestion implied in the *Irish Press* article that the determination for the present quarter was the result of something done or omitted to be done on the part of the Irish Government is wholly unwarranted'.[117] While the *Irish Press* was obviously a Fianna Fáil-supporting paper and had, as part of its agenda, a need to attack the Inter-Party Government as often as possible, its comments highlighted the apprehension that existed within Government circles, both political and administrative, on the loan-versus-grant issue. Although the Fianna Fáil Government had not been given a firm commitment to the effect that Ireland would receive a grant, the failure of the Inter-Party Government to secure a grant as distinct from a loan would leave it in a precarious political position and open to all manner of attack by the opposition and its supporters in the press.

When the news eventually came that Ireland was to receive a loan, MacBride quickly went into action, flying to New York and warning that the Irish Government might not be able to participate in the ERP as it did 'not like entering into obligations that we see no prospect of being able to meet'.[118] While the US, to an extent, wanted to include Ireland in the Marshall Plan – believing that Ireland had the potential to aid European recovery by producing more 'food for export' to Europe, thus reducing America's burden – they were unimpressed by MacBride's bravado. Despite intensive lobbying by MacBride, it was clear by June 1948 that the chances of any sort of a grant were slim. J.O. Brennan of the Irish embassy in Washington wrote to Boland on 15 June outlining a conversation he had had with Hoffman on the loan/grant question:

> He emphasised again that Ireland was, in his opinion, a loan-country and much though we had his sympathy and as personally inclined as he might be to accede to our desire for a grant, he felt that as administrator of this investment-banker business – ECA – he could not conscientiously tell me that we would be given a grant. He went on to say, in reply to a question from me, that if we declined a loan 'that would be our funeral', because there were any number of other people to accept the money if we failed to do so.[119]

## CHICKENS COME HOME TO ROOST?

Alan Milward suggests that Ireland failed to be awarded grants in the plan's first year because of its neutrality during the war, with Washington showing little 'sympathy' for the Government's position.[120]

Moreover, de Valera and Fianna Fáil did not have a monopoly on grievances over partition; MacBride had campaigned vigorously in the first half of 1948 to persuade the ECA not to acknowledge the partition of Ireland in the allocation of aid. This also made little impression on the Americans, but MacBride continued to harbour hopes that the OEEC might emerge as a genuinely supra-national organisation and evolve into an apparatus within which partition could be ended.

MacBride was also coming under increasing pressure from his own party on the partition question. J.P. Brennan, for instance, harangued MacBride in the Dáil on the question of the interlinking of Marshall Aid and partition in March 1948, and asked for a reassurance that at a meeting of the OEEC to be held on 14 March, MacBride would not discuss:

> ... any political matter other than economic until (A) the partition of the country will have been solved to the complete satisfaction of the people of Ireland, and (B) opportunities for freedom of speech will have been conceded to the inhabitants in the territory of Northern Ireland.

Considering that no progress had been made on partition since the foundation of the state, it was questionable whether any Irish minister could discuss political matters on the international stage at all if Brennan's maxim was to be held. In any event, MacBride replied to the demand by deflecting the political ramifications of the acceptance of Marshall Aid:

> The matters to be discussed at the resumed meeting of the OEEC on March 14 appertain primarily to the economic sphere. In so far as the Deputy's question is intended to elicit the Government's attitude to the partition of our country, I should like to add that the Government

regards the continuance of partition as the most significant obstacle to the political and economic welfare of our people.[121]

MacBride's use of the word 'primarily', however, can in essence be seen as a tacit admission that there was a link between politics and economics contained within the Marshall Plan.

MacBride's political problems masked to an extent the ongoing administrative row between the Departments of External Affairs and Finance during these months. For External Affairs, the ERP had huge importance for Ireland both economically and politically. In a submission to the Government towards the end of April 1948, the department pleaded for more staff as it was 'unable to reply to important communications from the US Government as promptly as we should', and 'any inefficiency, delay or lack of attention in dealing with the ERP may have very serious results for our national economy'.[122] External Affairs also asserted that without Marshall Aid, Ireland would find it practically impossible to obtain most of its requirements from the dollar area, whereas with Marshall Aid, the country would be able to obtain the raw materials and capital goods it required. Moreover, it argued that Marshall Aid, properly administered, would enable the Government to develop foreign trade – essential, given the vast surplus of Irish imports over exports – and absorb both the capital and labour that Ireland was exporting. Most important of all, according to External Affairs, was the political dimension:

> From a political point of view, ERP is of great importance as it is the first time that so many nations in Europe have banded themselves together for the purpose of complete economic co-operation. It is intended that the organisation should continue after the four years of American aid under the Marshall Plan. It is also the first time that Ireland has had an opportunity of co-operating in an international European organisation

in which the members of the British Commonwealth of Nations were not also participating.[123]

## FOR A FEW DOLLARS LESS

On the other side of the administrative fence, both Joseph Brennan – the acerbic governor of the Central Bank – and J.J. McElligott – the equally combative secretary of the Department of Finance – argued against accepting any form of aid unless it was given in grant form. Dollars, they argued, could not be repaid as Ireland earned too few of them. At one stage, McElligott remarked to his minister that 'we cannot expect any measure of salvation from the so-called Marshall Plan'.[124] Moreover, both Brennan and McElligott were concerned that the expansionary Department of External Affairs had too much control over the ERP process. McElligott wrote to Boland outlining Finance's worries after Boland had circulated a memorandum in which he argued that all ERP issues should be co-ordinated through External Affairs:

It seems inherent in your proposals that the Minister for External Affairs should assume all responsibility vis-à-vis the Government in relation to European Recovery Programme matters. We are here, as you know, in favour of you playing a preponderant role in regard to ERP in view not only of the position of your Department but of your own special knowledge in regard to the matter. But I presume your memorandum does not mean that no Department should approach the Government on a subject relating to ERP except via the Department of External Affairs. Occasion will arise when interests of the Minister of Finance are paramount and it seems to me desirable that he should be the vehicle for the submission of all proposals and memoranda of a financial character to the Government, subject of course to prior consultation with other Ministers concerned.[125]

Finance had no real idea as to what should be done with Marshall Aid other than using it to reduce the national debt, and essentially opposed it on the grounds that politicians would squander the money on inflationary expenditure. As Patrick Lynch has pointed out of McElligott:

> While he was extremely able and great credit is due to him for the benefits he conferred on the country, he was very cynical. He distrusted politicians and believed that their sole aim was to impose a bigger role in public spending for taxpayers' money. He saw the role of Finance as to reduce expenditure and while he was successful in this, his thinking was unduly influenced by Whitehall. In those years, Merrion Street was like a small Whitehall. It believed that financial policy should travel absolutely in line with British thinking.[126]

Seán Cromien has also talked of Brennan and McElligott's belief that politicians of the two main parties were extravagant spenders:

> Both of them were non-political and that is why they took offence when politicians disagreed with them. Brennan was particularly bad. There was a saying about him that when he used go to visit the Minister for Finance 'gloom followed as he walked along the corridor'. He was known to be gloomy and had no vision at all. In essence he stayed on too long.[127]

Cromien recalls both Brennan and McElligott as being very wary of Marshall Aid, and appalled at the idea that it eventually came in a loan form: 'both found the idea of Americans trawling through the civil service and demanding masses of documents detailing how we were going to spend Marshall Aid as abhorrent'.[128] External Affairs, however, did not see the Americans in the same light. Boland recalled that:

[The] Americans appointed in each country what was called a technical advisor, but he was really a supervisor to see to what extent we were carrying out the plan ... We had a fellow called Carrigan who was Professor of Agriculture at the University of Connecticut, or some place like that [he was actually dean of the University of Vermont]. He was a thoroughly decent fellow; we never did things without asking his advice. So the thing went on; we got through the thing all right. By the time it was finished, I was on the way to London.[129]

In any event, by December 1948 McElligott was telling his minister, Patrick McGilligan, that loans were a more preferable option than grants, as 'you are subject to less snooping by the Americans'.[130]

In essence, the Department of Finance's decision was related to its agreement with the British Treasury to do everything possible to reduce the strain on the sterling pool. A year later, Finance was continuing to question the validity of Marshall Aid. This time the attack came from Whitaker when he wrote a scathing critique of expansionary policy, focusing on the dangers of using such aid to fund new spending programmes. Insisting that the level of public debt was a direct result of excessive social expenditures, Whitaker asserted that taxation was too high and a disincentive to private enterprise, and claimed that infrastructural and industrial expenditures were also too high.[131] Whitaker has since recalled that 'Marshall Aid was not the beginning of planning in any systematic sense but the pursuit of an indigenous experience to get the right result'.[132] For him, at this stage, the right result was that Marshall Aid would be used to ease the public debt, not fund an increase in socially productive spending. George Duncan, professor of economics at Trinity College, Dublin – and of the same classical school of economics as Brennan and McElligott – succinctly summed up the taxation problem facing the country in a lecture in May 1950 to the Dublin Chamber of Commerce:

[Firstly] concealed taxation is found in every state, but in a small and highly protected state like ours it is of much greater relative significance. Secondly average income here is lower than in many neighbouring countries, some 117 [pounds] per head as compared with 200 per head in the United Kingdom and a given percentage extraction is more painful at the lower level. Also a large part of that income accruing in kind to farmers is not amenable to taxation and the burden falling on the rest is correspondingly increased.[133]

Thus, for Whitaker and his colleagues in Finance, it seemed sensible that Marshall Aid be used to ease public spending and reform the taxation system rather than becoming simply a spending tool for the authorities.

Marshall Aid, though it did fall well short of what the Government and particularly External Affairs hoped for, was eventually to account for about 50 per cent of total state investment during the Inter-Party administration. Over the total period of the ERP, Ireland received $146.2 million, made up of $128.2 million in loan aid and a rather measly $18 million in grant aid. Brian Girvin has argued that this result shows that Irish diplomacy in respect of the Marshall Plan was, to say the least, misjudged if not actually incompetent.[134] Yet for External Affairs, the Marshall Plan and the monies it provided had to be seen in a wider political context.

Beyond the interdepartmental and political nexus, the plan was condemned by the radical socialist, Peadar O'Donnell: writing in *The Bell*, he complained that Marshall Aid was part of a capitalist Pax Americana. Ireland, O'Donnell wrote, should 'remedy underdevelopment and stand for peace, or failing peace, neutrality, [rather] than … seek alms and surrender to war plans on which we can have no influence'.[135] While this was precisely the communist line at that stage of the Cold War, O'Donnell's was a lone voice in the Irish wilderness.

What the Marshall Plan did was to initially allow Ireland to re-join the community of Western European states to which External Affairs, in particular, felt the country belonged. It ended the country's diplomatic isolation after the end of the Second World War by allowing it a discursive place at the initial proceedings and by involving it in an already mapped-out course for the immediate economic future of Western Europe. The Irish Government did, however, concede little ground over intra-European trade liberalisation, and remained extremely apprehensive about US ideas for a multilateral customs union, which would have entailed joining a free trade area with a common external tariff.[136] Moreover, the Government was obsessed with partition, which to everyone else at the original conference was nothing but a nuisance. Coming at a time when the world was trying to reinvigorate itself after the horrors of the war, Irish complaints about partition were both incoherent and unrealistic.[137] Nevertheless, the agenda advanced by the Department of External Affairs in this crucial period of Irish foreign policy did set an important precedent for the direction that the Irish state would take – albeit torturously at times – in the following two decades.

# 2

# THIS DARK AND DISMAL LAND

Patrick McGilligan introduced Ireland's first capital budget in May 1950, declaring:

> One of the primary responsibilities of a Government is to promote, by an enlightened budgetary and investment policy, the continuous and efficient use of national resources in men and materials.[1]

Described by Patrick Lynch as the first explicit expression of Keynes in an Irish budget, and drafted by Lynch in association with Alexis Fitzgerald, the budget sought to allocate a certain part of the nation's finances to public purposes, and to ensure that the nation's resources were utilised to advance the interests of the community as a whole. Lynch – very much influenced by the Swedish and Norwegian systems – saw the capital budget purely as a matter of capital investment. He argued that the only way in which the repatriation of sterling assets could be achieved would be by a deficit in the current Government budget; the proceeds would go into productive investment.

McGilligan had undergone what could be described as a Pauline conversion from his very conservative, 'reactionary even' days of the late 1920s, from which the 'Irish people might have to starve' comment continued to hang albatross-like around his neck.[2] Lynch put this conversion down to the fact that McGilligan was a man of wide reading; he had read Keynes and was influenced by him. Keynes' comments during the Finlay Lecture (at University College, Dublin) of 1933 – during which he argued that if he was an Irishman, he would see very great merit in the policy being pursued by the Fianna Fáil Government that had just taken office – 'undoubtedly influenced a thinking man like McGilligan'. Thus, by the time he became Minister for Finance in 1948, McGilligan was very receptive to Lynch's advice – much more so than anybody in Finance with the exception of T.K. Whitaker and one or two other young officials.[3] Whitaker had taken the traditional Finance line on social spending, but was an official with a remarkably adept mind and someone not willing to simply sit still. While he continued to display conservative sympathies at this stage, he was looking to other countries to see how they pursued economic development. He studied in detail the 1942 Beveridge Report in Britain, and closely analysed the performance of the Tennessee Valley Authority during Franklin Roosevelt's New Deal of the 1930s. He was also influenced by the Monet Plan in France and the Vanoni Plan in Italy after the Second World War. Thus, Whitaker was no dogmatic or doctrinaire economist rigidly adhering to a particular theory, but, rather, one who was receptive to advice and willing to look to other jurisdictions to procure economic security and advance for the Irish state.

The first Inter-Party Government's economic policy was outlined by John A. Costello in a speech to the Institute of Bankers in Ireland. Written by Lynch and Fitzgerald, it argued that only by large-scale investment could the national wealth of the country be increased. Costello's address was unique in that it was the first time in the history of the state that the head of Government had devoted a major speech exclusively to the principles underlying his Government's economic policy. Lynch believed that Costello's Government had an unrivalled opportunity to install Keynesian principles firmly at the heart of Irish economic-policy formulation.[4] What ultimately distinguished the Inter-Party Government from Fianna Fáil, according to Lynch, was 'a belief that capital investment by the state based on the theories of John Maynard Keynes could best solve the basic Irish economic problem of providing jobs for the thousands who were unemployed or who emigrated'.[5] McGilligan outlined the Government's policy in a letter to Joseph Brennan, of the Central Bank:

> It is the intention of the Government to draw a more strict line of demar-cation than that hitherto followed between capital and non-capital services. The need for this arises from the greatly expanded programme of capital development which we have in hand. Our intentions were announced as long as last November when the Taoiseach made a pronouncement on the subject at the annual dinner of the Institute of Bankers.[6]

## KEYNESIANISM UNDER FIRE

The main opposition to this shift to Keynesianism came from Finance. Most of its senior officials, led by McElligott, vehemently opposed Costello's speech and the Government's economic stance. McGilligan, however, was an impressive proponent of a moderate Keynesianism adapted to Irish circumstances, and had actively approved of Costello's speech. The first Finance minister who could match McElligott intel-lectually and a formidable exponent of whatever viewpoint he chose to represent, McGilligan could not be brought into line by tradi-tional Finance thinking.[7] With McGilligan driving this new shift in Government thinking, bureaucratic opposition to his policy came from the Central Bank. In its 1949–50 annual report, the bank implicitly criticised the inflationary potential of Government policy and expressed serious concerns regarding the monetary consequences of the 'extensive programme of capital works on which the state is engaged'.[8]

The 1950–51 annual report contained a scathing attack by Joseph Brennan on the whole thrust of Government policy, causing political uproar. Published in October after the Costello Government had lost office – and after Marshall Aid had come to an end and the Government was faced with an acute balance-of-payments crisis – it incensed incumbent ministers, among them Lemass, and ex-ministers, particularly McGilligan and MacBride. The report expressed grave misgivings about the financial state of the nation, uncertainties that were shared by the majority of senior officials in Finance. It claimed the nation was living beyond its means, and criticised increased Government expenditure, especially on public works and subsidies. It urged fiscal measures to curb inflation, balance the budget and restrict improvident spending. It called for restraint in wage policy and restriction of bank credit.[9] The report starkly illustrated the deep conflict of opinion between those who sincerely believed that Ireland could be stirred out of economic stagnation only by massive public investment – for which adequate resources could be found solely by borrowing – and those in the Central Bank and elsewhere who believed with equal sincerity that such a policy would eventually defeat its own purpose.[10]

Reaction to the report varied. The *Irish Press* stated that the independent monetary authority had confirmed the warnings of Fianna Fáil ministers, and the paper condemned policies that were particularly associated with the preceding Government.[11] The Government published a White Paper in 1951 entitled *Trend of External Trade and Payments* – just before the Central Bank's report – in an effort to show that the Government and the bank were united in their attempts to enforce conservative economic policies.[12] Lemass, however, distanced himself from the Central Bank report. In the Dáil, he declared that the report was not a statement of the Government's views on economic policy. He pointed out that the bank had emphasised the facts of the economic situation and had alerted the public to the fact that there was a problem to be solved. He added that the Government nevertheless intended to follow a policy that was 'diametrically opposite to that which the Central Bank suggests'.[13] The Government's solution, according to Lemass, was to increase production, not cut down consumption. The Dáil and the country would have to choose between two sources of finance – borrowing or additional taxation – to pay for such increased production. To the extent that it could not borrow the money, stated Lemass, the Government thought it worthwhile to get it by increased taxation. Thus, the Central Bank report had been publicly repudiated by the Tanaiste – other than de Valera, the most senior member of the Government.

MacEntee – who later clashed bitterly with Lemass on economic policy – defended the Central Bank's independent position and its responsibility for the safeguarding of the national currency. As Minister for Finance, MacEntee wholeheartedly endorsed the views of McElligott and Brennan, and pursued a conservative approach, making a mockery of Lemass' promises in the process.

The response from the opposition was typically scathing. MacBride – an enthusiastic advocate of a large-scale investment policy – criticised Brennan for advising the Government to pursue a policy that opposed national development and that could only result in increased emigration and a lowering of living conditions.[14] Dillon and McGilligan were equally harsh. Dillon charged that Brennan's investment policy had been responsible for more than half of the external deficit of 1950, and that 'if the report was accepted, the wisest thing young people could do would be to fly the country as quickly as possible'.[15]

Beyond the Dáil, the ITUC rejected the report's proposals, claiming that they would result in higher unemployment, a cut in consumption, lower real wages, increased taxation, removal or reduction of subsidies, a restriction of the capital-investment programme and a standstill on wages. It asserted that building work being carried out under the public-works programme was of vital importance and should not be singled out as affording considerable scope for retrenchment in the economy, as the report had stated. On the whole, the ITUC declared, deflation would exacerbate the nation's problems, not solve them.[16]

A letter from McElligott to McGilligan in February 1951 illustrates the worries the conservative group had regarding the financial situation. In it, McElligott claimed that he had repeatedly drawn attention to the:

> … progressive deterioration in our public finances, the rapid growth in public expenditure and in public debt and the inadequate degree of taxation resulting in a series of budget deficits, the growth of which has been camouflaged by deductions for so-called 'capital' services, by capitalising subsidies for housing and rural electrification and charging as capital many recurrent items on various votes of a totally unproductive character such as various public works and buildings, harbour grants, airports, employment and emergency schemes, works under the Local Authorities Works Acts and others.[17]

For McElligott, removing services from the category of capital services was the only way of securing a realistic approach to what was one of the nation's more intractable problems. That year – 1950 – saw a deficit in the balance of payments for the fourth year in succession, and Finance forecast that it would continue over the following three years unless remedial actions were instituted. The minimum requirement, according to McElligott, was:

> … a considerable increase in taxation if the present scale of expansion is to be maintained. There seems no prospect of reducing the latter. Indeed

all the indications are for an increase. We have already, in my opinion, allowed the situation to drift too far without taking proper financial measures, but we cannot delay any longer except at great peril to our national economy.[18]

Brennan and McElligott had by this time become legendary for their adamant refusal to contemplate Government intervention in the market, and were staunch believers in a low-taxation, low-spending economy. A month later they were using an OEEC report on the Irish economy, which had made the point that the Irish state was not using enough resources for capital purposes but was instead putting too much money into day to day spending, to implore the Government to change its course of economic action. A memorandum for the Government prepared by McElligott on this report suggests that McGilligan had come around to the thinking of his secretary and that of the governor of the Central Bank:

> Too much money is being devoted to consumption and too little is being saved for capital purposes. The corrective measures are rightly stated to be such as would reduce the consumption (primarily of non-essentials) and expand current savings … The Minister for External Affairs does not consider that the present level of consumption reflects an unduly high standard of living. Neither does the Minister for Finance. But like the European Recovery Programme committee, he cannot evade the evidence that as a nation we are at present living beyond our current income, that is our standard of living is higher than we can afford. Of this the heavy external disinvestment for consumption purposes is living proof.[19]

Thus, McGilligan could not see how consumption could remain at its prevailing level unless there was a great increase in production – which was unlikely – if, at the same time, the Government desired to expand domestic investment by the promotion of savings. Savings, he argued, inevitably entailed abstention from consumption.

While one can only speculate as to whether McGilligan would have gone down the more conservative road if the Inter-Party Government had continued in office, the comment of Noël Browne, Minister for Health in that Government, suggests the affirmative; according to Browne, McGilligan was a traditionalist in matters of finance: 'Balance the books, pay your way, cut capital expenditure, prime the private enterprise pump and all will be well'.[20] Although McGilligan could be a formidable advocate of Keynesianism in the Irish context, and was genuinely disposed to a more expansionary financial approach, it does seem that he was willing to revert to a more cautious outlook on financial policy when, early in 1951, McElligott finally persuaded him of the merits of this approach to economic policy. Seán Cromien suggests that McGilligan – in part because of poor health and in part because he was not enamoured of MacBride's constant interference in matters that were entirely economic – was not entirely happy in Finance, and talks of him avoiding meetings with McElligott in particular, and generally keeping a very low profile.[21] This supports Browne's theory that:

> [Once] it came to the end of the financial year, and the budget approached, he [McGilligan] appeared to melt into an orgy of inaction and self-pity, skipping Cabinet meetings or arriving late. He clearly dreaded the 'loaves and fishes' job of trying to reconcile our many conflicting claims in such a multi-party Government.[22]

This was one of the kinder comments from the Cabinet-portraits section of Browne's autobiography, from which McGilligan is one of but two politicians to emerge with any credit.[23]

There were, indeed, many conflicting claims within this Government, with powerful figures like Dillon and MacBride urging their own views on McGilligan. There is little doubt that McGilligan's 'shrewd, critical, questioning approach was hampered by the tensions of the Inter-Party Government'.[24] Of the ministers in charge of the main spending departments, all had different agendas to that of McGilligan. While in essence it appears that he was not willing to follow an expansionary policy simply for the sake of it, and took the view that it had to pay its way, the demands made upon him from all sides would inevitably put a strain on the Government. Of the important spending ministries in the Government, William Norton, James Everett and T.J. Murphy of the Labour Party were Ministers of Social Welfare, Posts and Telegraphs, and Local Government, respectively; Dan Morrissey – a member of Fine Gael at this stage but formally of Labour – held Industry and Commerce; and James Dillon – not at this stage a formal member of Fine Gael – held Agriculture. As Ronan Fanning points out, none could be accounted party colleagues of McGilligan's in the fullest sense.[25] McGilligan was not as radical, and did not go as far as some of his colleagues – most particularly MacBride – would have liked in curbing the extreme caution of his department. Yet his period as minister was the first in which Finance was subjected to a questioning political master who was not afraid to challenge its orthodoxy. In the cautious atmosphere of administrative Ireland, that was an achievement in itself.

## 'WE SHALL RELY ON OUR OWN PEOPLE'

By the time Fianna Fáil regained power in June 1951, Finance had identified the three problems it considered to be at the root of the financial crisis: primarily, the Government was not covering 'even the current outlay of spending by taxation'; secondly, the inflationary effect of this was accentuated by the fact that capital expenditure by the Government was not being met to any adequate extent from current savings, and was predominantly of an unproductive character; finally, money incomes in the country were being raised 'not only irrespective of increases in output but even faster in many cases than corresponding increases in Britain, notwithstanding that taxation and living conditions are better here'.[26] The restoration of Fianna Fáil to Government and the balance-of-payments crisis that accompanied the party's return gave the mandarins in Finance the opportunity to revert to the virtuous way of economic orthodoxy. Seán MacEntee, back at Finance, was only too willing to help.

MacEntee's sympathies are aptly demonstrated by the infamous 1952 budget – introduced on 2 April, up to then the earliest in the history of the state. The budget removed subsidies on bread, butter, tea, sugar, alcohol and petrol, and raised income tax by a shilling in the pound. Price increases ranged from 28 per cent for butter to 63 per cent for sugar, and even Maurice Moynihan, official historian of the Central Bank, called it a budget of 'unusual severity'.[27] MacEntee justified the budget by pointing to the balance-of-payments situation. In the Dáil, he estimated that in the absence of corrective measures, a deficit of £50 million could be expected in 1952. He argued that:

[There] was no reason to think that the balance of payments will right itself spontaneously. The opening months of this year showed virtually no improvement ... and it seems clear that, without an improvement in personal savings and a reduction in inflationary Government finance, the deficit in the balance of payments will remain excessive.[28]

In the Seanad, he further argued that the possibility of a very severe slump could not be ruled out.[29] Yet the economy was already in recession when the budget was introduced, and budgetary policy undoubtedly worsened the position. Indeed, current expenditure rose only slightly, while current revenue increased considerably. Furthermore, the balance on the Government's current account went from a deficit of £4.7 million in 1951 to a surplus of £5.3 million in 1952, while the borrowing requirement fell from £35.5 million in 1951 to £32.2 million in 1952.

Budgetary policy had set out to reduce the current balance-of-payments deficit; in this, it succeeded and by the time of the 1953 budget, the balance-of-payments situation had been rectified. The economy was ready for a period of expansion, but the deflationists in the policy arena were not ready to change direction. There would be no somersault to an expansionary regime. MacEntee ended his budget statement with a note of what Tom Feeney calls 'almost Churchillian confidence in the Irish people':

> We shall rely on our own people to provide by their industry and thrift the capital necessary to build up the nation. We relied on them before during stringent and terrible days. They did not fail us then and they will not fail us now.[30]

Reading it more than fifty years after its delivery, it invites comparison with Brian Lenihan's concluding remarks during his October 2008 budgetary speech:

> This Budget serves no vested interest. Rather, it provides an opportunity for us all to pull together and play our part according to our means so that we can secure the gains which have been the achievement of the men and women of this country. It is, *a Cheann Comhairle*, no less than a call to patriotic action.[31]

The 1952 budget is remembered for its removal of subsidies on food. An interdepartmental committee on food subsidies set up in October 1951 concluded that:

[They were] nothing more than a general supplement to incomes provided out of general taxation; they are a costly social service in which, however, the entire community shares without regard to individual income or need. There is no real justification for continuing this policy and in principle it would be desirable to abolish the food subsidies, provided arrangements are made to ensure that the weakest sections of the community do not suffer as a consequence.[32]

The abolition of food subsidies offered numerous advantages, according to the committee. In the first instance, the difficulty of financing exchequer commitments would be greatly eased by relief from 'the enormous burden of food subsidies'. It would also restore more normal trading conditions, would foster efficiency, and help to 'remove economic rigidity'. By allowing real costs of production and distribution to be reflected by prices to the consumer, a more normal price structure and pattern of consumption would be created. The committee further argued that the abolition of food subsidies would help to counteract the inflationary effects of any wage increases granted in the public and private sectors. MacEntee subsequently used the committee's recommendations in a New Year's Eve memorandum to the Government, which he concluded by stating that:

It is essential that the budgetary problems of 1952, already grave enough on the basis of existing expenditure, should not be further aggravated by allowing new commitments to develop. The Minister is very conscious of the difficult problems which he will be called upon to face ... and he desires that every possible step should be taken to lighten his task in advance.[33]

Brennan, however, was not convinced that the Government was taking the financial position seriously enough, and contemplated retirement.

After seeing MacEntee early in March, he wrote that:

> [The minister] seemed to imply no intention on the part of the Govern-
> ment to arrest budgetary expansion of purchasing power. He said his
> budget would throw fresh light on the estimates which were meant to give
> the public a shock. When leaving I told him that I thought it would be far
> better to have someone else at the Central Bank ... Met de Valera at 5.15
> who talked about the political difficulties of handling of economic situ-
> ation and about need of avoiding unemployment. I said inflation would
> not cure unemployment but make it worse.[34]

There is no record in Brennan's personal papers of a specific response
to the budget, but there can be little doubt that he approved of most
of MacEntee's final budgetary package, as did the official principally
involved in the drafting of the budget – T.K. Whitaker – who wrote
to MacEntee, at a time when MacEntee was ill, stating:

> I could not let this opportunity pass without expressing my great admi-
> ration for the courage behind the 1952 budget and for your unsparing
> devotion to public duty when everyone would have had you executed.[35]

Tom Feeney – in his very fine biography of MacEntee (2009) – notes
that the relationship between MacEntee and his officials in Finance
was particularly strong, and makes the case that the quality of advice
proffered to him 'does not bear an overtly dissimilar philosophy to
that underpinning the much lauded *Economic Development* six years
later'.[36] Feeney also quotes Whitaker as noting that while MacEntee
intended the budget of 1952 to be severe, 'he did take on board the
draft prepared for him'.[37] The final draft, however, met with almost
unanimous disapproval from across the political spectrum, newspaper
commentary and interest groups, all of whom held MacEntee very

much responsible. *The Leader* initially saw it as 'a bombshell', and predicted that its after-effects would continue to dominate policy for the months ahead. Even more importantly, it saw Lemass as having been 'sidelined' in the economic policy debate that was being fought out within the party at the time.[38] Some months later, *The Leader* expressed its disenchantment with Government policy:

> An economy with such a history of defeat as ours needs the stimulus for enterprise of material progress, and private capital investment suffers if this is not given while measures adopted to reduce the standard of living incidentally tend to frighten away external capital.[39]

*The Statist* was also unhappy with the budget, but claimed that all was not doom and gloom, noting that there was great scope for industrial advancement, especially in the field of light secondary industries based on agriculture. Agricultural output, it asserted, was far from its potential maximum, and, furthermore, the manpower was available to run profitable industries. There was a sting in the tail for the Government, however, when *The Statist* proclaimed that:

> For British industrialists, with the capital to sink in new enterprises and the technical knowledge to run them, there would appear to be great opportunities for establishing themselves in Ireland to the mutual benefit of both countries.[40]

This was hardly a ringing endorsement of state policy in setting up indigenous industry.

## A SPANNER IN THE MACHINE

The budget enraged both the employers and the unions. Senator E.A.

McGuire – president of the FUE – complained that though nobody liked food subsidies, the point was that they should only be abolished when it was possible to do so with the least possible upset to the social and economic life of the country. While the object of the removal of food subsidies was to lift a weight from the exchequer, he argued that it should be done in such a way that the burden was passed on to the consumer at a time when consumers were earning more wages or receiving direct reliefs from the exchequer approximating to what they had lost by the removal of the subsidies. While the budget was likely to go some way to solving the financial woes of the country, he said, it was socially undesirable, and he argued that the economy could be improved by an increase in wages that raised the purchasing power of workers:

> Instead of siphoning purchasing power and drying it up, we should try to maintain and, if possible, increase purchasing power, I mean purchasing power on the part of the public. It is necessary to retain as much money as possible in circulation so as to develop and expand business, so as to create employment and keep our economy strong.[41]

MacEntee's reasoning was that curtailing domestic demand – leading to a possible reduction in prices – would boost exports. He was acting on the assumption that earnings had outstripped the cost of living; consequently, it was believed, there would be no demand for wage increases as a result of the removal of food subsidies. This most definitely was not the case. McGuire believed that the Government had failed to get its economic policy right, and had left the employers to pick up the pieces of its failed policies:

> What has happened is that the whole problem of the Budget has been thrown to the employers and into the arena of industrial relations

86

generally at a time when we are already occupied with bad trade, unemployment, rising costs and higher prices ... This is the problem that has been thrown to industry. It represents a very big spanner in the economic and industrial machine at the moment when employers are ... preoccupied with keeping the business and trade of the country going.[42]

The trade unions were equally embittered by the budget. They claimed that there had been a 10.5 per cent rise in the cost of living in the past year, from 102 to 114 on the consumer price index. With the removal of food subsidies, the total rise would be 18 per cent. The ITUC calculated that if the rise in the cost of tobacco, alcohol and other commodities were included, the figure would be 25 per cent. It argued that since there was already a definite trend towards deflationary fiscal policy, it was essential that the budget should not accentuate this trend but, on the contrary, attempt to counteract and reverse it. MacEntee's budget did, however, slash purchasing power, and followed almost religiously the policy advocated by the Central Bank in its 1951–52 report. Inevitably, the reduction in purchasing power hit the working classes hardest. The mirroring of the Central Bank report by MacEntee was noted by the opposition: James Larkin of the Labour Party declared 'it was no unfair criticism to say that if the board of the Central Bank had ... presented the budget, instead of the present Minister of Finance, there would hardly have been a comma changed'.[43] The ITUC was more vitriolic in its assessment:

A policy that results in increased unemployment is nationally suicidal and socially criminal. Yet this is precisely what will follow from the budget proposals. It may be that the Minister of Finance considers this preferable to running a deficit in our Balance of Payments and using up our external assets. If so we might remind him that all that needs to be done to wipe out the deficit entirely is to proceed to slash living standards still more savagely, it is as simple as that.[44]

The ITUC further argued that there was no reason why a Government budget deficit should have been completely ruled out, notwithstanding MacEntee's assumption that it was 'common ground' that the current budget must be balanced. The running of a budget deficit was justifiable in a deflationary situation such as existed in this period, particularly when there was a threat of more serious deflation and given that the Irish economy was susceptible to external economic movements and trends. Ultimately, it was the contention of the unions that the greater part of the additional taxation required to rectify the balance-of-payments difficulties could have been raised in other ways. They proposed, for example, a combination of tax on profits, higher rates of surtax and estate duties, and a purchase tax on luxuries. These, they maintained, would have spread the burden of taxation more equitably. Dismissing MacEntee's arguments, they insisted that:

> Deflation, far from solving our problems, will aggravate them. Experience has taught us that a policy of deflation once initiated is self perpetuating being uncontrollable by politicians and bankers, and leading to slump and depression and endless misery.[45]

Finance rejected the ITUC's arguments, stating that its case ignored the special benefits wage-earners derived from the Government's policy in regard to social services, subsidies and housing. It did acknowledge 'that even when a fall in the national standard of living is inevitable, certain classes in the community may be able to protect their own position or even better it at the expense of other classes'.[46]

Finance was extremely worried at any proposed wage increase, which it reckoned would add millions to personal expenditure, including expenditure on imports, thus making it impossible to check inflationary pressures, and which in the long run could only lead to a rise in unemployment. While this may have been true, this policy of deflation undoubtedly led to stagnation in the economy because the concern with maintaining external reserves took precedence over concern about unemployment and development.

The Central Bank maintained that the Government was on the correct financial track, and endorsed – albeit grudgingly – MacEntee's actions, and urged him to continue in the same vein.[47] This brought the bank some unwanted and trenchant criticism. *The Standard*, in an editorial entitled 'The Central Bank (mis) reports to you', accused the bank of going beyond its remit:

> It is difficult to avoid the view that the commentary has been given an emphasis which renders it largely political. Perhaps the most disquieting feature ... is its political trend. The political party has come to be the supreme unit for consideration in the state, not excluding the family, and the Central Bank has insured its own continued overlordship in the state's economy by the success it has achieved in setting off one political party against the other – divide and rule.[48]

There can be no doubt that Brennan was apolitical, and that his support of MacEntee's deflationary budgetary was based on economic considerations. Denis Gwynn, writing in the *Cork Examiner* after Brennan's retirement, offered what is surely the most perceptive interpretation: that Brennan and McElligott together 'have presided with shrewd judgement and highly trained experience over the management of Irish public finance without regard to party politics'.[49] *The Leader*, in a profile of Brennan, aptly summed up his relationship with politicians:

> He conceived it to be the special function of the civil servant to guard the professional politician against himself and his friends and, at the same time, to protect the interests of the people against both ... Brennan is one who has served his country more than usually well.[50]

In the Central Bank report, Brennan stated that the views expressed in the previous year's report had 'lost none of their appositeness and indeed have been reinforced in urgency by the heavy deficit in the balance of payments'.[51] The fact that the report for 1950–51 had criticised so outspokenly the Inter-Party Government's budgetary strategy while that for 1951–52 had supported Fianna Fáil policy does not reinforce *The Standard*'s position. No political party would ever have Brennan's unqualified support, as he distrusted them all. The report, however, came in for criticism from newspapers around the country. The *Cork Examiner* noted that the report 'seems to have been drawn up by or under the inspiration of a pessimist', and argued that the 'note of alarm in the report will not excite the Community, and not a few will hold that it has been overdone', while the *Evening Herald* commented that even though there was a mild recession in the autumn and winter of 1951, 'the industrial and commercial parts of the economy required careful nursing. Instead of which they have received very drastic treatment.'[52] In a political sense, de Valera during the 1954 general election campaign felt a need to publicly defend the aims of the 1952 budget, declaring that 'our aim … was the simple one of making ends meet – of balancing current expenditure by current revenue, as any prudent person would do in his own private affairs'.[53]

By March 1953 Brennan patently had enough of all Governments – Inter-Party or Fianna Fáil – and decided to resign. He wrote to E.C. Fussell of the Reserve Bank of New Zealand, with whom he was in regular correspondence, outlining his position:

I have been in fundamental disagreement with our Governments for some time past on matters of monetary and financial policy and as there has been no sign of improvement but rather the contrary, I felt … reluctantly to go out at the end of the financial year. My board has consistently supported my views and both the board and the Finance minister pressed me to stay on but I felt unable to retain any responsibility in the circumstances.[54]

There is little doubt that Brennan's resignation was felt deeply by his board. James Meenan, appointed in February 1949, considered Brennan's retirement 'a great loss to the public service, which, just now, has very few standards to judge policy by. But it is traditionally an ungrateful task to provide such standards'.[55] Brennan had intimated to the board and the Government in early 1953 that he wanted to step down. He told de Valera about his desire to resign. Both MacEntee and de Valera attempted to change his mind. MacEntee wrote to Brennan on the latter's meeting with de Valera telling him the prospect of resignation was 'as unwelcome to him [de Valera] as it is to me'.[56]

Brennan's resignation was a watershed. The Central Bank had become indelibly associated with him. Those on the conservative side of the economic fence saw his departure as inflicting a mortal blow against their own side. Lord Glenavy pleaded with him not to go:

> Even now I beg you to reconsider … to try to persuade you against what the members of the board consider will be a disastrous blow to the cause of monetary wisdom … The Central Bank is your creation. I do not think it would survive your going under present conditions. It may survive but it would have a long and maybe hopeless task in trying to recover from the blow of your departure. Two more years under you as Governor would make all the difference – knowing as well as you do what is involved can you not make the sacrifice of those years?[57]

Brennan, however, could not be dissuaded from his intended course of action. Once he perceived that his advice to Government was being disregarded, he felt he had no choice but to exit the public arena, and duly resigned on 31 March 1953. He was replaced by McElligott, with Owen Redmond becoming secretary of the Department of Finance.

Notwithstanding Brennan's departure, economic policy remained conservative in orientation. McElligott and MacEntee were kindred spirits. McElligott paid him the highest compliment a senior civil servant could possibly accord an active politician when he wrote to MacEntee, then recovering from illness, in 1954:

> You carry now as always my respect for your ingenuity and courage and my admiration for the single-minded manner in which you have served your country ever since I came to know you, nigh forty years ago and in different circumstances. If all Ireland's sons were so devoted to her service how different would be her recent history.[58]

## 'THE GLORIES OF PUERTO RICO'

While MacEntee may have earned the plaudits of similar-minded conservatives, Lemass took a somewhat different route. After the 1950–51 Central Bank report, he had attempted to distance himself and the Government from the bank.[59] MacEntee supported the thrust of Central Bank policy, as it was in accord with his own economic sympathies, and he managed to isolate Lemass. Prior to the budget, Lemass cautioned the Dáil about the possible dangers of pursuing deflationary policies, claiming that all developed countries were worried about the possibility of deflation:

> Almost every country in the world which, like ourselves, was concerned at the beginning of this year or towards the end of last year, at the danger of the inflationary forces, which were then active, are now no longer

worried, any more than we are, about the danger of runaway inflation. They are beginning to get much more worried about the possibility of deflation, of the downward spiral beginning to move.[60]

The dominance of MacEntee's restrictive economic policy marginalised Lemass. This affected his role with the unions, as they and his urban constituents had to face a disproportionate burden of the belt-tightening impact of the budget. During the Fianna Fáil Government of 1951–54, Lemass and MacEntee fought out a battle within Cabinet to direct Government economic policy. There was a fundamental difference in their economic philosophies: MacEntee was an ardent conservative preoccupied with the idea of sound money; Lemass was an expansionist who believed in using the power of the state to encourage demand and investment. In September 1952 they argued about the possibility of raising a national loan to be used to encourage investment in the country. In reply to Lemass' promptings on the necessity for such a loan, MacEntee asserted that his thesis lacked a sound basis: its premise was that Irish resources would support a much greater capital investment in Ireland if only the banks and other Irish institutions desisted from channelling them into British investments:

> This is a misconception, beloved of propagandists to which the Stacy May Report has given spurious respectability. It is absolutely absurd as a basis for policy. First it is not true that Irish resources, in the form of current savings, are adequate to support present levels of investment in Ireland. The fact that we have had to draw so heavily on external resources for years is proof of that.[61]

The Stacy May report to which MacEntee referred was produced by the IBEC Technical Services Corporation, which was favourable to Irish industrial policy and to the setting up of the IDA in particular, but which was also very hostile towards agricultural and especially fiscal policy.[62] It advocated that policies to attract foreign industry and build up native industry should be pursued, notwithstanding costing criticisms by Finance and the Central Bank. As to the former, the report suggested that the Government should attempt to attract US capital in particular, and drew specific attention to the approach adopted by Puerto Rico. The impact of this report on subsequent industrial policy has been criticised by some who were involved in the Department of Industry and Commerce:

> While the report put forward phrases like rifle selectivity rather than shotgun diffusiveness and held out the glories of Puerto Rico, where is Puerto Rico now? But everyone went for it. All you had to do was set up a suitable tax regime and foreign industries would come flooding in.[63]

While the expansion of native industry was stressed, in reality this aspect took a back seat to attracting foreign industry within the department. The attitude of 'get the foreigners in to give us the jobs, while protecting our own' became widespread. Stacy May, as the *Economist* pointed out in an article entitled 'The Irish troubles', noted:

> ... the astonishing degree of state control in the economy ... this is due as much to the failure of private enterprise as to ministerial ambitions. A review of the principal groups of Irish industries allows them in general a greater degree of efficiency than they usually get credit for though the yardstick of comparison with the United States hardly seems helpful.[64]

Whilst the *Economist* might have thought that Irish industry was somewhat hard done by in the Stacy May report, the Department of Finance was appalled at the whole thrust of the document:

Although the report contains some helpful comments on financial matters it also contains quite a number of statements based on misconceptions and misinterpretations. In particular, the allegation is repeated several times in the report that the Irish banking systems (and the Government) are channelling Irish savings into the British Capital market in preference to retaining them in Ireland for domestic investment. It is obviously undesirable that this fallacy should be given a spurious respectability and a renewed currency by publication of the Stacy May report.[65]

The Department of Finance demanded that the report not be published, but de Valera overruled its objections. It was a rare example of the 'Chief' allowing what amounted to hostile criticism of something indigenously Irish. He did not have to look into his heart to see that the industrial fabric of the country was not in a healthy state. De Valera famously wished that his people could live off the land, and lead happy, frugal lives – something he still seemed to believe was possible in the Ireland of the early 1950s. In 1951 he was adamant that:

Work is available at home, and in conditions infinitely better from the point of view of both health and morals … There is no doubt that many of those who emigrate could find better employment at home at as good, or better, wages – and with living conditions far better – than they find it Britain.[66]

Yet he must have realised that industrial development was a necessity if his country was to have any chance of keeping its place among the nations of the earth. That is the only possible explanation for his willingness to have the report issued. IBEC had drawn attention to the low productivity of Irish industry, and attributed this to the low level of investment in plant and machinery. The mandarins in Finance and their acerbic minister were not convinced.

This lack of conviction when it came to any type of capital spending was vividly on show in 1953 when Lemass put proposals before the Government to pursue an expanded capital programme by means of a national development fund of £5 million, to be replenished in each financial year. Finance was horrified. MacEntee's response shows him to have been in typical balanced-budget mode. As guardian of the nation's money, he was not willing to fund industrial development if it meant that his achievements of stability in prices and money values were to be sacrificed at the altar of capital investment:

> There is reason to fear that the decision of the cabinet committee in the field of expenditure have given rise to the belief that the 'lid is off' and that the economy is no longer to be seriously thought of in connection with existing services or with proposals for new ones. Such an attitude can only encourage avoidable spending. In the absence of increased tax, the additions of the current items in the £5 million, together with the interest charges for borrowing, makes it virtually certain that the 1953 budget will be in deficit. In any event, if next year's budget is to be balanced, additional taxation will be inevitable for the current items and to service the borrowing, including the carry over of temporary borrowing from this year. For all these reasons, the Minister for Finance views with the utmost anxiety the proposal to add £5 million to the borrowing programme.[67]

The Central Bank was equally upset by the proposals: 'is not the whole situation being approached from the wrong angle?' it asked. 'Government expenditure is no cure for unemployment. The lesson of past history is that the private sector of the economy is depressed by high rates and taxes.' The bank insisted that there was already evidence of inflation in the economy, and that the new proposals would add to inflationary pressures: 'the effect of new expenditure on employment is transitory but a dead weight debt and taxation are added too for a long time'.[68]

Lemass saw the national development fund operating within the protective sphere for Irish industry. As the architect of the Irish protective system set up in the 1930s, he was not yet willing to commit himself fully to completely abandoning it in favour of a policy of free trade. While he did realise the need for export-led growth, for the immediate future it would have to be within a protectionist framework. Furthermore, there was nobody in the Department of Industry and Commerce who was willing to question the very essence of protection. MacEntee, however, objected to the commitment to protection on the grounds that it prevented Irish industry from seeking export markets, and he believed that Lemass was mistaken in his view that Ireland could generate growth to absorb the unemployed. As we have seen, however, Irish industry in the early 1950s was not exactly excited by the option of aggressively pursuing export markets. Moreover, MacEntee did not put forward an alternative strategy for providing employment other than to call for low inflation, low taxation and low public spending in order to foster an enterprise culture. An injection of new money, he argued, would not be the cure for the country's economic ills. Ultimately, the Department of Finance and the Central Bank still saw agricultural exports as the mainstay of the Irish economy. What was needed, they argued, was an expansion of real production, particularly of agricultural produce that could be exported at competitive prices. The development fund, they protested, would only defeat the very purpose it was designed to serve.[69] The growth of capital expenditure, they believed, would have serious implications for the stability of the agricultural sector. Despite these strenuous objections, de Valera and the Government sided with Lemass and accepted the need for such a fund. It came into operation in December 1953, and lasted until March 1957.

The disagreement over the development fund was just one of a number of disputes over economic policy in the lifetime of the Fianna Fáil Government. In late 1952 Deputy Michael Moran urged that a 'special meeting be held in the near future for a full discussion of Government policy'.[70] A meeting of the full Fianna Fáil parliamentary party in January 1953 was consequently devoted entirely to economic policy. During the course of the discussion, de Valera explained that the policy of the Government was 'to pay its way and that any additional services called for by the people could only be paid for by taxation', and he stressed that 'increased production – principally from the land – was the remedy for most of our problems'.[71] While this was quintessential Fianna Fáil policy, it did not satisfy all within the party, and within six months a motion sponsored by twenty deputies was put before the parliamentary party; it declared:

> The party is of the opinion that in present circumstances a policy of financial austerity is no longer justified, and requests the Government to frame a progressive policy suited to the altered situation, with a view especially to putting an end to the undue restriction of credit by the banks, and making low interest loans available for farmers and house purchasers.[72]

The debate that followed this motion lasted through July, and – no decision having been reached – was postponed until after the summer recess. The topic, however, was not discussed again until January 1954. The minutes of this particular meeting are brief, simply declaring that:

> After a number of teachtaí had contributed to the debate, the acting Minister for Finance, Proinsias Mac Aogain, replied and An Taoiseach made a comprehensive statement on the party's general financial and economic policy, Deputy Carter withdrew the motion on behalf of the teachtaí who signed it.[73]

The minutes do not indicate whether Lemass was involved in backing the motion. What is clear, however, is that it echoed what he had been arguing since Fianna Fáil regained power in 1951. The development fund was a rare victory for Lemass during this period.

There is no record in the Fianna Fáil parliamentary party minutes of further discussion regarding economic policy until January 1957, by which time the second Inter-Party Government had almost run its course. The attempts by some deputies to place Government economic policy on an expansive footing did not succeed, as financial policy continued to be restrictive, notwithstanding the launching of the development fund.

## RECESSION? WHAT RECESSION?

As Lemass attempted to regain some of the policy initiative within Fianna Fáil – through the fund – he also set about rebuilding his relationship with the unions, which had taken a beating of sorts following MacEntee's 1952 budget. In July 1953 he and de Valera held a meeting with the ITUC and the Labour Party at which Lemass denied that Ireland faced a recession. He did, however, use the occasion to recommend to the Government the need for significantly increased public expenditure. His policy objectives in employment were strikingly similar to those of both the ITUC and the CIU, as was his preferred means of achieving them: massive state intervention.[74] For the next four years, Lemass – in opposition for most of them – was to retain his commitment to state-led economic intervention. Calling for a new expansionist programme that would challenge the Irish banking system to play a greater role in the economy, he offered a critique of restrictive practices and protectionism, and – most significantly – urged foreign capital to invest in Ireland. The latter was something that both the unions and the employers were calling for. Aodogan O'Rahilly, a major industrialist of the time, maintains that the aim of economic policy in the 1950s should have been to encourage all manufacturing enterprise, both Irish and foreign, and contends that Lemass-type inducements to outside investments could have been started earlier.[75] While some investment incentives had been put in place, at the domestic level Irish businessmen were still very reluctant to attempt anything new in either production or marketing terms. The files of the Department of Industry and Commerce are full of applications for more state protection and higher tariffs on imported goods up to the early 1960s.[76] Between 1952 and 1957, An Foras Tionscal received only 249 applications, of which seventy-five were approved and thirty-nine fully realised. It has been estimated that 1,700 jobs were created at an estimated cost of £460 per head.[77]

Throughout the 1950s, the IDA encountered considerable difficulty in encouraging foreign companies to locate in Ireland. Most of these companies had not considered the possibility of setting up in Ireland, while those who had were frequently discouraged by the Control of Manufactures Acts.[78] The IDA did, however, see that export-led growth in an increasingly competitive world was the only way to expand and develop the Irish economy. Lemass in opposition had, as we have seen, recognised this, but he also acknowledged the constraints that were placed on those trying to develop Irish industry; thus, he began to reformulate his ideas once back in Government in 1951. As Seán Cromien points out:

> Irish industrialists of the 1950s really were not very dynamic. They had low taxation, and at the slightest hint of competition they came back looking for a higher tariff. So there was a worry that these were not the type of people who were going to revitalise the Irish economy. That is why there was such an emphasis on bringing in investment from outside. There was quite a change of heart on the part of Lemass, who had been

the architect of protection but who had quickly come to realise that it was necessary to allow foreign industry in to participate in and own Irish industry.[79]

Yet state-led enterprise was not something the employers viewed with any great enthusiasm. It was valid that efforts be made to attract industry, but any infringement on private enterprise was to be avoided. As E.A. McGuire, writing in 1951, asserted:

> All efforts of Government should be directed to a widespread distribution of private ownership, and nothing should be done by the state that will unnecessarily penalise or discourage the ideal of large numbers of persons being engaged in small business, or individual enterprises of any kind ... it is essential that state control and interference be limited to the minimum, and that the fullest encouragement should be given to the formation of vocational groups in the community which will be urged to take an active part in the carrying on of the life of the nation.[80]

Whether any Government – be it Fianna Fáil or Inter-Party – would involve the various groups remained to be seen, yet it is noticeable that an economic realignment of sorts was being encouraged by industrialists such as McGuire. It would take some time for this idea to find its way into the mainstream of Irish political discourse, but it would have its day towards the end of the 1950s, when the Irish body politic grappled with yet another economic crisis.

# 3

# Opening Out

In January 1954 Lemass asked the IDA to review the policy of protectionism. He had by then become convinced that foreign capital could undoubtedly fill a much-required need. The evidence Lemass had gathered in his years in power suggested to him that indigenous Irish industry could not fulfil the objectives of economic and industrial growth. From as early as 1938, he was searching actively – if somewhat quietly – for new policy instruments to replace those of protectionism and restrictions on foreign investment that had characterised Fianna Fáil policy since it had first come to power in 1932. War and the difficulties it brought impeded any advance in the economic sphere, while Fianna Fáil's election defeat in 1948 was strangely interpreted by the party at large as being unrelated to the Government's policy inadequacies.[1]

Lemass had been persuaded to retain the IDA when he returned to office in 1951, and that body was adamant that the Control of Manufactures Acts would have to be amended, as they were a restriction on foreign capital entering the country.[2] Fianna Fáil's defeat in the 1954 election left Lemass in a position to do much thinking on this issue. While realising the shortcomings of protectionism, and the advantages that foreign capital offered, he was still reluctant to tamper with the Control of Manufactures Acts, as they had been the cornerstone of Fianna Fáil industrial policy since 1932. He was urged by some within the party to grasp the opportunity that foreign enterprise would give to the economy.[3] Nevertheless, if he was to amend the Control of Manufactures Acts, he would be turning Fianna Fáil industrial policy on its head.

The fundamental problem remained protectionism. As T. Desmond Williams perceptively noted:

> Fianna Fáil introduced it, Fine Gael continued it. Most people, however, including leading spokesmen in both administration and opposition, question the success of that policy ... But if protection were to be reduced many of these infant industries would collapse. Certain social consequences would then follow, involving damage to the interests of the worker and the employer. These interests in different ways cannot be ignored by the politician ... As representative of city and town they control the marginal vote which makes all the difference to the parties concerned. When a recent crisis threatened the textile industry, the immediate reaction on the part of the Minister was to impose a flat tariff of from 50 to 75 per cent on imports. This may have protected to some degree ... but it favoured the least efficient as much as the most efficient firms in the industries concerned; it also provided no genuine solution over a long term.[4]

This was the fulcrum of the problem for Lemass. As his economic philosophy on protection was developing, he had to balance how its removal would affect his urban constituents.

In any event, MacEntee's policies of economic orthodoxy were repudiated by the electorate. Fianna Fáil's share of the vote fell from

46.3 per cent in 1951 to 43.4 per cent in 1954, and it lost seven seats to fall to sixty-five. Fine Gael was the main winner in the election, gaining ten seats to bring its total to fifty, and increasing its vote by nearly 7 per cent, to 32 per cent. More worrying for Lemass was the slippage of the Fianna Fáil vote in Dublin to 39.3 per cent – down from 46.4 per cent in 1951. Fine Gael, Labour and Clann na Poblachta had all gained ground in Dublin at Fianna Fáil's expense. It would be essential for Lemass to stop this slippage from Fianna Fáil in urban areas if he was to gain a stranglehold on economic and industrial policy once Fianna Fáil returned to office. Patrick Lynch has spoken of Lemass remarking on how his interests stretched only to industrial development in Dublin, 'and as far as agricultural development in the west is concerned, the west is the wild west'.[5] In essence, what was important for Lemass was that he develop an economic programme whilst in opposition that he could put into operation once back in office, and – more importantly – that it would be a programme that would deliver results. In 1954 it was not clear if he would be able to do either.

## MISSED OPPORTUNITY

It was the second Inter-Party Government that had the first opportunity to develop a programme for economic expansion. It failed to take it. Fiscal policy continued to be restrictive under the new Minister for Finance, Gerard Sweetman – a man reported to be so conservative 'that if present at the creation of the world, he would have voted against it', and as having 'one of the keenest minds of the nineteenth century'.[6] He endorsed his department's orthodoxy, as had all his predecessors. While McGilligan had, to an extent, departed from these orthodoxies – most noticeably with the capital budget of 1950 – Sweetman took a conscious decision to revert to tradition. Yet the description of Sweetman as an arch conservative is somewhat misleading, as he would take a number of innovative steps in efforts to develop the country's industrial infrastructure. In fact, one of the second Inter-Party Government's principal aims on taking power was to increase industrial production:

> The Government believes that private enterprise should provide the country with the industrial development it requires. It recognises, however, that private enterprise may not be able alone adequately to develop the nation's resources, and that accordingly state encouragements and stimulation will be necessary. The State Capital Development Programme will be supplemental to and not in substitution for private investment, which it will be the Government's policy to safeguard as the mainspring of economic activity.[7]

Yet in the first two years of the Government's term of office, nothing was done in this regard.

After two grim economic years, Sweetman imposed in March 1956 special import levies and additional taxes. He followed these with further measures in May and July, thereby greatly widening the range of import levies and increasing the rates on items that had been subjected to an increase in March. The gravity of the economic situation is graphically illustrated by an episode early in 1956. Frederick Boland – who had moved from External Affairs in 1950 to be ambassador to Britain – commented on how he was summoned from London early in 1956 for a meeting with the Taoiseach, John A. Costello, the Tanaiste, William Norton, and the Minister for Finance, Gerard Sweetman:

> They told me that the state of the finances – the balance of payments – was bad, very bad and drastic measures would have to be taken to put it right, and that these measures would hit British exports to Ireland very severely. So I had to explain this as best I could to the British

Government, so I said 'What are they going to do?' 'We're going to put a duty of 60 per cent on all durables, machinery and so on, coming into the country.' Well I said, 'the British won't like that. Listen would you not make 60 per cent and 40 per cent preferential in favour of British and Commonwealth?' So Norton said, 'Yes we could do that, if you think it will make it any easier.' So they gave me a list of things they were going to put duty on and I set off.[8]

Boland discussed the issue with both the Chancellor of the Exchequer, Harold Macmillan, and the president of the Board of Trade, Peter Thorneycroft, and ultimately the British swallowed the unpalatable Irish duties without a 'ruffle of disagreement between the two Governments'.

The episode is indicative of the drastic state of the Irish economy, and also suggests a rather haphazard approach to trade-policy formulation. By 1956, four years of deflationary policies had taken their toll. In that year, industrial production fell by 3 per cent, agriculture by 7 per cent, GNP by 1.3 per cent, and employment by almost 2 per cent. Sweetman was insistent, however, that the measures he took were correct. He declared that 'what is at stake is our economic independence. If we should lose this the political independence we have achieved would be a mere facade. The Government are determined that both will be preserved'.[9]

Sweetman's economic policy was vigorously backed by the Department of Finance and the Central Bank, yet within the Govern-ment there was deep division. Costello himself had grave doubts as to the wisdom of such stringent economic measures, and there was serious dissatisfaction in the Labour Party. The Provisional United Trade Union Organisation (PUTUO) held two special conferences on the twin problems of unemployment and emigration, and actively criticised Labour for hurting its own supporters. In industrial policy, the Inter-

Party Government remained committed to a private-enterprise economy, but was willing to increase state involvement when private enterprises were unable to pursue various projects that might be viable:

> It has been accepted policy in this country that the state should not engage in industrial and commercial activity unless it was clear that private industries were either unwilling or did not possess the necessary resources to carry out a particular project. It might in fact be said that it was only as a last resort that the state entered any field of industry or commercial activity.[10]

## If Muhammad won't go to the mountain …

The Government did, however, set out to attract foreign investment to Ireland. If Irish enterprise was unwilling to take the risk of establishing native industries, William Norton – leader of the Labour Party and the new Minister for Industry and Commerce – was intent on the Government attracting foreign enterprise. Initially, the Government accepted the proposal of an Anglo-American oil combine to construct an oil refinery in Cork harbour. The deal – worth £12 million – was the largest sum invested in a single private enterprise in Ireland.[11] Following on from this success, Norton embarked on a European tour in spring 1955 in an attempt to persuade foreign investors to come to Ireland. Accompanied by the chairman of the IDA, J.P. Beddy, and Luke Duffy, a member of the IDA board, Norton extolled the virtues of Ireland for those who might be willing to invest foreign capital. In Sweden, for example, he claimed that Ireland was singularly free from trade disputes, and – curiously for the leader of the Labour Party – that 'our wage levels are very much lower than yours'. Beddy, for his part, reiterated that industry in the country was protected, but added that it would not have been feasible to set up native industries without such a policy. His primary argument was that indigenous firms would have had to face the competition of long-established manufacturers in Britain whose names and products would be very well known in Ireland. Without protection, it would not be possible to establish such new industries and face this competition. Beddy put particular stress on Ireland's advantages:

> We maintain absolute parity with sterling and there is no difficulty whatever in our arrangements with Britain. There is no credit restriction exercised by the Government through banks in Ireland in relation to industry … almost all industrial goods produced in Ireland enjoy the right to free entry to Great Britain … The Irish Government favours private enterprise and does not itself engage in industry unless in special circumstances.[12]

Ireland's close links with Britain were being put forward as one of the main reasons why foreign capital should invest in Ireland. Yet it should be recalled that Finance was following the British line in fiscal policy to the obvious detriment of any Irish industrial development, in that there was chronic under-investment in the Irish economy by the time the second Inter-Party Government assumed office.

Norton travelled to the US early in 1956, again with Beddy, in his continued attempts to attract foreign industry. He explained his motives for such visits:

> The steps now being taken to attract external investment to Ireland should not in any way deter our existing manufacturers from proceeding as rapidly as possible with their own plans for development. The whole purpose of stimulating external investment in Irish industry is to promote the establishment of new types of industries and to secure an

expansion that would not otherwise take place. Irish manufacturers, who are catering efficiently for the needs of the market, may, therefore, rest assured that their interests will be fully guarded.[13]

The problem with this was that it was bound to create quite an element of doubt amongst those industries catering only for the home market and not overly interested in finding new markets. These industries were not looking to share in the harvest of expansion, and were obviously worried as to how an influx of foreign capital would affect them. The more vibrant industrialists, however, had no doubt but that foreign investment was good for industry, and would help it expand and develop; as Aodogan O'Rahilly commented:

> As a country we needed more dynamism in an economic sense, whether we got it from at home or abroad was immaterial, we needed it or else we were not going to advance much further industrially or in any other sense either.[14]

Fianna Fáil opposed Norton's initiatives. It is tempting to see this as merely opposition for opposition's sake, particularly in the case of Lemass, who undoubtedly *was* in favour of bringing foreign capital into the country. In late 1955 and early 1956 Lemass was actively advocating large-scale schemes of expansion, but continued to insist that the Control of Manufactures Acts should not be repealed, though he admitted that they should be reviewed. De Valera and MacEntee, by contrast, still believed in the pre-eminence of agriculture over industry. While they realised that the Irish economy needed a vibrant industrial arm, there can be little doubt that they considered the future well-being of the Irish economy residing in its having a strong agricultural-export base. As the Irish economy was about to enter its worst depression since independence, there was as yet no likelihood that indigenous industry would lead the country out of its black trough and into a bright new dawn.

At this stage, Finance was still insisting that Ireland's recession was 'solely a monetary crisis'.[15] This was not the case. The parliamentary secretary to the Government, John O'Donovan, wrote to Sweetman on the perils of persisting with Finance orthodoxy:

> It is almost past understanding how arguments which have been proven wrong time and time again are still produced for the purpose of conditioning the members of Governments of this country to agree with courses which are contrary to their own firm convictions and their political advantage, and which experience has shown to be contrary to the good of the community in Ireland.[16]

In October 1956, Costello, under pressure from Norton and from some within his own party – including stalwarts such as McGilligan – launched a plan for national development covering every aspect of the Irish economy. For McGilligan, such a plan was essential, as without it the next election would be lost to Fianna Fáil, and the fortunes of the state depended on 'continuing control of Government by the present Inter-Party group'. He explained:

> It would be calamitous to allow Fianna Fáil again to be in control. They have been rejected by the people three times. In 1948 the electors did not so much vote *for* any specific party Government – there was no pre-election cohesion between those who opposed Fianna Fáil – but they did vote *against* Fianna Fáil. In 1951 the people still showed their antagonism to Fianna Fáil, and in 1954 there was as significant a landslide as is possible under proportional representation. This was accomplished against heavy odds – the *Irish Press*, *The Irish Times*, and many provincial papers, an industrialist section corrupted by tariff and

other favours, the boosting by Radio Éireann (which still continues in subtle ways) and the favouring influence upon their employees and again with some producers of Boards such as the Insurance Corporation, the Sugar Company, Bord na Mona, all built up in the likeness of Fianna Fáil clubs and left so to this day. There is, however, a danger that Fianna Fáil may come back not because the public really desire them but because those now in power have failed to come up to popular expectation.[17]

This was the context in which Costello announced a series of grants, tax reliefs and other incentives to industry and agriculture that were to become the hallmark of the new system of foreign-led industrialisation under free trade. The spur for this development was a paper entitled 'Capital formation, saving and economic progress' delivered by T.K. Whitaker to the Statistical and Social Inquiry Society of Ireland. Whitaker argued that national product in Ireland had to be enlarged and a greater proportion of it devoted to capital formation in order to avoid losing ground in incomes to other countries, particularly Britain. Failure to keep pace with Britain was a significant stimulus to emigration, which had blighted Ireland throughout the 1950s.[18] Furthermore, he argued that saving and production should be encouraged, and excessive consumption discouraged. This would stimulate capital development of a productive nature. He maintained that there should be a liberal attitude towards profits so as to encourage industrial expansion, arguing that assistance to agriculture should be directed specifically towards the development of productive capacity.

Whitaker voiced the belief that 'something had to be done or the achievement of national independence would prove to have been a futility'.[19] In this, we have an implicit assertion that by the mid-1950s conservative economic approaches undertaken since the foundation of the state were outmoded for a new generation.

On the industrial front, Costello's plan included a special incentive to encourage exports by a remission of 50 per cent on profits derived from increased exports – to be used for expansion of production – even more generous Government grants for certain types of new factories, tax exemptions for much of the profit of the mining industry, the immediate appointment of a Capital Investment Advisory Committee to advise on the best methods of financing new enterprises, and the establishment of an Industrial Advisory Council composed of industrialists and trade unionists to secure informed opinion on matters of welfare and development that did not come within the scope of existing bodies such as the Factories Act Advisory Council.[20] Costello also announced that the IDA had begun efforts to interest continental and US industrialists in the establishment of factories for the manufacture of goods outside the existing range of Governmental activity.

## 'A Challenge to our Manhood'

Despite these measures, Fine Gael lost ten seats in the March 1957 general election. The economy was the main issue in what was generally a lacklustre campaign, with Fianna Fáil claiming that the Inter-Party Government had failed to deal with the deteriorating economic situation, was responsible for the high level of unemployment, had no policy for recovery and, indeed, could not have had because its membership was divided. This division was not only at an inter-party level; Fine Gael itself was deeply divided over Sweetman's cutbacks, particularly his intention to eliminate food subsidies in the upcoming budget. Four members of the party's elite threatened to resign: the Minister for External Affairs, Liam Cosgrave, the Attorney General, Patrick McGilligan, the parliamentary secretary to the Government, John O'Donovan, and the Minister for Health, Tom O'Higgins.[21] Yet Sweetman himself fought a vigorous campaign. He claimed that Fine Gael had a progressive policy that 'built on the national solvency ensured by my tenure as Minister for Finance', and which would 'create an expanding economy with greater production and exports, particularly in agriculture and will enable us to have a higher standard of living'.[22]

Sweetman, however, did not have the opportunity to implement another budget, as people voted against the Government and the bleak economic situation. The electorate, weary of the harsh economic climate, chose Fianna Fáil as the party most likely to ease economic severity. Fianna Fáil, however, was equally divided. Lemass kept a low profile during the campaign, as the Fianna Fáil platform offered nothing in the way of a growth-oriented programme. If anything, it preached the old traditional patterns of economic organisation, particularly in agriculture, and offered no alternative policies. In reality, it mirrored a speech de Valera had given in Cork the previous July:

> Our past successes should be an inspiration to us. The whole doctrine of faith in ourselves, self reliance, self discipline and self support is today as energising nationally and as fruitful as ever in the past. The present difficulties should be regarded as no more than as a challenge to our manhood, our national character and determination, to our ability to organise, to work and to make good.[23]

MacEntee was the main spokesman for Fianna Fáil during the 1957 election. In typically caustic fashion, he accused Costello of having been an Irish Nazi who had 'studied Hitler's *Mein Kampf* and sat at the feet of the late Dr Goebbels'.[24] This bizarre attack was in response to an assertion by Costello that, with the exception of 1946, this was the first occasion in peacetime in over twenty-five years that Ireland's international-payments account was about to be brought into balance. This, according to MacEntee, was a shameful lie, as Fianna Fáil had a credit balance of over £2 million on the external account in 1938 despite the fact that it had been obliged to pay the British Government £10 million in liquidation claims with which the Irish Government had been saddled 'under secret arrangements which Costello's associates signed in 1923'.[25] MacEntee launched similar verbal assaults on Fine Gael throughout the campaign, but what is most interesting is that, to some extent, he sympathised with Sweetman's performance as minister. Showing his true conservative colours, MacEntee talked of supporting Sweetman:

> In the bitter struggle which I suspected he was waging with many of his colleagues to get them to accept the principle of a balanced budget. But I made it clear that the present burden of taxation was oppressive and that expenditure should be reduced so that the burden might be lightened. Such support that I gave Gerard Sweetman obviously annoyed his leader.[26]

This, claimed MacEntee, was in stark contrast to the position Costello had taken to the 1952 budget:

> Despite having reservations and with many doubts as to the wisdom of the measures which the Government was taking to deal with the grave situation which it had created, Fianna Fáil had given it such support as thought justified in doing in the nation's interest.[27]

While MacEntee could claim, with some justification, that he had the nation's interest at heart in his pursuit of a conservative economic policy, and would support such policies no matter who was in Government, there were others in Fianna Fáil who had a different economic agenda. A number of people had left the party in disgust after the 1952 budget, while others transferred their allegiance to Lemass' constituency of Dublin South-Central in the belief that he represented the authentic voice of Fianna Fáil and would eventually win this policy battle.[28]

Lemass himself was strangely subdued during the 1957 campaign. It may be that he felt the IDA was becoming more powerful, and that, even in Government, his influence would be curtailed at Industry and Commerce. Furthermore, he had clearly lost the economic-policy battle with MacEntee during the previous Fianna Fáil administration, and could well have feared that if MacEntee was reappointed Minister for Finance, the same would happen. MacEntee was highly critical of Lemass' 'Clery's 100,000 jobs speech' of 1 October 1955, and of a preceding memorandum on financial policy that Lemass had prepared for Fianna Fáil's central committee in mid-April 1955, which advocated greater Government intervention in the economy, and called for full employment.[29] In fact, Lemass originally submitted his Clery's speech in the form of a memorandum to the party, with a meeting of the party committee deciding that:

> Mr Lemass could speak in public in general terms on proposals set out in his memorandum but that reference to the Central Bank should be omitted; it could be pointed out, however, that our resources are ample to finance agriculture and industrial development.[30]

It would appear that the party was anxious not to get involved – or let Lemass become embroiled – in a public squabble with the Central Bank, as had happened in 1951. The Clery's speech was nothing less than a call for full employment. In part, it was based on the 1954 Italian Vanoni plan for post-war reconstruction, and was a public reiteration of Lemass' view that the state would be the primary driver in the quest to end Ireland's unemployment problem.

For its part, Fine Gael was scathing of Lemass' proposals, and noted that if a Fianna Fáil Government was returned to power at the next election, the taxpayer would be faced with additional tax burdens of up to £20 million:

115

Deputy Lemass is so enthusiastic about his proposal that he has stated that, if necessary, the budgetary surplus should be achieved regardless of the taxation measures found to be necessary. Private industry, as well as the ordinary taxpayer, has good reason to be dismayed by the deputy's proposal. It is undeniable that compulsory savings of this order, devoted to the state capital programme, would completely dry up the already inadequate pool of savings available for the financing of private industrial investment. Deputy Lemass has elsewhere shed some crocodile tears over the inadequacy of the capital funds available to industry. His present proposal would make sure that no capital funds at all would be available to industry.[31]

While Lemass was given a somewhat guarded go-ahead by the party for his speech, MacEntee took something of a back seat. In late 1954 Fianna Fáil had asked members of its central committee to submit memoranda on areas of major policy. While Lemass quite naturally focused on industry, it was Frank Aiken rather than MacEntee (who was recovering from illness) who undertook the task of attempting to shape Fianna Fáil's financial policy in opposition.[32] Nevertheless, by the time of the 1957 election, MacEntee had re-emerged as the main Fianna Fáil financial spokesman, and could reasonably have expected reappointment to Finance in any Fianna Fáil Government. This was not to happen.

## 'NO EASY EXPEDIENTS'

De Valera's decision not to reappoint MacEntee to Finance upon Fianna Fáil's return to power in 1957 undoubtedly left MacEntee disappointed. His diary entry for 8 March records that de Valera 'had already seen Ryan and Aiken before me. He was apparently committed to both.'[33] Finance actually went to Dr James Ryan, who had performed with distinction in Health after Noël Browne's problems with the 'mother and child scheme'. Aiken was appointed to External Affairs. Lemass returned to Industry and Commerce, with MacEntee being effectively demoted to Health. The 'Chief' – as de Valera was called in the Fianna Fáil parliamentary-party minutes of this period – had spoken.[34]

MacEntee was discredited by previous economic failure. Although his policies were in tune with de Valera's own beliefs, the electoral fortunes of Fianna Fáil were paramount. De Valera – astute politician that he was – had undoubtedly realised that Fianna Fáil had gone to the country in 1948 and 1954 with conservative economic records and had been defeated on both occasions. The economic crisis facing the Fianna Fáil Government in 1957 was so severe that there was every likelihood that a conservative approach would only exacerbate the problem, and, more importantly, return the party to opposition at the next election. De Valera thus decided that change was neces-sary – a change brought about by electoral fortunes, not a deliberate break with traditional Fianna Fáil economic policies. As Whitaker has speculated:

> First of all one must see that Dev recognised, through the eminence he gave to Lemass, the deficiency in his own viewpoint. De Valera was sup-plementing his idealistic view of things by a practical go-getter person in Lemass. Dev was still Taoiseach when they decided to publish this piece of official advice ... One is left thinking that it was his political instinct – it was a way out, a brilliant way out from being imprisoned in the old policies. Dev presumably had the perception to see that change was necessary.[35]

By the time Fianna Fáil won the 1957 election, de Valera was remote from much of the debate within the party. Yet he did recognise that the policies of economic retrenchment had resulted in defeat for his party twice in the previous nine years.

With Lemass at last having overcome the financial orthodoxy of MacEntee, what could Irish industry look forward to as the ideology of free trade began to take a foothold within the Irish civil service and body politic? Restored to Industry and Commerce, he immediately accelerated the process of opening up the state to new foreign investment, though without as yet removing tariff barriers. The economic instability that plagued Irish policy-makers throughout the 1950s led to serious unemployment and mass emigration. The relative success of the British economy at this time, and its labour shortage, provided a strong pull for emigration. Nearly 60,000 people left the country in 1957 alone, a quarter of a century after de Valera had first taken Fianna Fáil into Government.[36] Wage rates in Britain moved far ahead of those in Ireland, as did overall standards of living, facilitated by the developing welfare state. Historically, Ireland had compared its living standards with those of Britain, and the gap between them increased during the decade. Ireland's historic association with Britain caused mental as well as practical problems. Todd Andrews, for example, argued that a psychological sense of inferiority pervaded the country, and the farming community in particular. This was an important observation by one of the prime public servants and industrialists of the era. For Andrews and the policy-making community in general:

> The keynote of the national economy is agriculture and until we have fully utilised our national resources in agriculture nothing further in the way of substantial development is likely … I feel if the farmers want help they should get it if for nothing else than to show the goodwill of the country towards them and disabuse them of distrust.[37]

Policy-makers of all political hues and from across the civil service were at one with Andrews' description of the importance of agriculture to the economy. Yet one of the most significant features of the 1950s was the virtual collapse of the small-farming sector, leading to the demise of agriculture as a focus for employment or growth.

It is possible to identify a significant difference between Ireland and Europe up to the late 1950s. For the most part, Ireland restored its protectionist framework for industry after the war, while import substitution remained the policy goal for most political parties and successive Governments. Though industrial protection had brought limited success, its continuation contrasted sharply with policy in most other European states.[38] Lemass had never shared de Valera's dream of a small-farmers' utopia, and recognised that the sustenance of de Valera's pastoral society was heavily dependent on Ireland's privileged access to the British market, an objective which had been realised in the 1948 trade agreement and maintained subsequently. In comparison with its continental competitors, such as Denmark and the Netherlands, Irish farming was relatively high cost and inefficient. Its position in the British market was secured not through competitive advantage but was due to political negotiations between the two states and agreements that excluded continental competition. There was a well-founded fear in Ireland that any opening of British markets to European competition would lead to the weakening of the Irish advantage. Thus, the newly returned Fianna Fáil Government knew that it had to develop a strong industrial policy that could stand side by side with agriculture in developing the Irish economy.

By 1957 Fianna Fáil realised that it had to travel along a different economic path than it had previously taken while in Government. Lemass had hinted at this at a parliamentary party meeting in January 1957, where he made a statement dealing 'with certain short term proposals involving Government expenditure and retrenchment, which he felt were required to deal with the grave immediate problem of unemployment'.[39] In his first budget speech, Ryan unequivocally spelled out the economic objectives of the Government:

> It is clear that we have come to a critical stage in our economic affairs. The policies of the past though successful in some directions, have not so far given us what we want. Further progress on a worthwhile scale calls for a comprehensive review of our economic policy. The direction and rate of our future advance will depend on the decisions we take now. There are no easy expedients by which our difficulties can be solved.[40]

This speech fundamentally supported Whitaker's stance, and reassured the country's premier civil servant that the Government was committed to export-led growth. Lemass recognised that existing investment and output were not sufficient to maintain the level of demand he believed necessary to obtain full employment, and he became a wholehearted supporter of Whitaker's export-led ideas. Whitaker himself had instructed his officials that it was 'desirable that this Department should do some independent thinking and not wait simply for Industry and Commerce or the IDA to produce the ideas'.[41]

Thus, it was in the atmosphere of a new Government and a more active and interventionist Department of Finance that *Economic Development* was born. Whitaker has stated that it was Gerard Sweetman's tenure of office as Finance minister that did much to pave the way for *Economic Development*. Not only did Sweetman appoint Whitaker as secretary at the Department of Finance in breach of seniority principles, he also established the Capital Investment Advisory Committee and initiated the Irish application for membership of the International Monetary Fund and the World Bank. These innovations were intimately linked to the immediate origins of *Economic Development*. Sweetman also introduced tax reliefs for exports (in 1956) that emphasised the need for a substantial increase in volume and efficiency of national production.[42]

Whitaker advanced a three-pronged strategy: more planning, fewer tariffs and greater emphasis on productive investment. Lemass did not hesitate in joining him.

## 'THAT LEAST DISTINGUISHED DECADE'

Lemass and Whitaker were not alone. At a wider level, the mid-1950s saw developments that went some way towards solving the psychological problems Todd Andrews talked of in 1957:

> Psychologically speaking we have not fully severed the British connection and our economic and administrative reflexes were too much conditioned by our past historical and present economic association with Britain. We are inclined to rely too much on the British framework of reference for our ideas on policy. If we have the confidence in ourselves which we are entitled to have, and if we have a determination to act as well as to think, I believe it possible to achieve this wish ... A psychological blight seems to have descended on the country and the young people in particular seem to have lost confidence in our future.[43]

*Studies*, the influential Jesuit journal, devoted an entire issue in spring 1955 to 'Ireland Tomorrow'. The editor had made 'no attempt to tailor the essays to a rigid, preconceived pattern', and found it 'all the more remarkable, therefore, to discover the common undertone running through these pages: the plea for a more creative outlook'.[44] This was just one example of the discontent running through the various political journals. *The Leader* – under the editorship of UCD historian, T.D. Williams, and UCD economist, Patrick Lynch – *Hibernia* and *The Bell* – edited by the radical socialist, Peadar O'Donnell, from 1946 to its demise in 1954 – produced provocative and well-informed political and economic comment.[45]

At an official level, the degree of worry amongst public servants as to the welfare of the country was crystallised in the 1953 launch of the journal *Administration*, 'designed to give civil servants an outlet to express opinions on professional matters and eventually to form an institute of public administration'.[46] The previous year saw a number of younger officers in the civil service set up the Association of Higher Civil Servants, and it was through *Administration* that they 'could vent some spleen, as it were'.[47] The establishment of *Administration* was, as Garret FitzGerald points out:

> ... a remarkably brave venture in those dark days of the early 1950s, when uniquely amongst industrialised countries in the dynamic post war years, the Irish state, just three decades old, was sunk in the economic stagnation and intellectual torpor of that least distinguished decade of its history.[48]

Early in 1952 an inspired group of civil servants in the Department of Local Government at the Custom House, together with colleagues from some other departments, established an informal committee to organise meetings on issues of public policy. Headed originally by Patrick Doolan – collector of Customs and Excise – its first meetings drew an inordinate response, with Tom Barrington recalling that on some occasions 'up to five hundred people would turn up'. Doolan 'was fed up with the way the Association of Higher Civil Servants was bellyaching about pay rather than discussing policy-making initiatives. That was the driving force for him.'[49] The committee – which included Barrington, Brendan Herlihy and Des Roche – managed to persuade the association to finance the discussion group, and within six months of its first meeting, *Administration* appeared, publishing in journal-form papers that were read to the discussion group, together with other commissioned papers. *Administration* quickly saw its readership rise to 2,000. It received support not only from within the civil service but also from the local-Government service. Furthermore, academics – foremost among them Basil Chubb and Patrick Lynch – involved themselves from the start. Whitaker also used the journal as an outlet for his thoughts. The importance of the foundation of *Administration* was that it illustrated in a most fundamental way the restless discontent in parts of the civil service. This concern was reflected in pockets of influence throughout the country.

By the mid-1950s it seemed that if the civil service did not attempt to reform from within, it would become simply a bureaucratic monster going through the motions of Government, offering old solutions to new problems, and extremely reluctant to try anything even remotely tainted with novelty. There were many within the policy community who believed that the civil service needed to be drastically reformed. Todd Andrews in 1957 wanted to:

> ... divide local Government into eight or ten regions, run them by a small number of elected representatives plus a manager endowed with the same powers as at the present. I would remove from local adminis-tration some of the functions at present exercised by county councils ... I think we should change our ideas to permit the civil service to take a more active part in the affairs of the country than they are permitted to do at present ... Civil servants should be able to comment outside their department remit and should be permitted to serve on local councils.[50]

While these may have been radical proposals – later, Andrews ceased advocating such developments when he realised that the managers did not want an expansion in their role – the more significant point is that there was a body of opinion in public life that maintained that a stagnant civil service was serving the country poorly, and that change was urgently needed.[51]

The Catholic church also entered the debate on the country's economic affairs. Ruth Barrington maintains that the liberalisation of the Irish intellectual climate of the 1960s was seen in the fact that 'bishops asked for increased state intervention in the affairs of the community, not less'.[52] While this is broadly true, some individuals within the hierarchy were advocating such a policy years earlier, though they couched their arguments carefully. William Philbin, bishop of Clonfert, was one of the first into the fray when he delivered in August 1957 a lecture entitled 'Patriotism'. He argued that a highly developed national culture would give the world something to remember the Irish by other than 'our name carved on a tree':

> For such ends we may not neglect economic realities. If our numbers diminish much further we shall not have the strength or the interest left to develop the spiritual and cultural resources of our people and to offer the world evidence of an individuality justifying our struggle for independence.[53]

Equating the struggle to gain a healthy, expanding economy with the national struggle for independence was a notion subscribed to by Whitaker when he argued throughout 1957 and 1958 that without a progressive economy, political independence would be 'a mere facade'.[54] Philbin argued that national prosperity was vital if the country was to keep abreast of the rapidly increasing living standards in other countries. This, evidently, was the only way of:

> ... preventing our country of being drained of its most ambitious citizens. We cannot progress along these lines without the all out effort of all our people. There is need for the whole of our patriotic energy ... Surely a moral is easily drawn from the fact that our economic backwardness is being used more and more as an argument against the re-integration

of our country. A healthy economy is a presupposition of any political progress. To exist at all is more important than the political manner of one's existence ... Our patriotism needs to be realist, not escapist, practical not spectacular and romantic. If only a remnant of the Irish people is left at home, living on a run-down economy, it will matter little how we are governed, we shall be a negligible factor in human affairs.[55]

In this, one can see implicit criticism of de Valera's vision of the pastoral society. While this vision might have been entirely laudable, in economic terms it had failed, and there were those within the church willing to say so. A country not succeeding on the economic front had nowhere to go. Yet some within the clergy were enthusiastic followers of de Valera's Ireland. Father Terence Cosgrove, parish priest of Kilnamona, County Clare, for instance, stressed that:

We in the Republic have not fared too badly at all, taking due account of all the circumstances ... May Ireland be eminently successfully in her task, may she complete her work at home and may she be as she was in the Golden Age of history, an exemplar and a light to nations.[56]

Here, one can see illustrated two positions within the clergy on Ireland's economic problems. In essence, Catholic comment on the economic issues came down to a matter of individual choice. It is interesting that *Christus Rex* – which styled itself as a Catholic journal of sociology – opened its pages for critical comment on the economy to writers of various ilks; one did not necessarily have to be a member of the clergy to contribute. Thus, Whitaker's *Economic Development* came under much scrutiny. An anonymous contributor to the July 1959 edition wrote that while *Economic Development* gave a complete picture of national economic policy for the immediate future, and the diagnosis added up to a 'partial confession of failure, there may be some misgivings about the future. It does not seem likely that there will be any lessening of the Government grip on our economic life'.[57]

Government interference in the economy and in the life of the citizen was something that had preoccupied the clergy for some considerable time. In April 1952 William Conway – then professor of moral theology at Maynooth, and later to become cardinal and archbishop of Armagh – offered one of the more balanced statements of the time when he examined the reasons for the rapid growth of state power. While he demonstrated that this growth was a response to genuine needs, and was accepted by Catholic social theorists, he argued that:

> The growth and power of the state has become so sudden and so rapid that men of almost all shades of political and economic thought are beginning to wonder whether we have not loosed something which is getting out of control.[58]

Conway did acknowledge that the state 'had not merely the right but the duty to interfere in economic affairs when the common good demanded it', and declared that it was 'no part of the church's teachings … that state intervention is wrong in principle and therefore to be opposed in all cases'.[59] He insisted, however, that the church was right to be watchful and to oppose the Government when it felt that it had no other option. In essence, some in the Catholic church were prepared to comment individually on the economic situation and the role of Government, but, on the whole, the church formulated no concrete position on economic policy. This was the case with *Economic Development*: Whitaker deliberately quoted Philbin so as to lessen the possibility of its being damned with pejorative 'socialist' connotations of 'planning' – hence Whitaker's preference for 'economic programme' as opposed to 'economic plan'.[60]

*Christus Rex* also saw an important contribution on economic affairs from Labhras Ó Nuailláin, an economist from University College, Galway, who in April 1958 maintained that:

> The prospect of a substantial expansion of industry based on Irish private enterprise alone does not appear to be very bright for some time to come. In many parts of the country, the people with capital have no enterprise; the people of enterprise, in many cases have no capital, and a good many enterprising young people have left the country altogether. The introduction of foreign capital and foreign technicians is not a thing to be deplored, but to be welcomed, especially when they bring new skills and industries with a large male labour content.[61]

Bringing in foreign expertise was one of the fundamental tenets of the new economic strategy Whitaker was planning for the Irish economy. Moreover, for Ó Nuailláin, 'a long term comprehensive programme of planned development is imperative if we are ever to remedy the basic structural defects in our economy'. When these lines were written, Whitaker and his team were in the throes of completing *Economic Development*, and it does seem remarkable that within public commentary there was, to an extent, a convergence of minds on the solutions required to boost the Irish economy. Ó Nuailláin argued that the conventional notions and lines of approach adopted in the formulation of national economic policy since the foundation of the state would 'have to be cast aside before this state will be firmly on the road to rehabilitation'. He continued:

> One of such notions that must be abandoned is that the sole repository of wisdom lies in the headquarters of state departments. There are sections of the community, in the Professions, in the Trade Unions, in Industry and Commerce, in Agriculture and in the Universities, able and willing to give objective and competent advice and views on the essentials in

a programme of national rehabilitation. The Government that seeks out the advice and support of such people and learns to canalise that reservoir of national pride and self respect so far untapped, will be the Government, no matter its composition, that will set this nation on the road to national prosperity.[62]

While there is no evidence that anyone engaged in national policy-making was influenced by this article and the argument contained within it, it is nevertheless interesting to note that Ó Nuailláin's hypothesis calling for development of corporatist-style relationships between the economic interest groups and Government was, to a degree, taken on board in the years after the publication of *Economic Development*, when the various professional bodies were consulted during the making of national policy as the Government put in place a conscious political structure that integrated the organised socio-economic producing groups through a system of representation and co-operative mutual interaction.[63]

The role of the civil service was receiving more attention by the late 1950s. Todd Andrews in 1957 maintained that it would be better for the country if those individuals who entered the civil service out of monetary and job-security considerations went into industry instead, and argued that they would if national industrial development proceeded at a rapid rate.[64] A number of years earlier, a parliamentary party meeting of Fianna Fáil adopted a motion calling on the Minister for Finance 'to take immediate steps to effect a gradual reduction in the number of civil servants so as to bring them into line with what the country can afford'. MacEntee, as minister, responded by explaining that 'a special effort was being made to effect such a reduction'.[65] In essence, the argument about the civil service mirrored the debate about interacting with the economic-interest groups in that both were part of a re-examination of the way Government conducted its business in the period.

## A RADICAL REAPPRAISAL

The appointment of Whitaker as secretary at the Department of Finance in 1956 is normally considered to have been a radical departure for the civil service in the sense that traditional hierarchical expectations were ignored. More fundamentally, Whitaker came to the post with different expectations and an intellectual development distinct from many of his predecessors or colleagues. His challenge would be to take his senior colleagues with him in moving the Irish economy out of the desert and into the promised land. He realised that in addition to the economic element, this land would have social and political implications. It was within this context, and under Whitaker's impetus, that the Irish Government looked to Europe for a way out of the economic morass that the country found itself in.

*Economic Development* emerged from a crisis of national self-confidence provoked by the economic difficulties of 1956–57. Garret FitzGerald, for one, commented:

> It seems scarcely probable that the authors whether politicians, civil servants, businessmen or economists would have felt able, or, in other cases, have been given the opportunity to put forward such radical reappraisals of traditional national policies, had this psychological crisis not taken place.[66]

This reinforces Whitaker's view that the years 1955–56 had plumbed the depths of hopelessness, with the balance-of-payments crises overcome only at the cost of stagnation, high unemployment and emigration. In such a situation, a broad consensus of interested parties was needed in order to facilitate a new departure in economic policy that would transcend party politics. If the White Paper entitled *The Programme for Economic Expansion* had been launched without reference to the document on which it was based – *Economic Development*

– there was a danger that it might not have received the bipartisan treatment that was necessary if it was to provide an agreed basis for the development of the Irish economy.[67]

*Economic Development* – completed in May 1958 – became the basis for the White Paper published on 11 November 1958. The fact that *Economic Development* was published at all and a full eleven days after the *Programme for Economic Expansion* is significant: *Economic Development* was published in order to stimulate national interest and make available to the general public the blueprint for a form of national recovery – something a White Paper could simply not do. In essence, it was a national policy programme prepared by the head of the civil service. Its most critical feature was the proposal to sharply accelerate the shift from protectionism towards free trade, and from discouragement to encouragement of foreign investment in Ireland. This involved a dramatic reversal of the rhetoric and, to a large extent, the practice of all policy, but especially Fianna Fáil policy, since 1932.[68] Whitaker argued that the Government should encourage industries that would be competitive in world markets and provide a continuing source of employment at home:

> We can no longer rely for industrial development on extensive tariff and quota protection. Foreign industrialists will bring skills and techniques we need, and continuous and widespread publicity abroad is essential to attract them. If foreign industrial investment does not rapidly increase, a more radical removal of statutory restrictions on such investments should take place.[69]

The main theme of both documents, as was pointed out at the time, was that an increase in investment and an expansion in demand – coming from agriculture – would set in motion a general expansion in the national product.[70] In conjunction with this was the aim of attracting foreign industry. Whitaker outlined two ways of attracting foreign corporations: removing restrictions and giving incentives for foreign firms to establish bases in Ireland. The Control of Manufactures Acts were amended, and a series of proposals intended to attract outside investors to Ireland were recommended. He proposed that the IDA should expand its staff, particularly in North America, in an intensification of its efforts to attract foreign capital. He further proposed increasing the capital available for outright industrial grants. This was a point echoed by Todd Andrews:

> I cannot see any quick way, or indeed any way of providing these 20,000 jobs out of our own resources; the capital must be brought in from outside ... I do not think that we have enough trained people technically and commercially to enable us to spend £100 million per annum. We must try to induce established industries to set themselves up in the country.[71]

Andrews had in mind such novel proposals as setting up casinos in the country. He was particularly worried about the poor state of Irish tourism, and stated that only one new hotel had been opened since the foundation of the state. Moreover, some commentators were insisting that:

> The need to maintain some margin of tax advantage over more developed countries in north-western Europe seems evident, if we are to attract foreign investment and foreign enterprise, for even if it can be argued with some reason that the level of taxation may not, perhaps, have such a significant effect upon domestic investment as is sometimes suggested, it is clearly of paramount importance where foreign investors are concerned.[72]

An essential element in this new approach to economic policy was a redressing of the balance between economic and social investment in the public-capital programme. This programme gained support from a rising level of domestic savings based on steady growth in real national income, and domestic savings could be supplemented by reasonable recourse to foreign borrowing to promote productive home investment. Thus, a decision was taken to accelerate Ireland's economic progress through an inflow of external capital directed to types of development that would increase the country's productive capacity, and which would bring with it new techniques and methods. Economic policy thus became more expansionary – an appropriate Keynesian response, according to Whitaker, at a time when Irish costs were competitive and world trade was buoyant.[73]

While there were some significant differences between *Economic Development* and the *Programme for Economic Expansion* – which arose out of their different parentage – such differences were for the most part cosmetic, as the main thrust of both documents was the same. Where Whitaker had argued for intensive cattle production as the foundation of agricultural prosperity, the White Paper did not want to abandon completely Fianna Fáil's traditional preference for tillage. Whitaker's proposal to locate new factories in large urban centres was omitted from the White Paper owing to Fianna Fáil's policy of decentralisation of industry, despite Lemass' own doubts about the party line. While the political document did advance a firm commitment to a 2 per-cent annual growth in GNP over each of the ensuing five years, *Economic Development* – in time-honoured civil-service fashion – was suitably vague about targets. Yet on the whole the two documents were remarkably similar.

*Economic Development* remains probably the most seminal document in the independent Irish state. A recent popular history of Irish documents notes that for a rather dry policy document, it has now taken on an iconic status.[74] Bryan Fanning has argued that, as 'a post-independence cultural event, the nativity of *Economic Development* was rivalled in the telling only by the story of the conflict surrounding the 'mother and child scheme' in 1951'.[75] Yet *Economic Development* did not impinge on the consciousness of the body politic immediately. The major newspapers gave it only cursory treatment, while the political parties showed a similar lack of interest. The Fianna Fáil parliamentary party minutes of the period are fascinating for its discussion – or, rather, lack of it – of *Economic Development*. In its first discussion of the document, it was recorded that 'the Party be given a directive on the implications of the recent White Paper on Economic Expansion'. Ryan gave this meeting, at which Lemass was not present, a general résumé of the contents of the paper, which was then followed by the rather bizarre spectacle of a discussion 'in which arterial drainage and of certain very necessary drainage schemes was stressed by several members'.[76] A planned session devoted to the White Paper on 6 January was deferred until 28 January, when Lemass 'explained that the proposals in the White Paper were to be regarded as an outline of minimum requirements for the future and do not exclude further proposals'.[77] The agricultural effects of *Economic Development* were not discussed until March. While this seems to have occupied the party somewhat more as the debate ran into April, the minutes of these discussions are even more sparse than usual, although they state that the debate continued with contributions from various deputies.[78] It would appear that few politicians – whether in Fianna Fáil, as the evidence indicates, or elsewhere – were greatly struck by the attempt to revolutionise national economic policy-making.

One of the major problems faced by Lemass in his attempts to develop the Irish economy lay in the visible unwillingness of the Department of Industry and Commerce to embrace the new agenda for industrial expansion based on the active development of export markets coupled with a reduction in tariffs. Associated with this was the need to push Irish industry into a less complacent frame of mind, and to attack inefficiencies and the lack of competitiveness that had come to characterise an industrial base for so long sheltered behind tariff walls. Adding to this was the country's chronic dependence on the UK market for industrial as well as agricultural goods. A report from the Department of Industry and Commerce in February 1957 predicted that in the event of protection disappearing, a significant section of Irish industry would simply cease to exist. It estimated that up to 60 per cent of industrial employment would be lost if unrestricted entry of foreign goods were permitted: 'whatever the outcome, we must face the disemployment [*sic*] of from 80,000 to 100,000 persons, to say nothing about consequential disemployment that may be expected in other directions'.[79] Yet emigration between 1946 and 1956 was in the region of 300,000, while employment in manufacturing industry in the period increased by only 34,000. For Industry and Commerce, the question of protection was in many ways linked to the loyalty that the department showed to those industrialists who had set up businesses under the protective shelter. As one former senior civil servant who was highly involved throughout this period has surmised:

> Industry and Commerce would have felt an obligation to a lot of those people who had set up Irish industry and did so on encouragement and word of Industry and Commerce and also because they got protection. I don't think there's any question that they were obstructing the advent of free trade, but they definitely felt an obligation to those already in industry. Thus they argued their views strongly.[80]

The main impetus for changing the way manufacturing industry operated emanated from the Department of Finance. The formation of the EEC in 1957 and the reaction of non-OECD (Organisation for

Economic Co-operation and Development) members to this important development was one of the major factors giving rise to *Economic Development*.

## 'MORE CATHOLIC THAN THE POPE'

After the publication of *Economic Development* and the *First Programme for Economic Expansion*, Whitaker went on the offensive against protectionism and its supporters within the civil service. In December 1959 he issued a memorandum entitled 'Reasons for reducing protection'.[81] Its first line came straight to the point: 'The inadequacy of a policy of protection as a remedy for the problems of unemployment and emigration has become obvious in recent years with the increasing saturation of the limited home market.' The average number engaged in manufacturing industry had increased by only 2,000 between 1951 and 1958. The Department of Finance thus argued that it was only through enlarging its sales on export markets that Irish industry could in future provide jobs in increasing numbers for those who sought a livelihood in Ireland. For this to happen, a steady increase in exports would be needed to support greater internal activity and the higher expenditure on imports that would have to coincide with a general improvement in employment and living standards.

It was recognised by all sides that external purchasers would not turn increasingly towards Irish products unless these products were fully competitive in price and quality. By the end of the 1950s only a few Irish industrial products would have passed this test.[82] By contrast, most of the other countries of Western Europe already had large and efficient industrial sectors. Furthermore, between 1949 and 1958 the volume of Irish industrial production went up by only 23 per cent, whereas in OEEC countries taken as a whole, the increase was 73 per cent. Thus, to Finance it was obvious that the country could not hope to share in the economic advance of Europe if it were merely to try to safeguard the industrial status quo. Finance therefore argued for a determined drive to increase efficiency and lower unit costs to enlarge sales in export markets against the growing competition. The non-competitiveness of many Irish industries was related to the small size of the home market, the inadequate utilisation of productive capacity, and the lack of opportunities for economies of scale and specialisation. The only remedy for these deficiencies was to bring about an expansion of effective demand for the products of Irish industry. Finance saw two ways in which this could be achieved: firstly, by attracting external purchasers through the offer of high-quality goods at competitive prices, and, secondly, by raising real incomes and purchasing power in the non-industrial sector of the economy, as was the aim of policy in relation to agricultural exports and tourism. In essence, progress under the first option depended on raising productivity. This, however, would be greatly increased by success under the second.

The need for urgent action to bring down the cost and improve the quality of Irish-manufactured goods was made all the greater by the emergence of two distinct trading blocs in Europe. Competition in export markets would undoubtedly grow as the major countries of Europe – through tariff reductions and freer trade – achieved greater specialisation, higher output and lower costs. Ultimately, the high protective tariffs associated with Irish industry reinforced the non-competitiveness of Irish goods. In the case of the vast bulk of protected industries, exports formed only a small proportion of output:

The scale of protection is such that in many industries there is no effective competition at present. There are over 400 protective tariff references and of these over 100 provide for tariffs of more than 50 per cent *ad valorem* (full) or 33⅓ per cent (preferential). A gradually increasing element of competition on the home market would be a much more general and effective spur to improvements in efficiency than special aids and incentives to which only the progressive undertakings will respond. As long as high protection is maintained there will be no compulsion to get into shape for export markets. Sheltered against the normal consequences of inertia, unprogressive managements can use the high protection they enjoy to make inefficiency profitable.[83]

So said Whitaker. The aim of the Department of Finance was to gradually lower protection in the context of an agricultural-exports arrangement that would increase purchasing power on the home market. Tariffs, Whitaker claimed, were justifiable economically only as a temporary help for 'infant industries', while he maintained that a growing number of countries were formally recognising, by their participation in common markets and free trade areas, the mutual benefits to be derived from freer trade. Whitaker argued that with the support of the Federation of Irish Industries (FII), state aid in the transitional period – when the 'sheltering screen' of protection was being gradually lowered – could take the form of loan capital on reasonable terms, technical-assistance grants and other such incentives. This would be made available to assist in the process of adaptation and modernisation of industry. Ultimately, Finance wanted to be associated with some form of economic trading group that would enable the country to share more certainly in the economic advance of countries more favoured than Ireland:

A closer degree of association with the international economy, through reduced protection and participation in a free trade arrangement, would help to compensate for the narrowness of the domestic market, more especially if it also promised a surer and better market for agricultural exports. It is only by gearing ourselves for a growing trade with the rest of the world that we can tackle, with real prospect of success, the problems of unemployment and emigration.[84]

Whitaker's memorandum sent a shock wave through some sections of the civil service, with Industry and Commerce particularly aghast. J.C.B. MacCarthy, its secretary, replied tersely that he could not accept the views set out in the memorandum as anything other than a somewhat idealistic approach that was not backed by anything more than faith in the operation of the economic laws that were expounded – namely, free trade:

> The harsh realities of the situation are that we have our industries, with many thousands of people employed in them, and we cannot really afford to use them as guinea-pigs. You say protectionism is only for 'infant' industries but ours are not yet out of their teens and still need a measure of paternalism. It is well to remember that if the war years and their immediate aftermath are excluded, as they ought to be, our industries have not had much more than a decade of protection. Even the adult industries of the great industrial nations need and get protection.[85]

In essence, Industry and Commerce was warning about the dangers of Irish industries being involuntarily led from Whitaker's advocacy of the discipline of tariff reductions to advocacy of complete free trade. MacCarthy claimed that this might be an easy transition to make in the abstract, but would be entirely different in practice. He conceded that industries could be subjected to well-thought-out, prudent cuts in protection as an incentive to efficiency, but these would have to be made very carefully and 'on a basis that would not leave us without the power speedily to reverse engines as and when experience dictated'. He concluded by saying that he hoped Whitaker would have a chance of 'tempering economic theory to the facts of our industrial life' before they next met, while adding that he hoped that Whitaker's memorandum was intended to be 'provocative rather than doctrinaire'.[86]

Whitaker was enraged. He accused MacCarthy of forcing him to accept either one of two denigratory epithets: provocative or doctrinaire. He claimed that his original document contained the essence of realism, and was not, as MacCarthy had insinuated, an advocacy of complete free trade. Whitaker's paper basically advocated a progressive discipline of tariff reductions with the right to arrest the process where any major industry came under dangerous stress. Clearly stung by MacCarthy's riposte, Whitaker responded with his own denigratory epithet:

> We both of us know people who are more Catholic than the Pope; should Industry and Commerce not guard against becoming more protectionist than the Federation of Irish Industries ... I am personally convinced that the issue is not one of economic theory but one that bears directly on our hopes of future economic development.[87]

The FII had always been the most protectionist of organisations, and by comparing Industry and Commerce to it, Whitaker was undoubtedly giving the impression that the department was some sort of administrative dinosaur harking for a bygone age. MacCarthy swiftly responded. In what can be seen perhaps as a softening of the hard-edged tone evident in the correspondence of both men, he began with 'Dear Ken' rather than the customary 'Dear Whitaker'. This may have been because it was Christmas Eve, but in any event there can be little doubt that Whitaker's jibe about the FII had annoyed MacCarthy. He asserted that it was his duty to point out the pitfalls that lay ahead in free trade conditions for industry, and said that there was a tendency to underestimate these risks, whilst adding:

> I am sure that you would not wish to be unfair in any comment but I do think that the third paragraph of your letter of the 23rd December

hits a little below the belt. After all, it is the Government and not the Federation of Irish Industries that has to take the decision.[88]

While this may, indeed, have been true, MacCarthy went on to reiterate the old Industry and Commerce mantra that protectionism had served Ireland well. Ultimately, the debate came down to the future direction of the Irish economy. While Whitaker stressed that industrialisation, under protection, had not solved the unemployment problem, and that the continuation of the policy of industrialisation under protection would not provide the expansion the country required, MacCarthy preferred to take the view that:

> As far as employment is concerned, if we had not had the protective policy and, even if it is not a cure for all our ills, is it logical to toss it overboard, unless it is clear that something better can be substituted which will not only maintain employment at the existing level but give the scope for expansion which is desired? All I am seeking is to get the alternatives clearly stated so that a considered choice can be recommended.[89]

There was nothing in MacCarthy's remarks that could give solace to the thousands who had emigrated throughout the decade, and those still without jobs as the 1950s came to an end. Protectionism had clearly failed them, yet MacCarthy was insisting that it remain. His pessimism can be contrasted with the optimism of someone like Todd Andrews, who was asking the country to leave the dark days of the past behind it and begin afresh. As he told one audience:

> I ask you to disabuse your minds of the pessimism so terribly expressed by Patrick Kavanagh: 'It will never be spring always autumn, after a harvest always lost, When Drake was winning seas for England, we sailed in puddles of the past, seeking the ghost of Brendan's mast'.[90]

Whitaker, however, was not seeking the complete abandonment of protection. For him, the problem was that protected manufacture for the home market offered little prospect of increased employment, and in a highly competitive world, continued protection could not guarantee the maintenance of existing employment at acceptable real wages. Thus, if employment opportunities were to be created for the fresh thousands who sought work every year, industry had quickly to become more efficient so that its products could be sold on an increasing scale in export markets. This could be achieved by accepting an external commitment to reducing tariffs, accompanied by appropriate industrial incentives and aids towards industrial adaptation and modernisation.

Whitaker advanced these arguments to MacCarthy in his reply (written on New Year's Eve), but also attempted to launch a new line of attack. The Christmas spirit had not quelled his sharp instincts. He declared that it was over a decade since Industry and Commerce had felt it necessary to seek to establish the Industrial Efficiency Bureau to 'force the pace of progress in industrial efficiency'. While this legislation had not been proceeded with, responsibility for making periodic reviews of existing tariffs was subsequently imposed on the IDA. Whitaker argued that these reviews had been infrequent, with very few tariffs being reduced:

> There can be no doubt that an externally applied discipline, provided it is not too severe, will arouse less opposition, appear less discriminatory, and be more effective than a system operated entirely at the discretion of the domestic administration. The best way to get costs down to competitive levels is to face industrialists with the certainty that tariffs are going to be lowered. In their present mood and in an external trade relationship, I believe they will accept this pressure and react favourably to it.[91]

While this may indeed have been true, the reference to the IDA was bound to upset MacCarthy. Like Lemass originally, MacCarthy had opposed the setting up of the IDA, and had always suspected that the IDA was in some way trying to pre-empt the work of Industry and Commerce. In any event, he did not take kindly to Whitaker's remark. Declaring that he could 'never' agree that the introduction of an externally applied discipline of tariff reductions would be sufficient justification in and of itself for entering a free trade association, he took Whitaker to task for arguing that there was a possibility of the country being left stranded on a high and narrow protectionist plateau on which acceptable living standards could be provided only temporarily and for a diminishing number of our people:

> It is at least equally important ... that we should not so minimise the risks of 'Free Trade' as to obscure the possibility that the plateau or whatever replaces it would be occupied by a diminished number of our people even though their living standards, because there were fewer of them, might be enhanced. We must remember that ... increased emigration would, in our circumstances, be an almost inevitable consequence of reduction of industrial employment.[92]

Whitaker's comment had been made in a letter to Con Cremin, secretary of External Affairs, which was copied to Industry and Commerce, Agriculture and the Taoiseach's office. The Whitaker–MacCarthy correspondence was also copied to the other main departments, and would have been seen by Lemass.[93] It was a battle by proxy, and had political implications in that the mind of Lemass, the draftsman of the policy of protectionism in the 1930s, was there to be won. Cremin had responded to Whitaker's original memorandum in a positive mode, but did have some significant objections. Yet it is noteworthy that he could validate criticisms of Whitaker's document without starting a major administrative row, as was the case with the MacCarthy–Whitaker correspondence. Cremin was particularly worried about the possibility of a setback in industrial production as a result of the reduction of protection and a consequential outflow of redundant manpower. He did, however, maintain:

> A good case appears to be made for modifying our protection policy and for bringing to bear an international commitment. It is a question, however, whether there is not a tendency to discount, on the basis of abstract reasoning which may not be entirely applicable in practice, the possible adverse effects of the removal of protection. It could be contended that, in the economic field, the circumstances prevailing are in some ways so unusual as to weaken, or at least introduce serious qualifications to, otherwise sound theoretical conclusions even when they can be supported by evidence elsewhere.[94]

Whitaker responded to Cremin's comments by stating that he did not think:

> The force of our reasoning is lessened by describing it as 'abstract' or by referring to our conclusions as 'theoretical'. I have yet to see any convincing argument, on practical or theoretical grounds, for the opposite thesis, i.e. that the maintenance of a policy of high protection will raise employment and living standards and reduce emigration.[95]

While it was between Whitaker and MacCarthy that the cut and thrust of debate about protectionism was at its fiercest, Cremin's involvement can be seen as descending from the days when Frederick Boland was intimately involved with Marshall Aid. Cremin also played an active role in the Government's application to join the EEC in 1961.

## 'I WANT YOU TO SIT AT THIS DESK'

MacCarthy's response to the original memorandum did not impress Whitaker. Whitaker had three points that he wanted MacCarthy to address if, as MacCarthy kept implying, there were no worthwhile prospects for the expansion of industrial exports to a European free-trading area. He pressed MacCarthy as to whether his pessimism was due to the non-competitive character of most of Irish industrial production; how it was proposed to overcome this, if the discipline of gradual tariff reduction was not applied; and what grounds were there for expecting that existing industrial output and employment could be maintained – never mind expanded – unless industry was somehow made to become more efficient in the near future. Whitaker clearly had no intention of giving up his attempts of swaying MacCarthy to a free trade position: 'despite your rather forbidding reiteration of "I could never agree", I have not abandoned the hope of persuading you to see matters from a dynamic rather than a static viewpoint'.[96] MacCarthy, however, was not in the business of seeing things from a dynamic viewpoint. Industry and Commerce under his leadership had by the late 1950s become a 'department of disillusionment, without any backbone and not intellectually well endowed'.[97] A former official of the department has described the correspondence between Whitaker and MacCarthy in the following terms:

> Industry and Commerce did not have any faith in what they were doing anyway. They were only going through the motions of putting up this resistance but it was easier for them to do that. MacCarthy had lost faith in the protectionist mindset. He was a very able man … yet he would go with the tide. He adopted the institutional position in that correspondence defending the traditional departmental view … The problem with Industry and Commerce was that the start of everything was a view expressed by the Minister.[98]

The power exercised by Lemass in Cabinet would seem to have had a detrimental influence on his officials in Industry and Commerce in that they did not really have to do any independent thinking. This mastery, however, made his officials in some way a lacklustre group in comparison to the other senior departments, most notably Finance. In any case, MacCarthy replied in kind to Whitaker, claiming that it grieved him:

> ... to note that our correspondence seems to have done little to bring this discussion down to earth. The view expressed in your letter that our industries would gain more from expanded exports than they would lose in the home market, and that there is no need to fuss about getting an adequate *quid pro quo* for joining either EFTA [European Free Trade Association] or Britain in a free trade association is so far removed from our viewpoint that ... there is no point in continuing this correspondence.[99]

The implication at the nadir of the correspondence that Whitaker was talking economic theory rather than economic practicalities was undoubtedly calculated to leave MacCarthy holding the moral high ground. He, being the defender of traditional Irish industries, was not going to feed them to the wolves of free trade orthodoxy, while Whitaker was the shepherd who would abandon his flock to such economic precepts. Whitaker did have the final word, arguing that MacCarthy's response could not be accepted as being a 'fair or reasonable summary of the views expressed in my previous letters'.[100] This rather anodyne response did not disguise Whitaker's anger at having failed to move Industry and Commerce towards a free trade perspective. The essence of the debate is best summed up Tadhg Ó Cearbhaill:

> During the free trade negotiations, I was secretary of the committee

of four secretaries and you talk about strong views, well whatever you think about their views being strong in writing they were far stronger in person ... There is no doubt about it, a lot of roaring and shouting went on when protectionism was discussed.[101]

Meanwhile, Lemass – the apostle of protectionism – was sharpening his own thinking on the free trade question and on entry into a European trading bloc. He told a correspondent in July 1959:

> It is of course true that the Irish economy at its present state of development is not producing enough resources to maintain all our population at the standard of living we desire them to enjoy. The fundamental task facing this country is to expand its total production so that this situation will be brought quickly to an end. This cannot be done, however, by just wishing for it but by sustained hard work in support of an intelligent development programme. The *Programme for Economic Expansion* provides one element and we are now trying to generate the other.[102]

This second element was to enter a free-trading body in an attempt to develop Irish industry and subsequently Irish exports. It went hand in hand with bringing new industry to Ireland. There is an inconsistency between the dynamic Lemass grasping the nettle of free trade as Taoiseach and that of his old department providing the main opposition to membership of a European trading bloc. The role of J.C.B. MacCarthy was hugely significant. He had entered the civil service at Finance in 1927, had served in Industry and Commerce from 1945, and had continued that department's orthodoxy in terms of protection when he succeeded John Leydon as secretary in 1956. Moreover, most of the thinking in Industry and Commerce came from the top down. Thus, with Lemass' exit it was vital that the department be infused with political strength. In this context, Lemass' appointment of Jack Lynch to succeed him as Minister for Industry and Commerce was an important one.[103] He summoned Lynch to his office in the department and told him: 'I want you to sit at this desk'. As Dermot Keogh points out in his recent biography of Lynch, the appointment was for the precise purpose of bringing about a shift to free trade.[104] Having been appointed by de Valera in 1957 as a minister at the Department of Education (with added responsibility for the *Gaeltacht*), Lynch was seen as progressive on economic issues. He had also had dealings with Lemass when he was responsible for the running of the Underdeveloped Areas Act in 1951 as parliamentary secretary to the Government and to the Minister for Lands. He had evidently impressed Lemass, and upon his appointment was told by the Taoiseach that Industry and Commerce was now his responsibility. While Lemass would be captain of the ship, Lynch had assumed the position of trusted lieutenant. Thus, Lynch – to an extent – took on the mantle of guiding Industry and Commerce away from a policy of protectionism, a policy that had been ingrained in its philosophy for a generation.

Lemass was key in persuading MacCarthy to accept the inevitability of tariff cuts. Once he, along with Lynch, had politically sided with the free trade position, MacCarthy was left in an administrative limbo. When Lemass was Minister for Industry and Commerce, and had explicitly supported the policy of protectionism, it was easy for MacCarthy to support him from within the administrative framework. With Lemass, as Taoiseach, now attempting to get Ireland into a European trading bloc, and supported eagerly by his own handpicked Minister for Industry and Commerce, MacCarthy was persuaded of the necessity of free trade and tariff cuts.

By the end of the 1950s, the Irish body politic had launched the way for an export-led industrialisation policy that was to dominate industrial and economic policy in the 1960s. *Economic Development* and the *First Programme for Economic Expansion* had both been extremely conscious of the changing nature of economic relations in the late 1950s. While neither declared the explicit aim of entering a free trade bloc, the initial steps to that outcome had been put in place. The formation of the EEC and EFTA would create two important trading blocs, and could offer economic opportunity or pose new threats. While the Government was not directly looking to Europe with the publication of *Economic Development*, there can be little doubt that it set in train the decision to apply to the EEC, and the further decision to reduce tariffs within that context.

The 1950s had ended with Irish industrial development policy in a state of confusion. At an administrative level, Finance was leading the way, arguing for substantial changes in the protected sector. Supported by External Affairs, Agriculture and the IDA, it was determined to bring Ireland into a European trading bloc, and thereby expand the country's economic frontiers. In this, it first met intransigent hostility from Industry and Commerce, but a wind of change was blowing across Irish industry itself, which, under a new leadership, was to play an important role in getting the department to face up to the challenges of free trade. Ultimately, Industry and Commerce was playing a losing game. Changes in the Control of Manufactures Acts and new incentives to induce foreign industry to locate in Ireland were evidence that the Department of Industry and Commerce had found itself on the losing side in the battle of ideas.[105]

# 4

# A NATIONAL GOVERNMENT FOR IRELAND?

In late 2008 and early 2009 numerous letters to *The Irish Times* called on the political parties to form a Government of national unity given the spiralling out of control of the national finances, the nationalisation of Anglo-Irish Bank, the collapse in the share price of the other major banks, significant increases in unemployment and a burgeoning public-sector pay bill. One correspondent to *The Irish Times* maintained:

> [A] Government of National Unity is the only way forward if we want to manage the crisis. It makes more sense than social partnership, now proving so costly. A resolute national Government can face down those who would protect their own situation regardless of the plight of the country despite weasel words of sharing their concern for the nation's vulnerable citizens.[1]

Such calls for a national Government echo similar appeals made in the 1950s, when a supposedly outlandish political proposal to merge

Fianna Fáil and Fine Gael was given much credence by numerous political commentators.

National Governments in democracies usually arise during extraordinary crises, such as world wars and political revolutions. In Ireland, there had been significant calls for a national Government at various times during the Emergency, but these were always repudiated, most particularly by de Valera, who *The Irish Times* accused of being blinkered in his approach to the idea:

> Mr De Valera is Sir Oracle. When he opens his mouth, let no dog bark. He exercises complete dictatorial prowess over his Ministers, and *a fortiori* over the rank and file of Fianna Fáil. That is why he will have nothing to do with the idea of a National Government.[2]

De Valera's views are important, as his position in Fianna Fáil was central to the question of a national Government and political competition in the 1950s. The background to the 1957 election is one of the more intriguing in twentieth-century Irish history, in that the idea of a national Government was mooted very seriously in a number of political back channels and media outlets. Given the precarious economic situation at the time, several national newspapers – including *The Irish Times*, *Irish Independent* and the *Cork Examiner* – expressed support for the idea of a national Government to address the mounting crisis facing a country with spiralling debt and massive emigration. Despite dismissals at the time from de Valera and, much later, from Lemass, both the British and US embassies insisted in reports to their respective Foreign Office and State Department that discussions about a national Government were serious and ongoing, and that they were inextricably linked with the succession in Fianna Fáil to de Valera.

At the heart of any speculation regarding the formation of a national Government was the political context of significant policy disputes within Fianna Fáil after it lost the 1948 election. Out of office for the first time in sixteen years, Fianna Fáil felt slightly victimised by an ungrateful electorate that did not appreciate its stewardship of the country through the Emergency. As Niamh Puirséil points out, the election had not been contested on any significant policy differences, with most of the Fianna Fáil candidates contenting themselves with 'talking up Dev and down coalition'.[3] This led to a widely held belief within Fianna Fáil that its policies had played no part in its defeat, and therefore required no significant revision. Instead, the party focused on its administrative machine, believing that all it needed to do was keep its superior organisation intact and wait for the hotchpotch Government to collapse, as it inevitably would.[4] Unfortunately for Fianna Fáil, the Inter-Party Government proved somewhat more durable than envisaged, and managed to struggle on for over three years.

When Fianna Fáil regained office in 1951, de Valera appointed MacEntee to Finance against Lemass' wishes; according to de Valera's official biographers, it was a deliberately *conservative* choice.[5] MacEntee's return to Finance put an unequivocally conservative stamp on the new administration from the outset, and signalled that Lemass' influence was on the wane: in 1939 de Valera had apparently acceded to Lemass' demand (on pain of resignation) that MacEntee be removed from that post.[6] By putting MacEntee back there, the Taoiseach was making it abundantly clear that economically this would not be a progressive administration.

In 1954 Fianna Fáil went to the country in search of a new mandate based on its conservative economic record. During this election, MacEntee had emphasised:

If the wise and far seeing economic and financial policy of the Fianna Fáil Government were continued the value of our currency would continue to increase ... The financial and economic policy of the

Fianna Fáil Government had given the country a balanced budget, expanded social services and increased employment. It had enabled the country to conserve its reserves so that today every pound of them was increasing in value and it had enabled all our obligations abroad to be met.[7]

While this was classical economic orthodoxy – and MacEntee could *legitimately* claim that he had pulled the country back from the brink of economic collapse – what it did not say was that Fianna Fáil's performance in industrial policy was rather abysmal. Between 1951 and 1954, MacEntee and Finance attempted to reject on grounds of cost, all the main initiatives promoted by Lemass for developing industry. In any event, the 1954 election saw MacEntee's policies of economic orthodoxy repudiated by the electorate. Held on 18 May, it saw Fianna Fáil lose power again. Fianna Fáil's loss led to a flurry of correspondence across de Valera's desk on the idea of a national Government. Five days after the election, the Clann na Poblachta leader, Seán MacBride, wrote to de Valera with suggestions for the formation of a national Government, and offered his assistance. Should the proposals 'commend themselves to you and your party and should my services be of any assistance as an intermediary to bring about the formation of such a national Government I shall be entirely at your disposal', he declared.[8]

MacBride's view was that since the election was inconclusive, all parties should form a national Government similar to Switzerland's, with the main planks of encouraging reunification and full employment, increasing productivity, reducing emigration, and preserving the Gaeltacht. He argued that there was a general desire in the country for a national Government, but unless this desire 'is expressed in concrete form it is likely to remain an abstract wish'.[9] In this context, he took it upon himself to offer just such concrete proposals. Yet his overture also contained a clear attack on Fianna Fáil: 'it would be difficult for such a Government to be less satisfactory than the type of one party Governments we have experienced'. The trouble with the idea of a national Government was the sheer difficulty of operability. For MacBride, the Dáil would in the normal manner elect one of its members as Taoiseach, who, after consulting with the other political leaders, would appoint ministers and parliamentary secretaries in proportion to the strength of the various parties in the Dáil:

> The Ministers in charge of the main economic departments and of any department whose policy was of a sharply contested nature would be filled by members of the parties supporting the Taoiseach in the Dáil. The policy of the Government would also be the policy of the parties supporting the *Taoiseach* in the Dáil. The leader of the opposition, in present circumstances, would be one of the leaders of the Fianna Fáil party who was not a member of the Government. Whenever no question of major policy was involved the party whips should be withdrawn to allow a free discussion and vote.[10]

He conceded that 'by reason of the small representation of my party in the Dáil, I would not seek or expect representation in such a national Government'.[11] A more fundamental reason for not seeking representation may lie in the fact that such a scheme would be nothing short of a political disaster, given that the opposition – so-called – would consist of members of a party with members in the Government as well.

## 'I FOUGHT WITH YOU IN 1916'

MacBride was not the only individual enamoured with the idea of a national Government. One partisan supporter of de Valera, Liam Kavanagh, wrote to him in the following impassioned terms:

The results of the election tonight make it fairly clear that the people have decided against Government by our party Fianna Fáil as such. I have been a consistent supporter of Fianna Fáil since its inception and have no reason to change my allegiance now in its moment of defeat, but looking on the position in a broader way I feel that it ought to be possible for the sake of the common good of our country to bring about an understanding between the two big parties … In mentioning this I am only reflecting what the ordinary people of these parties and others outside are thinking. The alternative is an unsatisfactory coalition with some of the sectional parties … It is not easy for me to write this, I fought with you in 1916, and during the War of Independence, and on the republican side in 1922/23, and suffered at the hands of those who mainly control the Fine Gael party, but I have tried particularly since the Constitution was enacted to do away with the bitterness which 1922/23 engendered … I may not have put my feeling before you in a very satisfactory manner, but I would ask you for God's sake not to misunderstand my motives, and pray that God may guide you in your decision on the matter.[12]

De Valera was not too impressed with this impassioned plea:

Pardon me for not replying sooner to your letter. I have been very busy. I understand your feelings, but it seems to me you have not thought the matter out sufficiently and that your heart has simply got the better of your judgement. It would take too long in writing to show you how mistaken I think you are. I know, besides, that you do not want an argumentative reply from me.[13]

Even more critical of de Valera, however, was the Revd M. Slattery SMA, of St Xavier's University Hall, Doughcloyne, who suggested the following heresy: 'what about this solution: you hand over the leadership of your party to Mr Lemass who may have less repugnance than you to a coalition'. He went on to suggest that a coalition of Fianna Fáil under Lemass and Labour under Norton would be 'a real coalition, the union of the common humble people of Ireland.'[14] Another correspondent asked de Valera:

> In the new situation now cited is there any chance of your forming a National Government and so once and for all eliminating those ancient political differences ... Wouldn't it be a grand and glorious achievement and a fitting conclusion to your many statesmanlike accomplishments, if you succeeded in evolving a happy reconciliation between these old enemies?[15]

De Valera was again not too taken with this approach:

> I received your letter. I am afraid you have not given to this matter all the thought that is necessary. Had you done so, I doubt if you would have sent me your letter. I know you do not expect a long argumentative reply from me, so I will merely say – just think it over.[16]

One of de Valera's more interesting correspondents was the pharmaceutical entrepreneur, Sam McCauley, who suggested to him:

> Like the rest of us you must have mellowed with the years, and I am sure your genuine feelings towards your main political opponents are no different than towards the 'Hibernians' of 1918. The Civil War occurred thirty-two years ago, and the younger generation are not interested as to who was responsible. The majority of the older generation (in my opinion) who participated in the Struggle 1916–21 would like to see a re-unification of the people who made the conditions of today possible ... I can claim neutrality, and if the leaders of 'Fianna Fáil' and 'Fine Gael', would consider an informal conference for an exchange of

views, with a view to unification, I would be delighted to arrange venue and preside at an inaugural meeting. I am writing Dick Mulcahy, and outside that no one is aware of the matter. Should the proposed meeting fail, no one need know anything about it.[17]

De Valera simply acknowledged receipt of this request, but McCauley was not deterred, and followed up his original note by declaring:

In taking the liberty of writing you and Dick Mulcahy last week, I felt sure the present political set afforded an ideal opportunity for healing the wound of the Civil War. In the interval I have discussed the present set-up with many Fianna Fáil and Fine Gael friends without giving a hint or clue of the initiative I had taken, and I am more satisfied than ever that there is an overwhelming majority in favour of unity. There seemed to be a general feeling, however, that you were the stumbling block, and as I have so often done before, I recalled on such occasions the incidents that arose during your visit to Downpatrick in 1918. Amongst many of your friends you are affectionately referred to as the 'big fellow', and that isn't just a matter of height. Zero hour is approaching, and unless some move is made today, it will be too late. I suggest you are 'Big' enough to make that move, and to be generous to the other side. If unification eventuates it will undoubtedly involve dropping certain personalities, but to my mind, unity is of greater importance than any individual.[18]

This heartfelt appeal to the 'big fellow' failed to elicit a response, and rather than enter any type of national Government or engage in coalition bargaining, Fianna Fáil duly opted for opposition.

In opposition, Lemass considered it essential to stem the loss of support for Fianna Fáil in urban Ireland if he was to gain a stranglehold on economic and industrial policy once Fianna Fáil returned to office. Bew and Patterson have commented on how Fianna Fáil's failure in urban areas presented Lemass with a golden opportunity to identify the party with economic expansion.[19] This, however, is more a case of reading history backwards. In 1954 there was no certainty of Fianna Fáil having a quick return to office, and emphatically no certainty that Lemass would succeed de Valera as party leader. A profile of Lemass in *The Irish Times* in July 1953 remarked: 'when the time comes it is assumed he will succeed his chief. But will it be as easy as that?'[20] Furthermore, *The Leader*, in a commentary on the 1952 budget, noted:

> The *Taoiseach* himself is temperamentally disposed towards 'austerity' and he has himself thrived in applying it in his own case. The 'modest frugal' life has generally been the ideal advocated by him for Ireland, while he has rarely shown the same exuberant enthusiasm for an industrialised and prosperous Ireland which the Tanaiste has always endeavoured to promote.[21]

The priority for Lemass was to develop an economic programme that he could put into operation once he and his party were back in office, and – more importantly – that his programme would deliver results. In 1954 it was not clear whether either objective could be met.

## AN 'IMPOSSIBLE' PROPOSAL

The second Inter-Party Government was unable to make any dent in the country's economic woes, and in the general election of March 1957 Fianna Fáil won an overall majority. The ageing and increasingly blind de Valera was once again Taoiseach. Within three months, the US embassy was reporting that de Valera was contemplating retirement, and had decided that James Ryan, the newly appointed Minister for Finance, should succeed him. The reasons for de Valera's choice, according to the reporting officer, John La Fréniere, makes for what can only be called interesting reading. The election had been called when the Inter-Party Government of 1954–57 folded after Clann na Poblachta withdrew its support over the Government's failure to formulate and implement any long-term economic development plan to ensure full employment, together with its failure to make any effort towards the reunification of Ireland. Fine Gael had attempted to avert an election when it approached Fianna Fáil on 5 February with a view to forming an alliance. Rumours of Fine Gael's overtures caused de Valera to issue a statement on 10 February wherein he admitted to receiving two members of Fine Gael and 'listening' to a proposal that he found 'impossible'. According to de Valera, when he mentioned it to the Fianna Fáil committee 'as a matter of course', the committee dismissed the proposal, and he informed the Fine Gael representatives accordingly. Nevertheless, La Fréniere reported to the State Department on 18 February that a merger was still a possibility:

> The reporting officer has learned reliably that a rapprochement between Fianna Fáil and Fine Gael might occur should Fianna Fáil not obtain a working majority out of the election. It is reported that Seán MacEntee and Seán Lemass, lieutenants of de Valera, very much favour combining with Fine Gael to form a Government, if this becomes necessary. It was learned that the two parties would be prepared to come to an agreement on basic economic principles and on national commitments; however it seems unlikely that de Valera and General Richard Mulcahy, the Fine Gael leader, would serve in the same cabinet because of long and deep seated animosities.[22]

There is some limited evidence that Fine Gael made approaches to Fianna Fáil, and it certainly had considered the mechanics of a national

Government. Alex Bolster, a Fine Gael member, had submitted a policy document to Mulcahy in which he outlined various proposals as to how a national Government would be constituted. Mulcahy went public on 18 February, calling for a spirit of co-operation in Government between Ireland's political parties.[23] This was not a call for unification between Fianna Fáil and Fine Gael, or a merging of the two, but would mean 'working together as separate entities but bringing their own special contribution of thought and work to public affairs'. Bolster was particularly keen on the idea of a vocational council that would work in co-ordination with Dáil Éireann:

> As Dáil Éireann would provide the ultimate expression of political thought and practice the Vocational Council would provide the ultimate in experience and practice of all the other activities which go to make up the entire national structure. Apart altogether from the experience of the past, it is both natural and essential that the country should reap the benefit of the advice and guidance of those best fitted to provide such in all matters concerning the everyday life of the people. Certainly it can be said that with complete truth that the lack of co-ordination and amicable co-operation between political party Government and vocational bodies up to the present has contributed in great measure to the condition of our country today.[24]

Bolster's memorandum, however, also called for nothing short of a renunciation of the constitution, advocating as it did the abolition of the proportional-representation system of elections, a significant decrease in the numbers of TDs, suspension of the office of president of Ireland, the substitution of the Seanad with a vocational council, and the abolition of the compulsory teaching of Irish. Notwithstanding these rather surreal proposals – given that the constitution was only twenty years in existence – there is a piece of evidence in the MacEntee papers alluding to the idea of a national Government; in a diary entry of 4 February 1957 he notes:

> Jas Crosbie asked to see me urgently. I saw him for about 20 minutes, arriving about 5.50 and leaving about 6.10. He told me that what he had to say was off the record and strictly confidential. He then expressed the uneasiness of himself and some others regarding the continuance of the existing situation in which a majority of persons on both sides of the House who had the same fundamental views on most matters were kept divided. They wondered whether they could not be brought together either before or after the election. He recognised the difficulties inherent in his proposal, but was anxious to avoid any repetition of weak Governments. He proposed to continue to sound opinion.[25]

We do not have MacEntee's response, but there is no evidence that he – however putatively – in any way supported the idea of a national Government involving Fianna Fáil and Fine Gael before the 1957 election. Moreover, Lemass – in an interview with John F. McCarthy in 1969 – maintained that though the possibility of a national Government had been raised by Fine Gael, and that he had indeed met a member of Fine Gael (who he refused to name) in the Shelbourne Hotel, he had informed this individual that the idea was 'completely impractical'.[26]

For its part, Fine Gael had mooted on a number of occasions the idea of unifying the opposition to Fianna Fáil within a single political party. Such moves – involving at various times Clann na Poblachta and Clann na Talmhan – were driven by significant Fine Gael figures such as T.F. O'Higgins, James Dillon and its first Taoiseach, John A. Costello, who on a visit to Canada in September 1948 told the Canadian prime minister, Mackenzie King, that he thought he 'had the goodwill of all five parties in his Government. He believed by a certain amount of talk he would be able to get them welded into one party.'[27]

## THE VIEW FROM THE FOURTH ESTATE

Calls for a national Government found their loudest public expression in the main newspapers. In the run-up to the 1951 election, the *Irish Independent* advocated an all-party Government that would include Fianna Fáil: 'The best brains for governing the country and guiding it through the difficult years ahead are not to be found in any one party.'[28] Two days later, it advocated 'a Government representing all parties because in our opinion Fianna Fáil should have agreed to participate with the other parties in 1948 and should agree to do so now'.[29] In the immediate aftermath of the election – in which Fianna Fáil failed to secure an overall majority – it interpreted the result as a 'mandate for an all-party Government'.[30]

On the eve of the 1954 election, the *Irish Independent* expressed the view that 'one-party rule has not solved the nation's problems; it has kept alive old feuds and personal spleens'.[31] It is noteworthy, however, that its calls for Fianna Fáil participation in all-party Government tended to be loudest when outgoing Inter-Party Governments appeared to be on the ropes.[32] This could be seen as a tactic designed to ensure the continuance in Government of Fine Gael, or even as an outgrowth of a certain type of corporatism involving not only interest groups but political parties as well; it is certainly not the voice of the Civil War victors. Indeed, in his verdict on the 1957 election – in which Fianna Fáil defeated the Fine Gael-led Inter-Party administration – the *Irish Independent*'s editor, Frank Geary, noted severely that in some respects the verdict on Costello was a fitting one:

> In our view it was a negative but very effective way of showing their dissatisfaction with the conduct of national affairs in the last three years. On numerous occasions this newspaper has warned the ministers that their administration was extravagant, that public expenditure was excessive, and that the people were being asked to maintain a welfare

state that we cannot afford. The ministers did not heed our warnings and they have paid the price.[33]

Although Geary retired in September 1961,[34] the editorial line in the general election the following month was almost a replica of the one he had adopted in earlier years: if anything, it was even more middle of the road. All party leaders were invited to contribute articles to the paper, and did so: a similar facility, for instance, would not be accorded by the *Irish Press*.[35] On the day before the poll, the *Independent* expressed the hope that the result, 'whatever it may be, will be such as to dispose of any suggestion that it is inconclusive or incomplete'.[36] As the result of the election became clear – Fianna Fáil were four seats short of an overall majority – it argued strongly that the politicians should accept the intelligence and wisdom they professed to discern in the electorate, and 'get together in the united fashion that the public has so manifestly demanded'.[37]

*The Irish Times* – which had oscillated between support for Fianna Fáil and Fine Gael since the ending of the Second World War – plumped in 1957 for supporting both, and called for 'long-term Government'; in other words, 'a merger of Fine Gael and Fianna Fáil'. When Fianna Fáil was returned to Government, *The Irish Times* declared that it would have:

... greatly preferred an inconclusive verdict which would have forced the two major parties – even at the cost of a second general election – first to merge, and then to regroup into the elements of a clearly defined Right and Left, with the philosophically differing approaches towards national problems that are the essence of parliamentary democracy in most countries.[38]

## 'WHEN IS A STEW NOT A STEW?'

The idea of a national Government was not on de Valera's agenda. During the election campaign of 1957, he spoke of the evils of coalition, and – even worse – how the idea of a national Government had seeped into the public consciousness. For de Valera, these were two signs of the same busted coin, with people telling Fianna Fáil that an all-party Government – a 'national Government' – would not be a coalition:

> We have, however, new people who tell us that this All-Party Government, they say, and a Coalition 'are poles apart'. We have now the answer to the question, 'when is a stew not a stew'? According to the reasoning of those who claim that an All Party Government is not a Coalition the answer must be, a stew is not a stew when further ingredients are added. The purpose of this whole scheme is, of course, simply that they want Fianna Fáil to be in the swim with the rest. Fianna Fáil is, however, not in the market. Surely, it must be obvious to every thinking person that the addition of Fianna Fáil to the Coalition combination would be to add a further divergent element, making for still more Governmental hesitation and delay – still more indecision and inaction. Is the position not bad enough as it is? People who are asking for this so-called 'National Government' should remember that an Opposition would arise in any case. It would be created overnight, and certainly at the first controversial measure this 'National Government' would introduce. As Mr Lemass has said, this talk of National Government is unrealistic. It is just foolish.

He became all philosophical on representative democracy, and the importance of the party system:

> Politics is no new science or art. Its story did not begin yesterday. Representative democracy and the party systems associated with it are

not new. Their workings and behaviour in history can be observed by any interested student, and the evils attendant on coalitions, whether they be made up of only some parties or all parties in the state are evident and well known. They could be anticipated by any thinking man who would face up to the realities of politics. The people are being told that a number of Fianna Fáil supporters are in favour of this All Party combination. I have yet to meet them. To those not of our Party who are playing with this idea of a National Government I commend to them the words of Edmund Burke: 'What no men could set with effect who did not set in concert; That no men could set in concert who did not set with confidence; and That no men could act with confidence, who were not bound together by common opinions, common affections, and common interests'. If you want to have a National Government you must give to the National Party the over-all majority that is required.[39]

Many were not convinced by de Valera's protestations. In March 1957 the British embassy picked up on the views of the fourth estate. For the British, the issue revolved around the succession of de Valera, with the British ambassador, Alexander Clutterbuck, noting: 'there are rumours that some of the old guard such as Mr Aiken would not be prepared to serve under Mr Lemass, who is the heir apparent'.[40] Later, the embassy would see these personality problems as opening the way for James Ryan to succeed de Valera as a compromise choice. By August, however, John La Fréniere of the US embassy was relating to the State Department how an informed source was now reporting that both Lemass and MacEntee had fallen out of favour with de Valera, causing him to lean toward Ryan as his likely successor:

This change of attitude by de Valera toward his two able lieutenants is said to have come about in early February 1957 when the then

Inter-Party Government was trying to avert the general election that was threatening, and members of Fine Gael approached members of Fianna Fáil with a view to forming an alliance with Fianna Fáil or even a national Government ... According to the source mentioned above, President Seán T. O'Kelly was secretly conducting the 'merger' negotiations between the Fine Gael leaders and Lemass and MacEntee ... It is reported that the above-mentioned negotiations had proceeded to an almost final stage when Lemass and MacEntee decided it was time to include de Valera in their plans. Mr de Valera's reaction was one of extreme annoyance and displeasure with his two colleagues and he bluntly rejected the proposals. The chief had spoken and that was that. The source states that since then Mr de Valera has indicated that he considers Dr Ryan as the person in the party who should succeed him.[41]

Some months earlier – when de Valera was forming his Cabinet – he had Ryan appointed to Finance at Lemass' insistence, with MacEntee moving to Health.[42] Brian Farrell maintains that 'in 1951 de Valera had refused his [Lemass] request not to reappoint MacEntee to Finance; in 1957 he acceded'.[43] Joe Lee's contention that MacEntee 'was discredited by his association with the unsuccessful policies of the previous Fianna Fáil administration' is a valid one but must be seen in the context that de Valera himself cannot escape the charge that he had wholeheartedly supported MacEntee's policies.[44] If anything, de Valera must stand equally as indicted. There is no evidence that de Valera was willing to listen to alternative advice. MacEntee's conservative economic views would not have seen the light of day if de Valera had opposed them. As noted earlier, Fianna Fáil parliamentary party minutes of this period referred to de Valera as the 'Chief',[45] and there can be no doubt about his status. As absolute head of the party and the Government, no major policy decision could be implemented without his approval. Tom

Feeney points out that MacEntee's move from Finance was deemed necessary given the political fallout of his previous stewardship there between 1951 and 1954, and maintains that his demotion – for that is what it was – should not be read as determination on behalf of the Government to change financial policy.[46] Feeney credits the change in economic management as coming from the civil service, and while there is some truth in this, it is nevertheless also true to say that without a change in the economic fortunes of the country, the next general election would almost certainly have seen Fianna Fáil return to opposition. This was something de Valera could not countenance. Thus, electoral considerations demanded that change was necessary. MacEntee was demoted, and Lemass moved centre stage as leader in waiting.

## VOTE FINE GAEL FOR A FIANNA FÁIL GOVERNMENT

The belief in the US embassy that Ryan was de Valera's chosen successor had some basis in reality in that a number of commentators were of the view that Ryan could emerge as a compromise candidate between Lemass and Frank Aiken, who did not come into the equation at all so far as the US embassy was concerned. While it is unlikely that any US official had much regard for Aiken's political nous given his stance on nuclear issues at the UN, his omission from embassy speculation is nonetheless surprising. The British embassy, by contrast, was convinced up to the end of 1958 that Ryan could emerge as a compromise candidate between Lemass and Aiken.[47]

MacEntee, as a result of his move to Health after the election of 1957, was never really a serious candidate to replace de Valera. Jack Lynch – appointed Minister for Education at thirty-nine, and the youngest member of the 1957 Fianna Fáil administration – had an interesting take on MacEntee:

Seán Lemass was obviously always regarded as Dev's immediate successor. Seán Lemass, having first become in the 1932 Fianna Fáil Government Minister for Industry and Commerce, showed such a bent for Industry and Commerce, showed such a capacity in economics generally, that I think Seán Lemass would have stayed there as long as he liked and did in fact until the war came and he was appointed Minister for Supplies and I think Seán MacEntee then became Minister for Industry and Commerce for a short period of time. But for that reason since Seán MacEntee obviously had no ambition, he may have had ambition but he saw no possibility, as long as Seán Lemass was there, being a younger man, of becoming the Deputy Taoiseach or Tanaiste as he [Lemass] ultimately became. Therefore he [MacEntee] was a man of such ability that Dev used him deliberately ... used him as a utility man so to speak in the Cabinet, but as I said it was first because of the fact that Lemass concentrated on the economic side that MacEntee had no objection in the event of being moved from what you might call a senior ministry in Finance to a less senior ministry in Health or Local Government so they were [the] two factors there combining in that part of Seán MacEntee's official life. I said earlier that Seán MacEntee was a man of great commitment and would fight for the cause in which he believed. He was a man of great commitment, he gave me great assistance; irrespective of whether he had a regard for me or not he had a regard for the leadership of Fianna Fáil. He supported that leadership in a most effective manner. He was a most potent factor in establishing the authority of the leader and therefore in maintaining the integrity of the party in every sense of the word integrity. This is something I will always remember Seán MacEntee for.[48]

There is a problem with Lynch's analysis given that MacEntee clearly subscribed to orthodox conservatism while at the helm of financial policy; in that context, it is very difficult to see how it could be a case of MacEntee willingly moving aside to leave Lemass control economic policy. MacEntee's commitment to what he was doing was far too strong for him to simply give way. While he may have ultimately lost the battle, it was one that he had fought out of a belief that the stability of the state – that he himself had done so much to establish – would be maintained by a conservative economic policy. For Fianna Fáil – and Lemass in particular – the trouble with this was that it was costing the party votes. In the fluid and politically unstable 1950s – with rumours of national Governments flying around the political elites – this was a situation Lemass could not countenance. He commenced weekly off-the-record briefing sessions with the political correspondents of the national newspapers – with de Valera's retirement among the subjects that frequently came up for mention – and was a regular source of leaks.

By August, when La Fréniere was writing his memorandum, Lemass had managed to sideline MacEntee where Government economic policy was concerned. By this stage, Lemass was in the process of reorienting relations with the various interest groups, and was fashioning a more active economic policy that eventually would have interdependence with Europe at its core. On the leadership front, an undated reference in the MacEntee papers – scribbled on his copy of Brian Farrell's biography of Lemass – refers in passing to 'Lemass' tirade to Margaret against Dev'. The personal closeness of the two political protagonists – as John Horgan points out in his biography of Lemass – is underlined by the fact that Margaret MacEntee could readily share this confidence with her husband without any feeling of disloyalty, and (though Horgan does not point this out) that Lemass could share it with Margaret MacEntee in the first place.[49]

While Lemass had his critics in the party – with many of the old guard often using Aiken as a means of access to de Valera in ways that bypassed the Government – Lemass was undoubtedly popular, and

Seán Lemass switches on the current at the new steel mill at Haulbowline in Cork in 1939. Originally privately operated, it was bought by the state in 1947 to secure some 240 jobs. Courtesy of the *Irish Examiner*.

As war looms in Europe, Lemass opens Irish Steel in Cork.
Courtesy of the *Irish Examiner*.

An anxious crowd look on at the opening of Irish Steel.
Courtesy of the *Irish Examiner*.

Voting in the general election of 1948 when Fianna Fáil lost office for the first
time since coming to power in 1932. Courtesy of the *Irish Examiner*.

Lord Mayor of Cork Seán McCarthy visits the Dunlop tyre plant at the Marina in Cork city in 1949. Courtesy of the *Irish Examiner*.

Crowds queuing for milk during the dairymen's strike in early 1953. Courtesy of the *Irish Examiner*.

Dockers at work on North Wall in Dublin in June 1954. The Inter-Party government had taken office in the previous month, but could do little to stem the tide of unemployment and emigration. Courtesy of Lensmen Press Agency.

General Richard Mulcahy of Fine Gael visits a traditional clothing factory in Ballingeary, Cork, in 1956. Courtesy of the *Irish Examiner*.

Seán Lemass in typical brusque pose as Taoiseach. Courtesy of Lensmen Press Agency.

An unemployment march in Dublin in April 1957. Fianna Fáil had regained office in the previous month, pledging to end both unemployment and emigration. Courtesy of Lensmen Press Agency.

The Ballinasloe Horse Fair in 1957. Rural life in Ireland was symbolised by numerous fairs. Courtesy of Lensmen Press Agency.

Workers' Union of Ireland seminar in Greystones, Wicklow, 1958. Front row (left to right): Donal Nevin (research officer, ICTU), Maj. Gen. Michael Joe Costello (general manager, Irish Sugar Company), Bishop James Kavanagh (aux. Bishop of Dublin), Jim Larkin jnr (general secretary, WUI) Louden Ryan (Prof. of Economics, TCD), T.K. Whitaker (secretary, Dept of Finance). Whitaker's *Economic Development* was ready for publication at this time. Courtesy of Aoife Breslin.

Eamon de Valera speaking in Cork in July 1959, a month after he had handed over the leadership of Fianna Fáil to Lemass and was elected President of Ireland. Courtesy of the *Irish Examiner*.

Sean T. O'Kelly, President of Ireland 1945–1959 pictured in July 1959, a month after leaving office. The American embassy was convinced that O'Kelly was conducting secret merger negotiations between Fianna Fáil and Fine Gael in 1957 without de Valera's knowledge. Courtesy of Lensmen Press Agency.

President John F. Kennedy, accompanied by Lemass, leaving Dáil Éireann after addressing a joint session of the Houses of the Oireachtas in June 1963. Kennedy was keen to see Ireland join the EEC. Courtesy of Lensmen Press Agency.

Lemass, Kennedy and de Valera in full regalia at a state banquet honouring Kennedy's visit in June 1963. Also pictured are Kathleen Lemass, Sinéad de Valera and Eunice Kennedy Shriver. Courtesy of Lensmen Press Agency.

Charles Haughey pictured in 1964. Lemass appointed Haughey Minister of Agriculture after the resignation of Paddy Smith. Courtesy of Lensmen Press Agency.

Lemass congratulates Jack Lynch on Lynch's appointment as Taoiseach in 1966. Lynch was Lemass' hand-picked successor as Minister for Industry and Commerce in 1959. Courtesy of the *Irish Examiner*.

offered the best avenue for political success in the party. De Valera eventually announced his decision to retire as Taoiseach and as president of Fianna Fáil at a party meeting on 15 January 1959. It would take six more months for him to finally resign. When the time came for the election of his successor by the Fianna Fáil parliamentary party, Lemass was nominated by his old rival, MacEntee, and after much tumultuous cheering was seconded by Aiken. Bar one or two discordant backbench voices, his election was greeted with wide acclaim by the parliamentary party. The rumours from the British embassy in particular that he would face significant opposition failed to materialise.[50] There seems to be no other evidence for any plotting by Lemass, MacEntee and O'Kelly in attempting to form a national Government. The British, for instance – while conscious of the approach by Fine Gael – were not aware of any attempt by senior figures in Fianna Fáil to move towards the formation of a national Government. For Fianna Fáil, the period from 1948 to 1957 was indeed a difficult one, and a belief remained amongst senior party members, including MacEntee, that without de Valera at the helm, the party would suffer electorally. There can be little doubt that de Valera had any stomach for the abandonment of protectionism and self-sufficiency. By the time Fianna Fáil won the 1957 election, he was remote from much of the debate within the party. Yet he did recognise that the policies of economic retrenchment had resulted in defeat for his party twice in the previous nine years. MacEntee's attempts in the 1950s to stabilise the state economically through a conservative financial policy had been repudiated by, firstly, the electorate, and, secondly, de Valera. The latter rejection must have been a tough blow to take, especially as Lemass went on to reorient economic policy in a more statist fashion. Nevertheless, all we know of Lemass, MacEntee and others in Fianna Fáil who had committed themselves to the service of the state suggests that no matter how severe the economic crisis, a national Government was not an alternative they were willing to embrace. In that context, it is perhaps fitting to end with the words of Lemass himself, for whom it was nothing but a 'scheme designed to give people the idea that they could vote Fine Gael, and almost by proxy get a Fianna Fáil led Government'.[51]

# 5

# OWNERS, WORKERS AND FARMERS: THE INTEREST-GROUP EXPERIENCE

Protectionism – which continued to operate after the war – was reinforced during the 1950s. The crisis in the Irish economy during that decade lay not so much within industry as within agriculture; due to the importance of agriculture for the economy as a whole, however, the crisis affected industry to much the same degree. Industrial employment continued to increase, though at a slower rate than before. Unlike the 1930s, it proved impossible for protected industry to provide enough employment for those leaving the land and for those entering the labour market for the first time. One consequence of this was an acceleration of emigration, which was to characterise 1950s Ireland. Nevertheless, the trade union movement was generally supportive of protectionism in the post-war era, since it was seen to have brought about some improvement in the industrial situation. The unions, however, remained concerned about low pay and women's unemployment. As Donal Nevin has commented:

The principle of protectionism was overriding. There was this residue of the idea of self-sufficiency, if we could produce all our own goods we would have full employment or that if we could keep out imports we would have plenty of work. There was no conception of developing a large export capacity like the big industrial companies. It was not as if anybody was talking about opening up protectionism and looking for new markets. Thus for both the union movement and the rest of the policy-making arena, there were two strong feelings: the need for protection to develop employment and the assumption that if you took self-sufficiency in that way you could create new jobs.[1]

Yet Irish wage rates – which had historically remained quite close to those prevailing in Britain – fell well behind in this period. By 1960 the average British worker earned at least 40 per cent more than his/her Irish counterpart.[2] This income gap served as a strong incentive for skilled workers to emigrate even when not threatened by unemployment. Comparatively, Ireland after 1945 failed to maximise its opportunities in the expanding European economy, and consequently did not share in the affluence that accompanied it. It was during the 1950s that Ireland went into relative decline against similar states in Western Europe. In most states, the process of post-war recovery was characterised by intensive industrialisation, the development of a strong export potential (often in manufacturing), and the acceptance of a broadly multilateral and free trade environment, expressed through the recognition of GATT rules.[3] Ireland clearly did not share in this experience – mainly because it made little attempt to. Economic policy-making continued to be restrictive, agriculture remained in a hegemonic position, and Ireland continued to be on Europe's periphery in a political sense. Unlike other European states, Ireland did not achieve self-sustained growth in the course of the 1950s. Serious balance-of-payments problems plagued policy-makers during the first half of the decade, followed by recession and then a depression in 1957.

## 'GRAPPLING WITH THIS NEW SITUATION'

Trade union influence on policy-making in Ireland was much less marked than in most other Western European countries, including Britain, where the Trade Union Council had considerable influence on the Conservative Government's economic policy.[4] Trade union influence in Ireland, however, was at best indirect and depended on Fianna Fáil being in office. The existence of two congresses caused great difficulties for unions, weakening their efforts, dissipating their resources, and making impossible a common front against the employer organisations, steadily growing more powerful. A divided trade union movement meant that any negotiations with the Government were destined to reach an unsatisfactory conclusion for one or other of the congresses, given the rivalry that existed between them. In practice, however, there were no serious ideological or organisational differences between the two congresses, while personal discord between the leaders had gradually disappeared by the mid-1950s.[5]

By the late 1950s, union leaders were well aware of the need for greater competitiveness and productivity. The International Confederation of Free Trade Unions, to which the PUTUO sent representatives, welcomed any movement that would harmonise European trading conditions:

Trade barriers between the participating countries in the form of tariffs and quotas will gradually be reduced and finally abolished during the transitional twelve year period and provide member countries with a market of 250 million people. It would lead therefore to a greater degree of industrial specialisation in the countries of Western Europe. The European trades unions are convinced that such co-operation would do much to raise and harmonise living standards, to improve social conditions generally and to extirpate national rivalries provided, however, that such co-operation is established in a realistic and progressive spirit.[6]

Trade unions throughout Europe saw the liberalisation of trade as a solution to the industrial problems of their nations, and suggested ways of making any such free trade area work. They rather unrealistically claimed that the abolition of unemployment was indispensable if a free trade area was to function properly. Thus, they sought changes in industrial structure and employment, a reduction of tariffs, gradual abolition of quotas, and the insertion of rules in a treaty on the setting up of such a free trade area. For the trade union movement, the fruits of new industrial methods could only be reaped by large economic units. Furthermore, the pace of technological change required an economic policy that would be based on a wider level than that of national borders.

There seems to have been a remarkable degree of acceptance of the desirability of establishing a free trade area, and what differences there were seemed negotiable. At a European industrial conference in London in 1958, the French did express concerns that the area's policies could be inconsistent with those of the Common Market, and that any proposed co-operation with the EEC would be illogical. They argued that it would be better to enlarge the six to include projected members of EFTA. Frank Cousins of the British Trades Union Congress, meanwhile, was emphasising the importance of retaining within participating countries 'the right to take action necessary to retain full employment', something of a holy grail for the trade union movement. Representatives of the Irish unions, employers' and farmers' organisations were present at this conference, and all made reference to the somewhat underdeveloped nature of the Irish economy, and mentioned that Ireland would need to receive some special assistance in such an industrial area. This was a route the Irish Government was itself taking in its negotiations to enter the area. The Irish case did receive some lukewarm endorsement; Ruaidhrí Roberts, in his report to the ITUC on the conference, commented:

It should be noted that endorsement of cases made by underdeveloped countries does not represent a specific endorsement of each proposal put forward but rather an endorsement of the view that these areas should receive adequate special privileges to enable them to participate.[7]

The attitude of the Irish trade union movement to joining a trading bloc was more circumspect. For its purposes, certain major economic conditions had to be addressed. Primarily, it believed that an increase in Irish exports was vital. Agricultural products still constituted three-quarters of trade exports, with the vast majority going to Britain. If Ireland remained outside a trading area that included Britain, this would create major obstacles in the way of maintaining exports to Britain. The unions further argued that there did not seem to be any real prospect of increasing trade by any considerable magnitude. In an important memorandum by Donal Nevin on the trade union movement's attitude to the free trade area, it was recognised that the industrial sector of the country was relatively weak. Some industries suffered from inefficiency and bad management, while others were inevitable victims of a small home market. Membership of an industrial area might, it argued, remedy some of the deficiencies, but for too many industries the problems arose out of geographical position, lack of resources, and the absence of traditional export markets for industrial goods.[8] The memorandum noted that there would be an increasing reliance on external aid in building up big export industries if the country was to make any significant advances in industrial development, while declaring that 'any uncertainty in relation to Ireland's participation in the free trade area would make it increasingly difficult to attract outside industries notwithstanding that labour costs in Ireland were among the lowest in Europe'.[9]

Ultimately, the unions saw Ireland as a small, underdeveloped country that did not represent a threat to other European states. It did, however, face enormous emigration and employment problems that they anticipated would not affect Ireland's chances of associating with EFTA, as the purpose of such a bloc was to improve economic conditions and living standards:

> It is clear that if our economic conditions were to be worsened and our living standards jeopardised by participation, other EEC countries would take cognisance of the fact. Anything else would be markedly contrary to expressed aim of movement to create European co-operation. Ireland cannot hope or expect, nor should she desire, to remain unaffected by these developments on the continent. Our weak economy, beset as it is by acute problems, will be profoundly affected by them. Whatever our ultimate attitude towards the free trade area, we must recognise the necessity for grappling with this new situation, the difficulties as well as the opportunities it presents.[10]

Thus, on the understanding that a free trade area was designed to improve the economic position of all participating countries, and that small, underdeveloped countries would be afforded the opportunity to reach a high level of economic development, the trade union movement in Ireland was, in principle, in favour of Ireland joining such an area. These remarks were prefaced by the usual union mantras of commitment to full employment and the elimination of the economic compulsion to emigrate, as the unions 'endeavour to ensure that the policy adopted by our Government will be in harmony with the objectives sought by the international trade union movement in supporting the principles of a free trade area in Europe'.[11] For the trade unions, better economic organisation had to be regarded as a means towards the end of improving social conditions, and they were insistent 'that this end not be lost sight of in the welter of economic proposals'. Laurence Hudson, president of the PUTUO, reiterated this point when he declared that alarm at the prospect of the collapse of the industrial arm of the country was not justified either by reason of the likely consequences of a free trade area or by reason of the state of the industrial sector:

> By international standards – and not merely the highest American standards – we are not as inefficient as some of our defeatists would suggest. Nor for that matter are the golden opportunities that some seem to think would face our agricultural industry in the event of our joining the free trade area at all certain to be realised.[12]

In this context, the unions were willing to enter into any trading bloc that brought improved conditions for their members.

There were some in the union movement who were willing to put a different slant on the European issue. John Swift, general secretary of the Irish Bakers', Confectioners' and Allied Workers' Amalgamated Union – a noted radical once described by the police as 'a dangerous agitator' – was more responsive to the idea, although from a different angle.[13] Swift thought that the response to any suggestion that Ireland join a European trading bloc was too timid, claiming that it stressed that the free trade area was still in its infancy and:

> Our knowledge of this particular infant is so meagre, the decent thing for us to do is to hold our hand lest rash moves to acclaim its birth might expose us to the risk of seeming to father or foster a spurious progeny. This is a misconception. The real progenitors of the projected body, the Free Trade Area, are the old pioneers of our own movement. That the seventeen Governments of the OEEC are now working out programmes for more production, full employment and higher living standards, for the people of its countries, is proof of the influence these old pioneers have come to yield in world affairs. Our trade union and labour pioneers taught us to clamour and fight for these things. We

have been clamouring so long for them we scarcely notice the portends of their coming among us.[14]

Notwithstanding the flourishing rhetoric, Swift argued that the trade union movement had to serve the European ideal in honour of the line of progenitors who had seen the vision of a united Europe and sought to make a practical reality of the idea. Basically, Swift was calling for the trade union movement internationally to be at the forefront of European economic unity. What was comparatively new was the realisation that the unity of the continent and its peoples could only be built on an economic basis, 'on a basis of production, distribution and exchange by people who work and who are free to live a full and cultured life'.[15] The goals of full employment and rising living standards could, he believed, only be achieved if the trade union movement came out strongly in favour of the idea of a free trade area, although he qualified this by stating that any such support would be conditional on the area serving the social purposes envisaged by the OEEC. Swift was not entirely captivated by the romantic prospect of an economically united Europe that would free the downtrodden working classes. He conceded that the process of adjusting to the area would bring serious problems of industrial change, and that some firms would cease to exist once exposed to competition. Thus, he advocated a thorough examination of vulnerable industries to see how they might adjust to the economic rigours of such competition. What was not in any doubt, however, was the fact that the ultimate aim of EFTA was economic integration, and that the union movement should play an active and central role in it.[16]

## A NEW ERA

In February 1959 the Irish Congress of Trade Unions (ICTU) was formally inaugurated, and in July the ITUC – founded in 1894 – and the CIU – founded in 1945 – were dissolved. This was due mainly to the work of a committee of the PUTUO consisting of James Larkin and Ruaidhrí Roberts of the ITUC, and John Conroy and Leo Crawford of the CIU, which had been set up to draft a constitution for a united Congress. The ninety trade unions affiliated to the new ICTU represented a membership of well over half a million workers, two-fifths of them in Northern Ireland.[17] The healing of the trade union split came at an appropriate time, for a unified body could provide advice and exert influence without contradiction from an alternative voice of labour. This was especially important as Lemass' views on economic policy were closer to that of the ICTU than those of MacEntee, who had embraced a more conservative economic outlook. A further development in 1959 was the completion of the seventh round of wage increases. This brought to manual workers increases ranging from ten to fifteen shillings in individually negotiated settlements. A number of further settlements were reached during 1960 amongst clerical and salaried workers. These provided for a general revision of the salary structure, but saw widely varying increases at different points of the scale.[18]

Shortly after becoming Taoiseach, Lemass invited the ICTU to meet him to discuss the question of development, and to consider how co-operation might be generated between the various economic actors. The ICTU, while broadly supporting the premise that Ireland enter a free trade body, called on the Government to adopt a planning strategy that would involve the expansion of the state sector.[19] In broad policy terms, the ICTU was adopting what Brian Girvin has termed a 'consumptionist strategy', which would increase purchasing power, thus increasing demand.[20] The trade union movement had in fact been stressing such a policy since the dark days of 1952. The ICTU also emphasised that the approach of the employers towards higher productivity was one of aiming at a constant production level with a reducing labour force, instead of increasing overall production and at least maintaining the labour force. It castigated the employers' approach as fatal to the long-term prospects of economic expansion, and as unlikely to win the support of workers for programmes of higher productivity.[21]

Expansion of the state sector was welcomed by some industrialists. Pádraic O'Halpin – a businessman and the chairman of the Engineering Development Council – in an address to a meeting of Tuairim (a sort of early think-tank established to examine the problems affecting Ireland), approved of the state's concern for the increased prosperity of the people:

> Where the national grounds for prosperity as our neighbours understand it do not exist here, that the people will press more and more for a better organisation of their existing assets. To obtain a clearer idea of what exactly is meant by organisation of existing assets, it is necessary only to think of the present-day circumstances which were the result of past Governmental actions and to consider how we should stand without them: the ESB, the industrial drive beginning in the early thirties, Bord na Mona and the Irish Sugar Company are examples. We must bear in mind that these advances were not forced on the people but in effect demanded by them through their elected representatives. It is safe to say also that the people have welcomed these events and that their expectation of Government includes the advocacy of similar organisations in the future.[22]

Lemass seemed to recognise the validity of this approach, but the ICTU argued that Government policy, while broadly correct, would not necessarily bring about quick results, either in employment or export terms. The ICTU insisted that Ireland should not merely wait for export-led expansion but should also infuse capital into the domestic economy to achieve growth. At this stage, the Government was pursuing a cautious fiscal policy, maintaining spending at existing levels but shifting investment from social to capital spending. The ICTU maintained that while capital investment was important, it would not on its own expand the economy. It argued that social spending should not be seen as non-productive, since it injected money into the economy that had a knock-on effect. It was during this meeting that Lemass dropped the first hint that he was unhappy about the EFTA negotiations. The ICTU report of the meeting states:

> As far as relationship with the seven [EFTA] was concerned we could come in at any time if we wanted to. He [Lemass] did not see it ever being to our advantage to do so. If an agreement was to come between the seven and the common market, we might change our policy.[23]

What Lemass was evidently worried about was that Irish industry and agriculture would not be able to expand significantly within such an area, and he thought that for the moment Ireland would be as well off pursuing a policy of maximising trade with Britain. Finance, however, was painfully aware of the country's over-reliance on Britain. The EEC offered the combined attractions of agricultural and industrial expansion. It also had in place a structure within which Ireland could maintain elements of its protectionist system for a number of years. For Finance, the bottom line was that Ireland should not join unless Britain did so as well.[24] A downside to any application to enter the EEC was that it would undermine the commitment to planning in any independent, systematic fashion. If Ireland was to accept that international competitiveness was the main aim of policy, then planning on a national basis would, to an extent, be redundant.[25]

## Making the National Cake Bigger

Notwithstanding this caution on Europe, Lemass had decided to abandon the economic policy he had inherited. Budgets were to expand, and increased investment become a Government priority:

> It is necessary that the state as such should participate in development activities to an even greater extent than heretofore, both as a promoter of industrial ventures, in spheres where private enterprise has as yet shown no interest, and as organiser of projects which, while not directly commercial, will contribute to the overall expansion of the country's economy and help manufacturers and farmers to achieve greater production and planning.[26]

In consultation with Whitaker, Lemass consequently decided to establish a planning branch within Finance where proposals for new state-investment activity would be examined.[27] It was to be headed by Charles Murray – Whitaker's chief collaborator in the writing of *Economic Development*. Thus, there was an explicit commitment from the Government to shift in a structured sense both output and exports from agriculture to industry. This reduced the impact on the entire economy of the considerable fluctuations in price and volume to which agricultural production was subject in the post-war period.

For both unions and industry, Ireland's drive to industrialise had enormous implications. At a meeting in May 1960 between the FII and ICTU, J.C. Tonge, president of the FII, argued that both sides 'should be concerned with making the national cake bigger rather than with the division of the present cake'.[28] This had been brought up by the unions during their meeting with Lemass the previous September. The lack of significant national economic progress was something each side blamed the other for. The ICTU stated that it was willing to discuss anything with anybody, but it is clear that it perceived the FII as anxious to increase profits in a free trade environment without a concomitant increase in living standards for workers. For example, when a draft agenda for this meeting was being worked out, the FII suggested that an item be added to the itinerary regarding 'the need for increased productivity and the problem of restrictive practices particularly in the context of changing conditions in Irish industry and the prospects for progressive reduction in protection and of eventual free trade'.[29] The ICTU rejected this out of hand. As far as the unions were concerned, discussions on Europe and the expansion of production could not be based on an analysis of Irish work practices.

While the Department of Industry and Commerce remained highly sceptical of any reduction in tariffs and of the general thrust of joining a European trading bloc, there was increasing debate within indigenous Irish industry on the European option. The FUE was enthusiastic about the possibility of Ireland entering a type of common market, and saw any moves to increase exports as positive. For the FIM, however, it was a little more complicated. In February 1957 an FIM conference on the proposed free trade area was held to discuss the merits of Ireland entering such a bloc. Divergent views were heard, with one speaker proclaiming: 'my personal attitude is wholly and entirely against the free trade area.' Another participant, however, declared that industry had to 'accept the Free Trade Area, and join with it, but at the same time fight for the best possible safeguards we can get'.[30] Most industrialists seemed to recognise that there would be a net benefit from Irish entry into a European trading bloc, although they understood that huge tariff cuts could not be withstood by the majority of Irish companies. In June 1957, for instance, A.N. Murray, chairman of the Cork regional group of the FIM, maintained:

> Within a very short time Ireland will be forced to join the Area because it will be economic suicide to stay out ... we are going to be forced to

export to survive commercially and we are going to face the most severe competition. It will truly be a case of survive or perish.[31]

Even *Irish Industry* – the journal of the FIM and an ardent advocate of indigenous industry – saw that the free trade issue had to be faced. It insisted in an editorial that manufacturers could give the lead in 'saving the country. If we must join this union the necessary safeguards must be forthcoming and the obvious concessions must be made to enable us to meet the competition of the European industrial giants.'[32] It did bemoan the fact that there seemed to be a lack of awareness among industrialists as to the importance of the free trade issue, but at a leadership level the FIM was preparing itself psychologically for a future without protectionism. Looked at from a global perspective, Irish industry was relatively weak, but it had been given some security by protection. This ethos was now being threatened, and native industry realised that it had to face what was going to be an uncertain future.

Ultimately, there was not a large enough economy to support firms who wished only to supply the home market, and a situation developed whereby industry split in two. Colm Barnes – one of the major industrialists of the time – has pointed out that 'those manufacturers who felt that they might survive had little incentive to unite with firms that were likely to fold'.[33] This was a point that had been inferred by Jack Fitzpatrick of the FII: writing in the Catholic journal, *Christus Rex*, in 1958, he declared that one could divide industry into two broad categories, namely those that were efficient and economic, and those that were efficient but not economic. The first group, he argued, was exporting competitively and selling goods in world markets, and its concern with regard to the free trade proposal was whether a protected home market would be required to facilitate continued exporting. The second category, represented:

... industries which were set up under the post 1932 policy of protectionism, including industries which were established by sincere men and women who were willing to invest their savings in the best interests, as they saw them, of the community ... It would obviously be unjust and immoral that these should be sacrificed without compensation. They must examine their position to see if they can survive, whether they could re-adapt their factories so as to make them competitive under such circumstances ... The problem is vast and complex but one thing emerges clearly and that is that a free trade treaty which makes no provision for dealing with the problem of industries which are efficient but, through no fault of their own, not economic, will not have dealt fairly with all aspects of the problem.[34]

The FII was, on the whole, eager for Irish entry into some form of trading bloc, and its annual report for 1959 suggested that the development of the industrial economy should in the future be considered in relation to three factors: firstly, the maintenance by existing industry of the home market, with a progressive reduction in protectionism, and eventually without protection against foreign competition; secondly, the development by existing industries of export markets with the same conditions in the home market; finally, the development of new types of industries without the expectation of the same measures of protection in the home market as had been available previously.[35] J.C. Tonge, president of the FII, was of the opinion that any changes should be directed towards improving the overall industrial position. He declared that the Government should accept responsibility for any radical change in policy, and was confident of the Government's attitude in this connection. The insinuation here was that the Government should grasp the nettle of free trade and consign the policy of protectionism to the dustbin of history. The FII was urging its individual member firms to make their own plans on the basis of free trade conditions in the future. Specifically, this meant urgent and constant attention to productivity in all its aspects, and particularly to the question of improving marketing policies and techniques, and to renewing efforts to find export markets:

> Confidence in our own ability and energetic action now on a planned basis by all individual firms and industries with the co-operation of the Government and the trades unions and of the public generally will ensure that these changes will be changes for the better. The Federation believes that the challenge which will be presented by the new conditions is also an opportunity for great developments in industry in Ireland.[36]

By 1960 the FII was firm but cautious about the benefits of entering EFTA. Tonge argued that if the Government was to enter the free trade area, it would be necessary to safeguard the industries built up under the protective system. He acknowledged that industrialists would have to study ways and means of survival under what would be new conditions, but stated that 'it will be extraordinarily difficult to adapt industry to free trade'.[37] He maintained that this could only be done with the co-operation of the Government and the trade unions. The FII was asking the Government to render special assistance during the transitional period, while it needed the contribution of the trade union movement as large numbers of workers were involved in industries that might be affected, and they would have to receive careful consideration in order to avoid hardship. The FII advised its members to be prepared for a progressive reduction in protective customs duties, and asked each firm to consider its own position and that of its respective industry in conditions of free trade. The FII also carried out its own pilot survey in the weaving industry, which suggested that while the concept of Europe was generally seen as fairly desirable, its consequences on Ireland could be disastrous. As Colm Barnes, who replaced Tonge as president in 1961, declared:

> There was definitely a fear in the minds of the traditional industrialists in particular that a reduction in tariffs would see most of them going to the wall. While some saw the advent of EFTA as a challenge to be met head on, because after all businessmen are supposed to be free traders, most members of the FII were horrified by the prospect.[38]

This attitude was summed up by Tonge when he declared that 'in general Irish industry does not want free trade, but at the same time it realises that Ireland cannot live in complete isolation from the rest of Europe'.[39] The FII, however, was determined that Irish industry would become more efficient and more cost-conscious, with productivity and marketing receiving prime consideration. It saw a way forward in Europe whereby its member firms would be encouraged to specialise in certain products, with less variety than had hitherto been the case. If overseas markets could be secured, the FII believed its member firms could make progress while facing an era of reduced tariffs:

> We are facing a challenge which should bring out the best, but if the best is not good enough the outlook for Irish industry, to say the least, will not be satisfactory. While not blaming our Government in any way for advocating a policy of reduction in tariffs, industry feels that the Government must bear full responsibility for the effects of any such reductions. Irish industry has confidence in the Government and is confident that its interests and indeed the interests of the country generally will be safeguarded in any difficult times that lie ahead in the EFTA era. Industrialists will endeavour to manage under Free Trade to the best of their ability, opposing no section but co-operating with all in the national interest.[40]

A problem for the FII – as Colm Barnes has since pointed out – was that it was a comparatively weak body, and although it might call on the Government to safeguard Irish industry, it did not do so from a position of strength:

> In 1960 when there was a lot of debate about EFTA the FII was dominated by the textile and clothing industries, yet the federation itself was very weak, hardly representing a third of those who were industrially employed. It lacked resources, effective membership and was on the whole a pretty feeble organisation. If one read about it at the time in the newspapers you would have got the impression that it was a strong body but that was not the case. Behind that apparent strength lay a great weakness. The consequence of this was that the Government of the day could do as it pleased within the industrial sector. It was only with the development of the CIO that they acquired more confidence and became more of an influence.[41]

## 'INVEST IN IRELAND INDEED'

The FII – while wanting increased trade for its members – was worried that those members would go to the wall through participation in the free trade area. This problem was exacerbated by the impact that foreign industry was having on home-based manufacturers – something the FII was acutely aware of. An example of the anxiety felt by individual members of the FII can be seen in a 1960 letter to the Taoiseach from a pottery manufacturer in Wexford:

> I received through the post a large coloured advertisement exhorting me, as an Irish individual, to 'invest in Ireland'. Allow me to point out that this additional indignity has been offered to me by a Government which has recently given a free capital grant of a quarter of a million pounds

to an American firm in order to subsidise that firm in the manufacture of peat moss plant potteries at Birr, in direct competition with my old established native Irish concern. It is futile for the Government to attempt to maintain that the Birr factory has been subsidised for the 'export market' because this is simply not so; the home market is already being very thoroughly canvassed in favour of Birr Potteries and what is more, the fact of the free Government grant is being used to suggest that only the new Birr factory has the confidence of the Government in the matter of peat potteries. This, of course, has every appearance of being true but for an Irish Government to allow an American firm to use such propaganda in its competition with an Irish firm is rather strange. Furthermore when I applied for some small assistance to help me meet the threat of Government subsidised foreign competition I was told by An Foras Tionscal that free capital grants are available to foreigners but not to native Irish industry. Invest in Ireland indeed.[42]

This is a striking example of the worries some in the FII felt in the face of the twin threats of free trade and the influx of foreign companies attempting to service the same markets.

Ultimately, the FII – though evidently worried about free trade – was willing to go along with the Government's strategy of generally phasing out protection, and Lemass was determined to bring the representative body with him on the journey towards free trade and competitiveness. The question of possible entrance of a trading bloc, however, was still to be broached by Lemass. He told the national export conference of the FII in January 1961 that Ireland was not a member of EFTA or the EEC:

... for the very good reason that there is no overall advantage to be gained at the present time by joining either group. In the case of the seven, Britain is by far the most important market for us and there

189

we already have, under our bilateral agreement, for practically all our industrial goods, the trade advantages which membership of that group would confer. As far as the other countries of the seven are concerned the obligations which we would have to assume in joining the European Free Trade Area including the dismantlement of industrial protection, not only against imports from the six continental members, but against Britain as well, would outweigh any trade advantages which we could hope to get from these countries.[43]

Whilst this speech suggested doubts about the European option and reinforced the importance of the British market for the Irish economy, the fact that there were intense discussions on possible entry into such a free-trading bloc implied that sooner or later the Government would seek to place the state within a free trade association.

The FII had recognised that fundamental changes in Irish economic policies were necessary and imminent, and would involve progressive reduction of protection for Irish industries, leading eventually to free trade conditions. Its national council issued a pamphlet entitled *European Free Trade and the Prospects for Irish Industry*, in which it argued that Irish industry was sufficiently strong and adaptable to meet the situation, and could develop and prosper 'provided that action is taken in time by individual firms and by industries and that the co-operation and assistance of the Government was forthcoming'.[44] The document represented a sea change in the attitude of the FII to protectionism. Up to the late 1950s, it had been an ardent supporter of protectionism; it realised now that new trading conditions required new attitudes. This new attitude in the FII was crystallised by the coming to power in the organisation of a younger breed of industrialists who believed that Irish industry could survive and flourish without protectionism if it was given the vigorous support of Government. But though the FII appeared confident, there was no guarantee that individual firms would put in the effort required to make a success of free trade.

As for the Government, it initially perceived the attitudes of industry to be too relaxed. At a meeting between the Department of Industry and Commerce and the PUTUO regarding the impact of a free trade area on industries, Tom Murray, an assistant secretary at the department, bluntly affirmed that the greatest possible expansion lay with those industries that were already doing an export trade, while the most vulnerable were those with highest tariff protection. He stated, however, that there seemed to be a fairly general attitude on the part of industry that it would not be too badly off within the free trade area. This outlook, he argued, was not a pragmatic one. Those industries with experience of exporting and who saw new markets on the horizon could obviously expect to benefit. But as to any special arrangements to assist industries likely to be adversely affected, Murray conceded that the convention setting up the area was not likely to provide assistance: 'the purpose of the Free Trade Area ... was to eliminate the unfit'.[45] The attitude pervading both the business and trade union communities on the length of time that industries could take to meet the full rigours of competition was not shared by the Government. Both the FUE and the FII thought in terms of a period of up to twenty years. The trade unions, on the other hand, thought that a period of twelve to fifteen years was more feasible. Lemass seemed to believe that Ireland had up to ten years to effect substantial change before having to face external competition. His officials were not as optimistic.

In May 1961 the Government decided not to join EFTA, and two months later formally applied to join the EEC after it became aware of Britain's intention to do so. In its application, the Irish Government stressed that there was no significant opposition to joining the Community, and that all the interest groups were broadly in favour of entry. For the purposes of examining the role of industry in the EEC, the Government had established the Committee on Industrial Organisation (CIO), on which the ICTU and the FII had direct representation. Originally, the ICTU was left out, and had to demand to be included. Garret FitzGerald – at this stage an advisor to the FII – argued that the FII had to work with the Government in a general review of economic policy, and approached Whitaker as to the feasibility of the study. This was truly a radical step for business to take. Whitaker readily agreed, and FitzGerald maintains that it was simply due to an oversight that the unions were left out:

> They proved to be most constructive partners. Indeed, insofar as tensions existed within the committee they proved – as I had anticipated – to be between the Department of Industry and Commerce on the one hand and the rest of us, with Finance, the CII and ICTU endeavouring as a troika to nudge that department into psychological acceptance of free trade.[46]

In the circumstances, it might have been more logical to have had a partnership with Industry and Commerce, but that department had remained protectionist-oriented, and FitzGerald anticipated that, on its own, it was unlikely to be an adequate partner in the contemplated exercise:

> Thus the committee was set up with the remit to make a critical appraisal of the measures that may have to be taken to adapt Irish industry to conditions of more intensive competition in home and export markets, to undertake an examination of the difficulties which may be created for particular industries and to formulate positive measures of adjustment and adaptation.[47]

*The Irish Times* welcomed the CIO, declaring that 'it could become the most important single organisation in the country, and will pilot industry through the transitional period'.[48] When the CIO reports began to appear in the autumn of 1962, however, they showed the weakness of Irish industry, especially when it came to export potential. Not all industrialists saw entry into the EEC as the solution. Aodogan O'Rahilly, for one, was deeply worried:

> While I welcomed foreign investment, I believed that if we were going to enter the EEC then our sovereignty would be lost and in a free trade environment we would quickly go under. I drew comparisons between entry to the EEC and the passing of the Act of Union at the time as I foresaw Irish industry dying, just as what happened in the early 1800s due to the operation of economic laws. In many ways I suppose I was an old style Fianna Fáil nationalist.[49]

More typical was the response of Jack Fitzpatrick of the FII, who told *Hibernia* that Ireland would join the EEC and the result would be the 'blossoming of our economy'.[50] Officially, the FII had become a supporter of Whitaker's policy of economic planning. It noted:

> In the midst of the activities in preparing for entry into the EEC it is good to see that the Government have not lost sight of their economic planning programme which will have an important bearing on our preparedness to face the challenge of the common market.[51]

The CIO was part of a continuing corporatist-style initiative by Lemass to involve unions and industry in developing the economy. The initiative sought to create political structures that integrated the organised socio-economic groups through a system of representation and co-operative mutual interaction at leadership level, and social control at the mass level. Moreover, Lemass' desire to incorporate the unions found an echo in the dominant trend of corporatist thinking within the trade union movement itself.[52] The Employer–Labour Conference came into existence in 1962, and the National Industrial and Economic Council (NIEC) was established a year later. These new agencies exemplified the state's commitment to economic planning, though if Ireland had succeeded in gaining entry into the EEC in 1963, it is doubtful whether subsequently they would have had much impact on policy formulation.

Not all observers were convinced by this rush of activity and the response of the economic actors. The US embassy, for instance, was none too impressed with these developments, maintaining that:

> [The] Government sets much store by this conference as a means of working out agreements between labour and management on long-term policies … However the embassy has not been especially impressed by the amount of enthusiasm with which the FUE or ICTU has been approaching the conference. Both parties have been diligently preparing for it, but neither side has indicated to the embassy that it has any great prospect of success.[53]

Patrick Lynch, however, recalled 'the freshness and vigour of trade union thinking on the desirability of a consensus on the broad economic issues such as income policies and economic planning'.[54] He described the representatives of the ICTU as being free from partisanship and as people who produced many original contributions directed solely to the common good, and he maintains that the support of the unions was essential for the success of economic planning that Whitaker was promoting. Donal Nevin has also talked of the importance of the unions' role in bodies such as the NIEC and the CIO, arguing that they could have taken the attitude that 'it is none of our business but instead played a positive role'.[55] While this may be so, the ICTU's first policy statement on entry into the EEC urged caution, and advised the

Government, rather unrealistically, to pursue alternative strategies such as searching for new markets.[56] More interestingly, Nevin maintains that Congress as a unified body left its negotiators – usually Ruaidhrí Roberts and himself – to formulate their own stance, and adopted their reports on various economic policies unanimously. Before the ICTU was united, many full-time craft-union officials involved in complex negotiations with Government and the employers on pay and other issues had little knowledge of economic problems. Nevin has stressed how the union movement – and himself in particular as research officer – relied on the advice of academic economists, such as Paddy Lynch, for their policy positions.[57]

## FREER TRADE IS COMING

The CIO was involved in incorporating the industrial-interest groups into Government structures, and within this framework Lemass met the FII and ICTU in January 1962 to discuss the implications of the application for industry. Lemass told the FII that it would have only a short period of time to adapt to the new conditions, and would then have to face the full brunt of competition. He recognised that some industries would not be able to make this transition easily, but said that the Government was aware of this and would seek some concessions from the EEC. Colm Barnes, president of the FII, protested that Irish industry could not survive what would amount to a 50 per-cent cut in tariffs. As he was to recall later:

> While we realised that the EEC would not tolerate stragglers, we thought it would be a massive act of self-deception on the part of the Government if they thought that industry could withstand such tariff cuts. Looking back now industry was very weak, but once you were in there was great security because you had a captive market and high

tariff walls which kept out imports. If we had entered in 1963 on these grounds native industry already weak would have been decimated.[58]

Lemass, in response, noted that the EEC would probably not give special concessions to Ireland, and that while negotiation was possible, the principle of a transition period leading to the elimination of tariffs had to be accepted. It was doubtful whether the EEC would agree to selective tariff cuts, but if there was a possibility of securing a special protocol, it would be necessary to specify the sensitive industries. He estimated that if Ireland joined in 1963, effective protection would be gone within three years of accession, and that, consequently, this was the time span to be dealt with. Within that period, and the longer transitional-period, adjustment might be made after consultation with the EEC, but he believed that the limits were well established.[59]

At another level, a former Government official has spoken of the frustration felt by those officials who undertook the CIO surveys:

> We would have an appointment to meet with the Managing Director of some firm down the country and we would arrive only to be told that he was gone playing golf or was off at the hunt, our experiences were literally of that kind. That was the mindset of industrialists at the time. They had no faith in the CIO.[60]

Countering this, Joseph McCullough – who was heavily involved in industry – comments:

> I was a general manager in a tyre manufacturing firm at the time. Civil servants from Industry and Commerce came down to see us but really they were hopelessly ill-equipped. The idea that these fellows could help us to organise when they were not even organised themselves was ludicrous. What happened was that civil servants were being transferred

from one section of Industry and Commerce to another but they were all really of the same mindset.[61]

Another industrialist has commented on how great opportunities were lost due to the attitudes of businessmen:

> Due to that lack of self confidence, which was largely within small business, and not having enough strong entrepreneurial spirit, major opportunities were lost. However, we had no business people to lead us, only politicians and civil servants. Yet there was a feeling that they did not know business, the nitty gritty of it, only the theory and as a result business people tended to try to ignore them. Their attitude to the CIO would be an example of that.[62]

Although the ICTU gave only lukewarm support to the original application, it offered no dissension to Lemass' strategy when it met him three days later. Lemass urged the trade unions to accept that changes were underway in Ireland's relationship with the wider world, and that existing preferential arrangements with Britain were already weakened. He reiterated his intention to seek membership under the best terms possible, but said that they would have to operate on the assumption that tariffs would have to be removed by the beginning of 1970. He stressed that it was his view that:

> State aids to industry designed to promote efficiency should be regarded as desirable ... though the form of aid in some cases would be modified ... In general it appeared likely that the question of adjustment to common market conditions would be a problem of the position of individual firms rather than industrial groups.[63]

This implied that even in the absence of EEC membership, considerable changes in the Irish economy would be necessary. The ICTU responded to the Government's stance by calling a consultative conference to debate the impact entry into the EEC would have on its movement. Though it issued no formal response to its meeting with Lemass, the ICTU could have been in no doubt that he was determined to bring Ireland into the EEC. *Hibernia* criticised the unions and the other economic actors for their general reluctance to comment publicly on economic issues: 'What is particularly lamentable is that the universities, the large business corporations, the trade unions, the private banks and the political parties make so little contribution to economic thought and discussion in Ireland'.[64]

It would seem that the ICTU was more concerned about the EEC than EFTA due to the political connotations associated with the former. Donal Nevin, for instance, told the 1961 annual conference that 'there is no doubt that entry into the Common Market would mean a surrender of control over economic policy', while the following year, John Carroll of the ITGWU told the conference that the ICTU had not done enough to 'point out to all of us the importance to our nation of the political ramifications of membership of the EEC'.[65] Some trade unionists, such as M. O'Donnell of the Irish National Union of Vintners', Grocers' and Allied Trades' Assistants, believed that 'the political aspect of this question is to a great extent a myth'.[66] Moreover, the question of the EEC being a bulwark against communism was raised by many speakers at the 1961 conference in Cork as a reason for entering the EEC. Irish entry into EFTA would not have the same political connotations as entry into the EEC, and the Cork conference showed that there was division over this issue within the ICTU.

The ICTU eventually responded to the EEC application by delivering a policy statement at the annual conference in Galway in July 1962. The main thrust of this was that the conversion of the Irish economy to conditions of free trade should proceed:

... at a pace, over a certain period of time and in such a manner that our object of securing a continuing increase in total employment shall be kept within such limits that redundant workers will be able to secure equally good employment in Ireland without adversely affecting the intake of new entrants into industry.[67]

Providing ample employment opportunities for redundant workers, while at the same time seeking similar opportunities for new entrants to the labour market, was inevitably going to prove difficult. While the ICTU conceded that this objective might not be attainable in the context of EEC membership, what it did not point out was that there would be no chance of achieving this aim in protective isolation. While the ICTU does appear from this to have had significant doubts about free trade, it was nevertheless willing to support the general thrust of Lemass' free trade intentions, which were inevitably focused on the EEC.

Inevitably, some unions were intransigently opposed to entry into the EEC – the Draughtsmens' and Allied Technicians' Association, for one, proclaiming 'we are definitely anti-Common Market'.[68] Yet while many unions – particularly in assembly and textiles – were worried about the effects of free trade, most realised that they had to face up to the fact that it was coming. In effect, it was the economic rather than the political ramifications of EEC entry that worried trade unionists, though a good many recognised the problems inherent in Irish industry. One ITGWU representative felt that the EEC could be the answer to the country's economic problems:

We have nothing to lose on the economic front. We have roughly 40,000 unemployed per year and 40,000 emigrate each year. Can it be very much worse than that, irrespective of what already adverse affects the Common Market has upon us? There are many protected industries in this country that refuse to install modern plant and machinery.[69]

At the 1963 congress, a member of the executive council remarked:

> It has been made abundantly clear to us now that what sufficed in the
> past will not do so in the future. A state of complacency does exist
> at all levels of industry whether it be with management or with the
> workers.[70]

It was with this awareness of complacency that the ICTU was willing,
however reluctantly, to join Lemass on the road to free trade.

The ICTU held a consultative conference in March 1963 to
discuss the preliminary reports issued by the CIO on the state of Irish
industry. The CIO had published reports on the leather, footwear,
paper and paperbond, cotton, linen and rayon, motor vehicle assembly
and fertiliser industries, and estimated that these could be faced with
considerable redundancies if EEC rules were applied to Ireland.
Unions representing workers in these industries communicated with
the ICTU to voice their fears and to ask that consideration be given
to policy in the light of these findings.[71] One ITGWU representative,
for instance, noted the seriousness of the reports, proclaiming that the
motor-assembly industry was likely to be drastically hit by free trade:

> These reports give serious food for thought because they indicate that
> unless many changes are made in our industrial set up we will be
> unable to meet the competition of free trade conditions. That these
> changes must be made all agree ... under the policy of protection many
> have failed to keep up with the changing times; failed to modernise;
> failed to introduce new techniques. Now following the CIO reports,
> these industries find themselves in serious difficulty. The changes that
> should have been made as a matter of course over the years were not
> made.[72]

Indeed, the motor industry would be hit substantially by EEC membership and the removal of protective support, though it took until July 1984 before Ford closed its manufacturing base in Cork.

For his part, Lemass saw the CIO reports as proof positive that 'the policy of protection has been clearly and officially shown in post-war circumstances to be defective in promoting or compelling the effort needed to ensure the continuing efficiency of industry'.[73] The ICTU recognised that if Irish industry was to survive, it had to export; to export, it had to be competitive. It would not be possible in the EEC to manufacture for export while receiving protection at home. Even if Ireland did not enter the EEC, there were two good reasons why this policy should not be continued, it argued: primarily, protected home industries tended not to export, and concealed the cost of inefficiency within high-priced products for the protected market; secondly, the consumer was subsidising the cost of inefficiency through higher prices, and this represented a drain on the national economy. The problem the ICTU faced was how to ensure that heavy reductions in employment did not result from the elimination of tariffs in the process of reorganising Irish industry. The manpower and social-affairs committee of the OECD had accepted recommendations that member countries should make an active labour-market policy an essential element in their economic policies for growth and development. The ICTU eventually adopted a somewhat catch-all position: it supported the reorganisation of industry as desirable, yet said that the extent of any reorganisation should be such that redundant workers could be absorbed. This could be achieved, it suggested, by the establishment of a planning body to gather employment information and adjust investment to overcome cyclical disturbances.[74] It is not clear, however, how the ICTU anticipated such a body working or if it really believed that it would solve the unemployment problems that would inevitably arise once Ireland entered the EEC.

The CIO, in its final report, concluded that the sectors it had examined were not adapting to the new economic environment, even though Ireland had not entered the EEC and was not likely to until 1970 at the earliest, and despite the Government offering to provide advice and finance to aid the transition. It found that most industrial sectors were not internationally competitive, that they concentrated on production for home consumption, and that unless adjustment took place there would be a considerable loss in employment.[75]

By the early 1960s the Government had decided that the future direction of the Irish economy lay in it being associated with the EEC. The trade union movement was initially lukewarm in its endorsement, but was co-opted by Lemass and subsequently involved in discussions on the future development of economic policy. The ICTU, it must be said, was not seduced by its important role in Government policy formulation; it realised that its main priority of protecting the welfare of its members could be best achieved by formally negotiating and working with the Government. The Lemass Governments of the early 1960s had actively sought the input of the trade union movement, as well as other interest groups, in what was effectively a realignment of Government economic policy in which agricultural and industrial policy was placed on an equal footing for the first time in the history of the state. The ICTU therefore concluded that workers' welfare could best be protected and enhanced from within a trading bloc, and by the union movement being in a position of influence – which it had not had before – rather that being isolated in the wilderness.

The Government, industry and the trade unions recognised that Irish industry would have to develop rapidly to meet the rigours of free trade. As the president of the ITGWU, John Conroy, pointed out:

Freer trade is coming and unless we all realise this and prepare we will find that every workshop and factory not fully and efficiently equipped will cease to produce to economic requirements and all the employees will find themselves unemployed.[76]

The CIO had pointed out the unpreparedness of industry for the transition from a protective framework to an interdependent economy. The ICTU, through its involvement in various Government-sponsored bodies, had entered the mainstream of economic policy formulation, and in the light of free trade conditions, it seemed that there could be no return to a protectionist position. Wage negotiations overlapped throughout this period with the evolution of an external economic stance, and the union movement recognised that higher wages and higher productivity depended on the expansion of the Irish economy. All parties involved recognised that there could be no return to protectionism, and resolved to adopt a trilateral approach in an attempt to revolutionise the Irish economy in the light of new free trade conditions. A consensus had formed to the effect that it was better to face an unpredictable world as a member of an economic alliance rather than persist as an isolated economy, and that export-led growth was required.

Ireland's economic interests had taken on a wider agenda – one that required the input of industry and the trade union movement. The European issue was vigorously debated at the ICTU's annual conferences in the early 1960s, yet while its position would change radically by the time of the referendum on entry into the EEC in 1972, there can be little doubt that as the CIO reports of the early 1960s were issued, the ICTU concluded that entry into Europe would be advantageous to its members. The ICTU and the majority of unions saw that protectionism had failed and that the challenge of free trade would have to be faced.

Union attitudes of the early 1970s were unquestionably much different than those of a decade previously. The intervening years had

seen a deterioration of relations between the ICTU and the Fianna
Fáil Government on a number of issues, not least on the direction
of the economy. After a lengthy examination of the European issue
in the early 1960s, Congress had tentatively embraced that 'spurious
progeny', but would soon spurn it once it took on a life that the union
movement could not agree with.[77]

## A PROSPEROUS RURAL COMMUNITY

One of the main beneficiaries of Ireland's entry into an economic
bloc would be the farming community – a sector of society central
to Lemass' attempts to realign Irish economic policy. The course of
state–farmer relations from the foundation of the National Farmers'
Association (NFA) in 1955 to the official formalising of relations
between the Government and that organisation in 1964 was a rocky
one. The 1950s saw a redefinition of state–farmer relations: the
specifically farmers' political parties of earlier decades had been unable
to establish Irish politics on a rural-versus-urban footing. The original
Farmers' Party did manage to win a handful of seats in 1922, but failed
to consolidate this modest achievement; its vote faded away within a
decade, with the remnants of the party subsumed into Fine Gael. In
1939 another farmers' party emerged: founded in Athenry, Clann na
Talmhan built a base amongst small farmers, and its policies included
land reclamation and redistribution. It performed spectacularly in
its inaugural election, in 1943, gaining over 100,000 first-preference
votes – close to 10 per cent of the first-preference vote. It was unable
to sustain this level of support despite participating in the 1948–51
and 1954–57 Inter-Party Governments, and its demise came about
in 1965.[78]

The absence of an influential agrarian party can be put down to the
relative political maturity of rural Ireland, wherein all parties espoused

some degree of interest in agriculture and made ritualistic references to traditional rural virtues.[79] From the 1950s on, farmers avoided party and parliamentary politics, organising instead in pressure groups and seeking to build up the muscle to take on the Government in pursuit of their demands.[80] Events were to show that the established political parties were slow to recognise the decoupling of farm issues from the party system. The organisation of such farmer groups had its genesis in the foundation of Macra na Feirme in 1944, whose original purpose was to bring young farmers together to discuss modern ideas on farming. Macra promoted the strategy of economic specialisation and organisation as a response to what it saw as the pressures to modernise Irish agriculture. One of these pressures was the increasingly fraught relationship between the farming community and the Government. Nevertheless, Macra was not prepared to transform itself into a producer group with a specific economic purpose and a mandate to negotiate with the Government to directly influence state agricultural policy;[81] instead, it promoted the formation of the Irish Creamery Milk Suppliers' Association (ICMSA) and the National Farmers' Association (NFA) as associations of farmers representing economic interests in Irish agriculture. In their capacity as economic-interest groups, the two organisations focused much of their attention on the way the state regulated the agricultural economy. From its inception, the ICMSA was a militant, agitating organisation concerned mainly with those who produced milk for manufacturing purposes. Early on, it defeated a Government proposal for a cut in the price paid to dairy farmers for milk, and in 1953 conducted the first milk strike in the country, which lasted sixteen days and was hailed a success as the farmers secured an increase of 1¾ pence per gallon for their milk.[82] Of even more significance was the emergence of the agricultural strike, a weapon hitherto the preserve of the trade unions.

The NFA was the main focus for negotiation with the Government during the period. Its influence spread rapidly in the years after its foundation, and it was far more aggressive in its championing of farmers' issues than any other organisation. While numerous attempts were made over many years to unite the NFA and ICMSA, this never happened. Once the ICMSA opted to remain independent, the NFA set about building up its own organisation on the lines of the Macra parish network, and by the autumn of 1955, it was reported that 350 branches had been set up.[83] Though impressive, there was an uneven spread of branches, with a marked weakness in the poorer farming areas of the west of Ireland. As for the leadership of the association, in general, most had been members of Macra, whose main farming interest was beef. For instance, Seán Healy, the first general secretary of the NFA, had served with Macra since 1948, becoming general secretary of that organisation in 1950, from where he played a crucial role in the setting up of the NFA.

The NFA's influence quickly spread, and by the late 1950s it had become the focal point through which farmer discontent could be aired. By this time, two issues had emerged that were to be of fundamental importance to the NFA and the farming community in general, and which were interrelated: the low level of agricultural income, and the impact Irish entry into any European economic grouping would have on those incomes. The NFA took a decided stance on both issues. In an address to NFA members in Kildare in 1958, the NFA's first president, Juan Greene, from Athy, asserted that 'the pulse by which we must assess the economic health of this country is to be found in a prosperous rural community'. He also maintained that farmers should enthusiastically support some form of European economic integration: 'European integration is more than our challenge, it will be our salvation if we wish it so … If we are to survive it will be as a partner in a larger viable economic unit of an international character.'[84] Regarding agricultural incomes, the NFA had since its inception been extremely critical of

206

Government policy in agriculture. There was an increasing perception within the agricultural community that Fianna Fáil under Seán Lemass' stewardship of the Department of Industry and Commerce had become a party driven by industrial considerations.[85] Things came to a head early in 1958 when a motion of no confidence in the Government was passed at a special meeting of the NFA's council. Greene wrote to the Taoiseach, Eamon de Valera, to say:

> The council of the NFA unanimously passes a motion of no confidence in the attitude of the Government towards the present agricultural situation and that the council asks that an interview be sought with the Taoiseach to place before him their views on the very serious crisis that has now arisen. The council further decided that it is vital that farmers throughout the country be more clearly acquainted with the situation and is to arrange for public meetings in each county.[86]

This was an important milestone in state–farmer relations, in that it was the first time that such a motion had been passed criticising the entire thrust of Governmental policy, and demanding a complete reworking of such. Relations between the NFA and Fianna Fáil had been fraught since the latter returned to office in 1957, and the motion of no confidence only heightened the tension. While the NFA mistrusted Fianna Fáil over general agricultural policy, Fianna Fáil's antipathy towards the NFA ran much deeper. In a speech in Wexford in 1958, the Minister for Finance, James Ryan, criticised the NFA, claiming that it was merely a pawn of the Fine Gael party:

> I can recollect three or four Farmers' unions in the last forty years; they all began by telling us they were non-political and non-sectarian but they all ended where they belonged in the ranks of Fine Gael.[87]

*The Irish Times* in an editorial entitled 'Politics and policy' came down in favour of the NFA, and criticised Government policy towards farming in general, stating that there was a complete lack of evidence that agricultural decisions were dictated by the balanced needs of a planned agricultural policy: 'When can we expect a Government which will begin to treat agriculture as what the party hacks are saying it is – our major industry on the planned prosperity of which our economic survival depends?'[88]

A former senior advisor to the NFA recollected that agriculture ministers of both parties thought of politics first and agriculture second: 'you had all sorts of accusations. Dillon used to say that the NFA was nothing but a Fianna Fáil rump while Ryan and others thought of the NFA as Blueshirts'.[89]

## DENIGRATE AND BESMIRCH THE DEPARTMENT

By September 1959 relations between the farm organisations and the Department of Agriculture had deteriorated to the point where Greene wrote to the minister, Paddy Smith, stating that 'if good relations cannot be established between the two, then I am at a loss to know where we are going'.[90] There were a number of reasons for the NFA's disenchantment. The NFA had come into existence with a clear set of priorities. High on the list, it claimed, was the establishment for the voice of organised farming of a more progressive relationship and understanding with ministers and their respective departments, in particular those most closely associated with the agricultural industry. The NFA declared itself determined to prove its worth as a partner with the Government in formulating a predetermined progressive agricultural policy for the country. For J.C. Nagle, a former secretary of the Department of Agriculture, there was in this phrase a hint of undemocratic thinking within the NFA, and he maintained that it 'did not seem to realise the full implications of a Government singling out one organisation as partner over another'.[91] Nagle – who became secretary at the Department in 1958 – played a key role in negotiations with the NFA in this period. He was described by the British Ministry of Agriculture as:

> ... at first sight a lugubrious-looking individual – responsibility for maintaining Irish agricultural aspects in the face of [the] European economic grouping from which the Republic is excluded is a daunting one – his gloomy appearance conceals a sharp intellect and a considerable flair for patient and astute negotiation.[92]

The NFA, in a 1959 *Quarterly Supplement,* asserted that its willingness to be a partner with Government would require more on its part than the mere passing of wishful resolutions that 'we wanted more cash per unit of production'. This the organisation was willing to do, but it should be armed with the reason why, and – more importantly – the answer as to how this was to be done in the context of the Irish economy.[93] It argued that in all its dealings at Governmental level, it had been confident in the knowledge that it had answered these questions. In attempting to gain a better deal for its members, the NFA stated that it recognised early on during its own activities that new attitudes would have to be developed if its membership and the country at large were to fare better than they had in the past, and that the NFA was supported in this by public opinion. This was important, as without it:

> ... there was almost nothing to hope for, for the very good reason that the future prospects of improving our whole economy are very largely dependent on vocational groups being willing, encouraged and even assisted, towards doing something for themselves. There is a duty for all of us now to determine what progress if any we are making in this

direction. NFA opinion is disappointed, often even discouraged, in having fallen short of the target we set ourselves.[94]

While claiming that its objective was to expose the deficiency rather than determine where the fault lay, the NFA had no doubt where the blame belonged for the failure to reach its targets. In this context, Juan Greene launched a stinging attack on the Department of Agriculture and, by implication, the other farming organisations:

> By default, in failing to produce from our own ranks many years ago a vocational unified voice for agriculture, we ourselves forced our Department to play a role in farming matters it was never designed to take. Further to this, with the development of a multiplicity of unco-ordinated and often contradictory voices speaking on behalf of the farmer, our Department was further forced to the all-powerful position of sole arbiter, ultimately developing into a closed shop mentality. For very many years the impression created in the public mind has been that of the farmers and their own State Department in a state of continuous rebellion and constantly at each other's throats. Anything less conducive to rational development of the industry could hardly be imagined.[95]

Stating that the NFA was well aware of the difficulties between the department and itself, Greene claimed that he was anxious that people in other quarters would become aware of it. This was seen in the department as some sort of veiled threat, and, if anything, made the Government, and the minister, Paddy Smith, more obdurate in its dealings with the NFA.[96] The NFA insisted, however, that it was determined to reach its self-imposed targets because if it was not to be regarded as a partner responsible to the industry, 'it would continue to remain a house divided against itself and might be as well written off as having no important place in the affairs of our country'.[97] The implication was that the department was wilfully ignoring the NFA, and had offered no response to approaches from it. Greene went so far as to suggest that it was interesting that no other vocational group was so obviously out of tune with its related Department of State than the farming organisations.

For its part, the Department of Agriculture felt that since its formation, the NFA had adopted a consistent policy of attempting to 'denigrate and besmirch the Department'.[98] At departmental level, the complaints of the NFA were treated cautiously, but there was a feeling that the association was engaged in a policy of trying to usurp the smaller farmer organisations, and attacked the department to show its strength.[99] At ministerial level, however, things were not so circumspect. Smith replied to Greene's complaints in a handwritten letter just over a week later, and resolutely defended his department's and his own record while launching a savage attack on the behaviour of the NFA. Claiming that there was absolutely no justification for the NFA criticisms, Smith mentioned that there had been forty-one meetings between the department and the NFA in the past year alone. Furthermore, many of these meetings had been convened on the initiative of the department, and some even at Smith's own behest:

> Some members of the NFA may take the line that such meetings are no use as the Minister has his mind made up beforehand. But it is just not true that reasonable recommendations and constructive criticisms are ignored by my Department or myself and I can give you a lot of examples of this if you wish. I can even remember a scheme which I accepted against my better judgement, shortly after becoming Minister, merely because discussions between my officials and the NFA which had been going on a long time were approaching final agreement.[100]

A point made by both Smith and J.C. Nagle regarding the NFA's grievances was that the department had many aspects to consider and weigh which the NFA did not have to concern itself with, but which were the Government's duty to examine. As Nagle pointed out:

> In practice some clashes between the Government and farming organ-isations have to a varying extent been inevitable, given the natural preoccupation of the latter with acquiring power to enable them to influence policy decisions by dint of continuing criticism without detailed and objective examination of the probable cost of their proposals to taxpayers. This is not to question the right of an organisation to use lawful means in pursuit of legitimate objectives, but it must remain a matter of opinion how far such rights should be tempered by reference to the public interest.[101]

Paddy Smith's assertion that his protestations 'should be taken in good part and not used for the purpose of misrepresentation and abusive attacks in the *Farmers' Journal* and elsewhere' was somewhat over-optimistic since the NFA was hardly likely to see it this way; nor was it entirely convinced by the department's protestations of putting the country first.[102] As a former NFA advisor, Louis Smith, remarked:

> All we were ever told at our meetings with the department was that they had to think about the country as well as agricultural policy. The point was that the NFA had become a serious threat to the department because we were putting forward policies and wanted serious reform.[103]

Paddy Smith also accused the NFA of using its contacts with the department for purely propaganda purposes, and 'purely misleading propaganda at that', and complained that 'while we have on several occasions been complimented and thanked privately by your organi-sation for various actions and services, I find it hard to remember occasions on which any public acknowledgement was bestowed on us'.[104] Smith further accused the NFA of using its position in the *Farmers' Journal* to put forward statements that had a 'strong political tinge'. This referred to a dispute over marketing for Donegal oats; the department issued a statement on the matter to the NFA, but this appeared in the *Farmers' Journal* 'under the guise of a mystery being cleared up and referred to misrepresentations and half truths coming from the minister'.[105] It was the minister's view that the NFA – and by implication the *Farmers' Journal* – was behaving as a pawn of Fine Gael in agricultural matters. However, there are inconsistencies in his stance on this position. He later informed Greene that he was not the first agricultural minister to encounter such problems with the NFA, and was aware that his predecessors also had difficulties with the association. Yet the only other agricultural minister to have had comprehensive dealings with the NFA since its foundation was Fine Gael's James Dillon.[106]

In truth, the NFA as a body was only interested in one thing: the betterment of its members' livelihoods; it could not really be described as anyone's pawn. Whether it was a Fianna Fáil or an Inter-Party Government, it was going to press its demands with as much strength and resolve as it could muster. Smith, however, claimed that his grievances against the NFA were valid. He acknowledged that the NFA must be seen to criticise when the occasion demanded, but insisted it stick to the facts as, otherwise, relations were bound to deteriorate. It is difficult to imagine relations being any worse than they were at this point, and Smith seemed intent on letting the NFA know exactly how low its stock was as far as his department was concerned. Relations between the two, he asserted, had been 90 per cent destructive, and he left no doubt as to where he considered the blame lay. He attacked the NFA's record as a vocational group, claiming that there was not a great deal of evidence of it taking on independently 'many functions which they could perform and which we would be delighted to see them perform'.[107] This is something of a moot point, as various farmers' organisations were in the process of developing policy initiatives on a whole range of farming issues. The department, however, was not so keen on some of the proposals put forward by these organisations. Smith, it would appear, was trying to have it both ways: condemning the farmers on issues of policy and their methods of trying to achieve their implementation, while excoriating them for not carrying out unnamed independent functions.

This correspondence did not deter the NFA from aggressively pursuing its agenda. It attempted to build up closer contacts with its European colleagues, and began applying with success to the department for funding to attend various agricultural conferences in such places as Italy, India and Yugoslavia.[108] Louis Smith claims that it was Lemass who cleared the way for the NFA to receive financial assistance, and that Paddy Smith was 'not one bit pleased with it'. He further argues that the department itself had no real wish to attend international agricultural gatherings, but rather relied on the British to keep it informed.[109] This was the beginning of a concerted effort by farmers to gain new markets for their produce. Their prime target was to be the EEC.

## THERE IS NO UTOPIA

By early 1960 the Irish farming community was very much alive to the benefits of participation in an EEC Common Agricultural Policy (CAP). In July of that year, the NFA issued a statement in which it requested the Government consider becoming a partner in the EEC. This move was provoked by its disappointment at the failure to improve the position of Irish farming during the review of the Anglo-Irish trade agreement of April 1960. The secretaries of Finance and Agriculture at the time have conceded that this agreement was somewhat of a disappointment, though both insist that it was the best that could have been achieved in the circumstances.[110] The NFA, most certainly, did not take the same view. Not only did it urge consideration of the EEC option, it also suggested that Ireland should join before Britain, and pursue its application whether Britain was admitted or not. The NFA considered that the historic trading link with Britain had been weakened, and that its advantage to Irish farmers had been eroded. CAP offered guaranteed high prices, access to an expanded consumer market and new trading opportunities. The NFA also suggested that Irish industry would be no worse off inside the EEC than it would be in the European Free Trade Area, and would certainly be better off in some trading bloc than persisting with isolationism.[111] In essence, what the farming lobby was interested in was the maintenance of its own income without consideration of other aspects of economic policy. There were two serious flaws in the NFA's argument. The first was central to the question of when and on what terms Ireland would join the EEC. Ireland's accession to the EEC would almost certainly be followed immediately by the abrogation of the Anglo-Irish trade agreements and the consequential elimination of the preferences, both industrial and agricultural, that Ireland enjoyed in the British market. The acquisition of any corresponding preferences in the EEC would only be achieved gradually over a transitional period that might be as long as ten years; thus, the intervening period would be fraught with difficulty, particularly for Irish industry. Secondly, there was the certainty that if Ireland joined the Common Market and raised a common external tariff against Britain, industrial exports to Britain would be penalised in a way that could not easily be compensated for through increased exports to the EEC.

For its part, the NFA could only see two possible disadvantages to joining the EEC: primarily, there was the traditional and close trading relations between Ireland and Britain. The failure of the Anglo-Irish trade agreement to offer due recognition to Irish agriculture, despite Ireland's almost complete dependence on this sector of the economy, made this special relationship redundant in the eyes of the NFA. Secondly, there was the problem that joining the EEC could mean that British industrial supremacy – valued at about £100 million a year in the Irish market – might be replaced by the EEC but with no greater benefit for the Irish economy.[112] The NFA, however, believed that returns from agriculture and other exports to EEC countries would increase substantially both in volume and in value; thus, entry into the EEC would offset any setbacks incurred by the loss of the British market. The farming lobby was strong throughout Europe at the time, and the NFA was emulating its European counterparts in advocating entry into the EEC as a means of harmonising access to the European market for all farmers.[113]

In response to the NFA statement, the Department of Agriculture warned the Government that there were disadvantages – which were more serious than the NFA had intimated – as well as advantages to joining the EEC. Among advantages for Irish farmers was the price-support mechanism offered by the EEC to protect farm prices from world competition, as well as the general principle that farm incomes would be maintained at specified levels. This would benefit Irish farmers as their price levels were lower than those prevailing within the Community. In specific areas, Irish farmers could hope to benefit from price adjustments elsewhere; Irish dairy produce might be competitive price-wise, but this would have to be considered in the context of surplus production within the EEC. In contrast to these advantages, the department suggested that Irish beef would be placed at a disadvantage in the British market, and that the British might not continue the favourable payments agreed for Irish cattle. In addition, continental markets were unlikely to absorb the surplus beef from Ireland. Entry into the EEC would also affect policy-making, as the bilateral aspects of the relationship with Britain would end, to be substituted by an expanded EEC within which the Irish Government would be much weaker. There were also social problems to consider, as there was every likelihood that the migration of labour from agriculture would continue, if not accelerate, under the EEC. The department concluded on a rather pessimistic note:

> In the absence of a large and growing home market, what is necessary from the farmer's point of view is to become associated with an industrial economy strong enough to give agricultural incomes the necessary degree of support and stability. It seems unrealistic to suppose that this can be achieved in the absence of some special economic understanding with Britain, whatever solution may ultimately be found for the Six–Seven problem.[114]

The Department of Agriculture was not, however, content to leave things as they stood, and was favourable towards entry as long as Britain entered as well. While the Government refused to be drawn on the question of its position if Britain did not secure membership, it is clear that the farming organisations were of the opinion that Ireland should nevertheless continue with its application. The department most certainly did not take such a view; it felt that the arguments advanced by the NFA for joining the EEC could be repeated with equal validity when advocating a similar arrangement with Britain. It was this appraisal of the economic situation that led the department in April 1959 to put forward the proposal for closer relations with Britain that were designed to tie Irish agriculture to British-supported prices over a wider front. The NFA, guided by similar considerations, was opting for integration with the EEC. In the view of the NFA, it had so far proved impracticable to get from Britain the kind of arrangement that Irish agriculture needed. For the department, it was appropriate in the circumstances that it should look to the country that took 80 per cent of Irish exports for such an arrangement.[115]

Fundamentally, the NFA agreed with the department's view that what agriculture required was to become associated with an industrial economy strong enough to give agricultural incomes the necessary degree of support and stability. The essential difference between the two bodies – the NFA and the Department of Agriculture – was the economy each wished to be associated with. Once again, the department displayed a cautious nature, declaring:

> There are few grounds for hoping that any worthwhile expansion of our agriculture can take place on the basis of compromise solutions between the six and seven which would not provide for a large degree of incorporation of our agriculture in the support arrangements of Britain or the Common Market. Tariff quotas or marginal increases in trade at world prices, even if they could be obtained, might be helpful but would not alter the fundamental situation of our agriculture.[116]

The NFA, however, was much more insistent that the Common Market was the place to be. Greene told an Institute of Public Administration conference on higher administration studies in late 1961 that:

> One is left with the impression that without becoming a partner in a larger, viable economic unit, that will seek to cater for agriculture in its wider community, there is little to be optimistic about for our agriculture over the next ten years. At all costs we must avoid the Common Market being used and becoming a fashion as the cure-all for our agricultural ills; there is no utopia for agriculture in the Common Market. All that can be said is that the Common Market will provide us with a greater opportunity … I think I would be right in saying that without the advent of the Common Market, the prospect facing Irish agriculture over the next ten years is pretty hopeless.[117]

A crucial meeting had been held the previous year in the Taoiseach's office between the Departments of Agriculture, Industry and Commerce and the Taoiseach, and the NFA, which was represented by Greene and Louis Smith. The primary aim of this encounter was to formulate a coherent position on the issue of the EEC satisfactory to both sides. The meeting resulted in deadlock. For the NFA, Greene felt that the ideal position for Ireland would be some sort of close agricultural association with Britain that would ensure that a worthwhile market was provided for all that was produced. This was clearly a utopian dream, and not realisable. The 1960 trade agreement with Britain did not bring any substantive change in agricultural relations, and Britain seemed committed to a cheap-food policy with high price-supports for its farmers. As far as the NFA was concerned, there was therefore no future in Ireland selling its agricultural surplus to Britain at a low price, and it was clear that the Irish Government could not afford the level of agricultural price support maintained in Britain. To the NFA, the situation was clear-cut:

> Agricultural incomes in Ireland were falling, costs were rising, and a number of farmers including big ones were selling out. By contrast agricultural output in Northern Ireland had increased very substantially … As Britain had refused to give us a reasonable agricultural deal we would be better off in the EEC where we could participate in all the benefits of the CAP which was based on the idea of equalising incomes of farmers with those of other sectors. Furthermore this would give us a strong bargaining position in relation to Britain.[118]

When questioned by the Taoiseach as to the seriousness of this proposal, Greene replied that it was a very serious and well-thought-out proposition around which the farming lobby was united. Lemass, on the other hand, spelled out the problems that EEC membership without the accession of Britain would have for the country. He proclaimed that he saw no reason why greater agricultural efficiency should not be developed in the country, and that while reasonable prices were important, they were not the only factor for improving the economic position of farmers. For Lemass, whether Ireland joined the EEC in the near future or not, increased farmer efficiency and productivity would have to be forthcoming from the farming community. Paddy Smith pointed out that the Government had not 'cried halt' to increases in production, and it had not said the limit of subsidisation had been reached. The NFA, however, was still to be convinced.[119]

For the Government, the economic argument for joining the EEC was paramount. As T.K. Whitaker put it:

> We have applied for membership of the EEC because it would be economic disaster for us to be outside of the community if Britain is in it. We cannot afford to have our advantageous position in the British market turned into one of exclusion by a tariff wall, particularly as our chief competitors would be inside the wall.[120]

While the NFA disagreed with the Government over the reason for applying, it was pleased when the Government decided to press ahead with its application in July 1961.

## El Dorado

At this stage, the key economic focus for the Irish Government remained agriculture, despite some recent commitments to industrial development. This point was made both internationally and at home. The Government's formal application paper in January 1962 proclaimed that 'for Ireland agriculture will always be of major importance.

We are naturally anxious that through membership of the European Economic Community, Ireland should be able to look forward to a balanced development of agriculture and industry.'[121] Lemass had also made this point over a year earlier when he told the Dáil:

> It is important to have it fully appreciated that the Government have never treated, and do not now treat, the interests of manufacturing industry as the predominant consideration in their approach to the question of association with either of the European trading groups, or in their trading policy generally, in the sense of having failed to attach due importance to agricultural interests.[122]

While industry was constantly discussed at official level, the main objective of government policy in the early 1960s was to obtain favourable membership of the EEC and to secure, if possible, continuing access to the British market for agricultural exports. This was made explicit in Lemass' statement to the Council of Ministers of the EEC in January 1962:

> Because of the close inter-relationship of the economy of Ireland and that of the United Kingdom, and the vital interest of Ireland in agricultural trade, the Irish Government would wish to have the discussions for the admission of Ireland to the Community completed at the same time as those for the United Kingdom.[123]

For the NFA, entry into the EEC would, it believed, alleviate the discrepancies between industrial and agricultural incomes in Ireland, and ensure a rise in living standards both in rural and urban Ireland. To Rickard Deasy, who had become the second president of the NFA in January 1962, the balancing of incomes between agriculture and industry in the early 1960s had become a matter of 'dominant urgency'.[124]

He claimed that it was irrational to ignore, as the Government was doing, the fact that:

> The prosperity of the nearly 40 per cent of our population who are engaged in agriculture is a major factor in determining the buoyancy of the home market for all our products both industrial and agricultural. It is absurd to pretend – against a background of falling prices for almost all agricultural products, round after round of wage increases and shorter working hours awarded to other sections – that this does not inevitably worsen the relative position of our greatest industry – farming.[125]

He calculated that it would take a Government subsidy of £83 million to restore agriculture to its 1953 relationship with other sectors of the Irish economic community. The agricultural lobby was worried by the eighth round of wage increases, which had been concluded in December 1961 by the Government, ICTU and the FUE. A campaign orchestrated by Deasy saw telegrams flood into the Department of Finance demanding that farmers' incomes be increased in line with other sections of the wider Irish community.[126] In essence, the NFA feared that agricultural incomes would fall further behind the rest of the community, and complained to the Government that every other class in the community was getting some improvement in income except the farmers. Furthermore, the farming community felt that the trade union movement had usurped its position in negotiating a further round of wage increases with the Government before it had an opportunity to advance a claim for greater state subsidisation. Moreover, the NFA was deeply suspicious of the urban Lemass, who had spent all his political life in Industry and Commerce, and who it regarded as no friend of the agricultural community.

The NFA's demand for a subsidy of £83 million gave rise to

indignation in parts of the civil service. A Department of Finance memorandum argued:

> It might even be said that the NFA claim goes beyond the socialistic doctrine 'from each according to his ability, to each according to his needs' and is based on a false notion of what is morally justifiable to transfer from one section of the community to another.[127]

The Central Statistics Office maintained that 'the Irish farmer is no worse off as compared with non-farm income than Belgian farmers and a lot better off than United States farmers',[128] while the Department of Agriculture made it clear that 'the NFA analysis of the situation is very faulty indeed, and that their requests are most extravagant'.[129] The Department of External Affairs was worried that if the Government assumed it had an obligation to ensure that the level of income of the different sections of the community must be more or less equal, it would involve 'transforming our economy into something approaching a totalitarian system where the state is all-powerful and the individual secondary'. At an economic level, External Affairs was critical of the NFA for postulating that the EEC represented:

> … as it were, an El Dorado and that the farming community here is entitled to claim all the advantages which any member of the Community may at present give to its farmers. This is quite a serious matter and unless the NFA quickly realise the fact that they must face keen and probably ruthless competition within the Community, their members are likely to suffer grave consequences.[130]

Lemass, in response, accepted that developments adverse to farmers had taken place. He argued at a meeting with the NFA in March 1962, however, that some of these could be countered by increased productivity. He did offer the farmers something of an olive branch by stating that the Government would review the provisions made for the farming community in light of the overall financial situation. This would ascertain whether productivity could be increased, and whether its direction could, with advantage, be changed. The NFA claimed in reply that its call for the subsidy was formulated at the time of the electricians' strike in September 1961 in the hope that its demand would be seen as a restraining influence on other sectors contemplating claims for higher incomes. This, however, was not the case, and the NFA – while sticking to its figure of £83 million – accepted that indiscriminate price support was not a practicable position.[131]

At this meeting, the NFA also raised the subject of relations with the Department of Agriculture. The NFA told Lemass bluntly that it deplored the unsatisfactory relations that existed between the two parties, and felt keenly that this should be remedied. As the NFA visualised it, the department and the NFA ought to pull together in harness, and the individual farmer should be convinced that the department was doing its best for him even though he might not be satisfied with the result at any particular time.[132] Lemass, however, was staunchly protective of the Department of Agriculture, and said that any suggestion that the department was not pulling its full weight in the interest of the agricultural sector was entirely without foundation. The *Irish Press* put the case for the Government:

To be sure the Government can always be counted on to give the farmers' case a sympathetic hearing but then they have to think of the health of the economy as a whole. But for the protection given to agriculture in the home market, the cost of living would be considerably lower. In farming as in everything else, we must aim at greater productivity. Protection has served the Irish farmer a very valuable home market but for any real increase in agricultural productivity the farmers must look beyond their own shores.[133]

The NFA was unlikely to be placated by this argument. It did indeed want to expand its markets by entering the EEC, but until this became a reality, it was looking to the Government to subsidise it through increased price support. Lemass, however, explicitly warned the NFA that if in pursuit of its aims it intended to disrupt public services, the Government would take appropriate action:

> If the NFA had in mind the staging of a political strike designed by economic pressure on the public, to secure concessions from the Government, they could take it that the Government would feel obliged, in the public interest, to take strong measures. Apart from the question whether the NFA case had merits or not, it would be contrary to the public interest that political strikes, which had not hitherto been resorted to in this country, should be tolerated.[134]

This harked back to recent reports in the media, and specifically an interview with Deasy in *The Irish Times* two days earlier, where he floated the idea that the NFA might have to look to new forms of protest in its disputes with the Government.[135] Lemass' warning can be interpreted as a sign of deep dissatisfaction within the Government as a whole with the threats emanating from the NFA. There was a feeling within the Government at this time that the agricultural lobby could not be pleased on any issue of policy. Lemass echoed this when he wrote to Paddy Smith about the NFA's demand for greater price support:

> There is a question whether any decision on which the Government may decide for the further assistance of agriculture should be announced and brought into effect separately or altogether. I suppose this will depend

to some extent on the character of our decisions, but rather than appear to relate our decisions to the impractical totals of the NFA proposals, I think it would be preferable to announce and apply them separately. We will get no credit from the NFA no matter what we do.[136]

The Government had since September 1961 accepted the principle that the farmers, as well as other sections of society, should share equitably in increases in the national income. Throughout 1962, however, the NFA saw no sign of its members gaining such an increase, and increased its attacks on Government agricultural policy. Lemass, for his part, was of the opinion that the agricultural lobby would never be satisfied. He made reference to state support for agriculture, stating:

The various aids and services provided for Irish agriculture already cost a great deal of money. In relation to national income, the Irish state supports its agriculture to a much greater extent than other European countries, even though the support rests on a smaller industrial base. Nevertheless it is unlikely that our taxpayers will not wish to support intelligent measures to raise small farm productivity and, in that way, to make them less dependent on public support. The problem of the small farm areas is one which has to be resolved before all our aims of national development are secured.[137]

Equating the ailments of the small farm sector with the aims of national development was quintessential Fianna Fáil. Yet it was the rhetoric of the Fianna Fáil of de Valera, not the rhetoric of Lemass the industrialiser. Whatever the merits of Lemass' sympathies regarding agricultural concerns, there is little doubt that he was acutely aware of the electoral support given to Fianna Fáil by this sector, and would seek to assuage the fears of those within in when addressing them. It is doubtful, however, if he believed his own oratory on this occasion.

For the Government, entry into the EEC would harness Ireland's national development in the long run by offering its industries and productive agriculture greater opportunities in an enlarged market, once industry had adapted to free trade conditions. While both indigenous and foreign-owned export industry was very weak at this stage, and seemed unlikely to gain much from EEC entry in the short term, for the Government entry was part of a long-term strategy within which industry would have to adapt.[138] Although a key element of EEC policy was the protection of small family farms throughout Western Europe, Lemass knew, as indeed did the NFA itself, that entry into the Community would not immediately alleviate the social and economic problems associated with the Irish small farm.

The NFA, however, was in no doubt that agricultural incomes still lagged well behind those of other sectors, and continued to predict that farmer unrest would grow unless the Government took meaningful action to alleviate the plight of farmers. The association's general secretary, Seán Healy, asserted:

> Average incomes in Irish agriculture had consistently been below incomes in other occupations for at least half a century and at the present time farmers the world over – a few excepted – had lower incomes than their non-farming counterparts.[139]

To Rickard Deasy, there were four main reasons for farmer unrest: the increasing rates burden, a persistent decline in farm incomes, a bleak future and, most importantly, a general lack of attention to the fundamental task of planning agricultural development more coherently:

> Successive Governments have dealt with industrial development with vigour and enthusiasm. Although we can expect to face in a few years, in conditions of free competition, the highly developed agricultural systems

of continental countries as well as the United Kingdom we have as yet not begun to assess and plan our agriculture. These plans must be comprehensive and embrace production, processing, marketing and trade policy. Farmers have been conscious of these planning deficiencies. They have for years been clamouring without avail for a fresh approach to the agricultural problem. It is precisely because nothing so far has been achieved and because there is little time left to achieve anything, that they have decided to make these deficiencies a major issue.[140]

Paddy Smith refuted Deasy's charges that the Government was inactive in relation to farmers, and claimed that the adverse farm-income trends were, in large measure, due to international protectionist policies and artificially depressed prices in Britain – developments over which he had no control. The *Irish Independent* attempted to find the middle ground between the two, and concluded that both could do better:

> The Common Market may provide a remedy to this problem by opening continental markets to Irish farm produce. But if this brightened prospect is to be adequately availed of, much more than at present will need to be done as regards research, particularly in marketing, and in improving quality standards. A more energetic approach to these aspects of farm policy is long overdue. Money spent this way will provide a real long term improvement rather than a temporary stop gap to the erosion of farm incomes.[141]

There was a perception within the farming community as a whole that the Government was placing industrial development at the top of its economic agenda, and that farmers were being left in a policy vacuum. It was within this context that they were campaigning for a redistribution of incomes. At a meeting with the Government in April 1962, Greene told Lemass that small farmers were putting pressure on the leadership over what they perceived to be a declining standard of living. He added that there was no political motivation behind any campaign that might develop, and agreed that it would be undesirable that political strikes should be introduced. He did not, however, rule this course of action out:

> Feelings of frustration and injustice were being built up and unless some concessions were made in the budget there might be local disturbances which the NFA might not be able to control ... apart from the merits of the case for some concessions to the farmers, it would be in the national interest to prevent anything which would tend to destroy the country's name abroad for political stability.[142]

Whether Lemass perceived what might be called Greene's 'advice' as anything other than a threat is not clear. Yet there can be little doubt that that is what it was. The subtext of the demand for concessions to farmers in the budget was that the NFA would use its considerable power to ensure that none of its members would strike. With the Government's application to join the EEC still on the European Commission's table, the last thing it would need would be a farmers' strike. Ever since Lemass had outlined the Government's position to the Commission at a meeting in Brussels on 18 January 1962, the Government had been attempting to ascertain the situation with regard to the application. A meeting was scheduled to take place in May 1962 between an Irish delegation and the permanent representatives of the member states, which the Government hoped would open the way for the formal discussion of the Irish application later in the summer. Thus, any strike could have ramifications for the Government's European strategy. Yet Greene's logic is somewhat confusing. A strike by farmers, though it might hurt the Government as regards its position with the European Commission, would thereby damage the main lobbying group for EEC membership for Ireland – the farmers themselves.

Whatever the implications of Greene's comments, what is clear is that the budget delivered four days later contained some concessions in rates and the abandonment of the proposed penny levy on milk delivered at creameries. The *Irish Press* reported the reaction of the NFA: 'the budget was a victory in principle for the case presented by the NFA on behalf of organised farmers'.[143] By late summer 1962 the *Connacht Tribune* was able to proclaim that relations between the Government and the NFA had improved considerably, with the Government being able to look upon the position of the farmers as 'reasonably satisfactory'.[144]

## To ride two horses at once

Failure to enter the EEC in the early 1960s brought bitter disappointment to the Irish farming community, as its hopes of increasing prosperity in the larger Common Market were dashed. Once the Government failed in 1963 to get inside protected continental markets through the EEC, the 1960s would become a period of increased farmer militancy as farmers protested at what they perceived to be their increasingly disadvantaged situation.[145] Relations with the Government soon deteriorated to their previous level. Serious differences between the Government and the NFA also arose in late 1963 over the withholding of rates in Kilkenny by a proportion of farmers who had the support of the NFA. For Lemass, if the NFA was involved in illegal activities, the Government would be compelled to take whatever measures the situation required. He told Deasy that the NFA could not expect 'to ride two horses at once and that a wish for closer co-operation with the Department of Agriculture could not be reconciled with a course of action which would make conflict with the Government inevitable'.[146]

In many ways, the withholding of rates in Kilkenny mirrored events of less than three decades earlier. Kilkenny was a strong farmer county, and had been one of the Blueshirts' strongholds in the 1930s; indeed, the emblematic 'blue shirt' made its first appearance in Kilkenny, in April 1933.[147] Moreover, Kilkenny was at the heart of an anti-rates campaign in the summer and autumn of 1934. The county council had a strong anti-Fianna Fáil majority, and refused to co-operate fully in the collection of rates. This resulted in the county council being dissolved by order of the Minister for Local Government.[148] Lemass and Smith, in all probability, would not have forgotten such incidents; thus, Lemass declared that a campaign of this kind struck at the very roots of representative Government:

> If agitation of this kind could succeed in any degree whatever, or even seem to succeed, or even so develop as being capable of being represented as having succeeded, it could bring the whole administration of local and central Government into disorder. This is the road to anarchy and I want to make the Government's position in this regard clear beyond any possibility of misunderstanding. We will not allow it to happen.[149]

Entering 1964, the Kilkenny rates controversy had still to be resolved. Yet by this time, the Government was in the process of redefining its relations with the agricultural lobby. The NFA was to receive formal Government recognition whereby, in future, the Government would welcome regular and full discussions and consultation with the NFA for the purpose of formulating agricultural policy, both broad and specific. For Paddy Smith, the Government's difficulty had been in finding:

> … [a] basis for fruitful co-operation while the NFA reserve the right to be destructively critical of every move made by me to help farmers, and

to use meetings with me and my officials as the basis of biased attacks on us and on Government policy.[150]

He therefore considered that the Government would be as well dealing with the NFA on a formal footing in the future. He was of the opinion that a well-organised farmers' organisation had a really valuable job to do, and that it was in his own interests to work with it and give a fair hearing to any proposal of a constructive nature that it might put before him. On 28 January 1964 Lemass sent a memorandum to the NFA stating that while the Government was concerned at the lack of unity and cohesion amongst farmers' organisations, it did recognise that:

> ... the NFA are interested in all branches of agriculture, and they welcome the prospect of regular and comprehensive discussions with the NFA in connection with the formulation of agricultural policy in the broadest sense, as well as their practical co-operation in respect of specific areas of agriculture ... It will be the ordinary practice of the Minister for Agriculture to inform the NFA about pending changes in his Department, proposed new schemes ... and to consider any repre-sentations they may wish to make to him in this regard.[151]

While the NFA received formal Government recognition, Smith was disturbed at the whole thrust of Lemass' economic policies. When Lemass took over as Taoiseach in 1959, Smith found it increasingly difficult to accommodate himself to Lemass' economic and social viewpoints. Smith – the archetypal countryman – had shared de Valera's conservative vision of Ireland as a largely pastoral society based on traditional values that would withstand socialist notions likely to promote a more dependent and less harmonious society.[152] Fundamental to Lemass' approach, however, was the development of an important industrial segment, a questioning of the efficiency and merits of existing industries, and a closer relationship between the Government and the trade unions in the interests of economic progress. Indeed, Lemass' co-opting of the farmers into a formal negotiating stance with the Government is mirrored in his attitudes to the unions. Smith, however, saw the courting of the unions as sacrificing rural to urban interest; thus, on 7 October 1964 he offered his resignation, the first Fianna Fáil minister to do so on a policy issue.[153] His resignation was the source of much controversy. The US embassy originally reported that Smith's resignation had caught his colleagues and the public by surprise, and was principled and courageous.[154] The following week, however, it was reporting a different story to Washington, maintaining:

> There are indications that Smith's action … may not have been as principled as was initially indicated. Various reports from generally reliable sources echo the theme that a cabinet reshuffle was contemplated and that Smith, along with one or two of his older colleagues, was to make way for the appointment of younger ministers.[155]

This was something that the newspapers of the time were widely reporting, with 'Backbencher' in *The Irish Times* noting 'the young men were preparing to take over with the blessing of Mr Lemass. The berths were all but allocated', while a later editorial in the same paper maintained that 'it is widely believed that he [Smith] anticipated only by a short time the end of his ministerial existence'.[156] Lemass was reported to have had up to seventeen resignation statements from Smith in his drawer, and it was only when he learned that Smith was attempting to get the press to announce his resignation that Lemass acted in accepting the resignation and appointing Charles Haughey to succeed Smith.[157] Despite the acrimonious relationship between Smith and the NFA, it expressed regret at his resignation from a position of influence that could have benefited the farming community.[158]

Ironically, for all his disputes with the NFA, Smith's views were those of the farming community in general. Once the trade union movement began to move to centre stage in the new debates on Irish economic and social development, it seemed to many farmers that they were in danger of being relegated if not exactly to the margins of Irish politics, at least to a more secondary role than they had traditionally enjoyed. Predictably, they felt threatened, and resolved to remind the Lemass Government that they were still a formidable power in the land.[159] Moreover, the NFA and the farming community in general were extremely wary of the urban Lemass. Essentially, as Todd Andrews points out of Lemass:

> He had little real rapport with rural Ireland and, considering the amount of travelling he did when building up the Fianna Fáil organisation, he had surprisingly little intimate knowledge of the countryside and its people. He was essentially the Dublin Jackeen with the ready wit and derisive humour so common in the city.[160]

Thus, one can see the protests of the NFA in the light of the growing strength of the unions' influence on the Lemass Government. While the NFA welcomed the Government's endeavours with regard to the EEC, it was deeply worried by Lemass' courtship of the unions, as ultimately it saw them as a threat to agricultural interests and feared that the agricultural community would be left behind in a rising tide of prosperity. Yet this period also saw the formal recognition by Government of the role of farmer organisations in the formulation of policy. It was perhaps naive of Lemass to expect that, having invited the farmers to sit at the policy table, they should abandon the confrontational approach that had, in their estimation, earned them that position.

For all its Blueshirt antecedents, by the early 1960s the NFA had come to be seen by Fianna Fáil ministers as a troublesome but essentially apolitical grouping: ten years earlier, it would have regarded it as no more than Fine Gael on tractors. Once inside the charmed circle of power, the NFA continued its aggressive championing of the cause of farmers. The road to the negotiating table had been a rocky one, but once there, the NFA remained steadfast in its goal of improving the position of its members.

Exposed to the emerging realities of European integration, the farming community did not simply view entry into the EEC in terms of prices and markets, but was able to comprehend the wider economic and social picture. Farm leaders were only too well aware of the social consequences of underemployment, poverty and mass emigration. Despite a continually fractious relationship with Government, and a view of themselves as poor relations vis-à-vis the trade unions and the employers, farmers rightly surmised that it was better to be inside the tent than outside.

The depoliticisation of interest-group politics, as seen in the formal-isation of relations between the Fianna Fáil Government and the NFA, can be viewed as an example of how far Lemass had gone in attempting to create new political relationships and structures in the Ireland of the 1960s. In that, it was a triumph of visionary leadership.

# 6

# EXPLORING FARAWAY LANDS

In January 1957 the US embassy in Dublin reported to Washington
that 'the Irish are beginning to think about the problems associated
with EFTA. The Taoiseach ... pointed out that Ireland could not hope
to remain unaffected by the plan and advised interested organisations
to study the plan'.[1] Such Western European moves towards European
integration were being actively followed by the main economic interest
groups, with farmers' organisations, trade unions and business interests
all adopting positions on both the European Free Trade Association
and the EEC.

The following month – when Lemass was thinking seriously
about issues of protectionism and free trade, and was hopeful that the
forthcoming general election would see the return to Government of
Fianna Fáil – the council of the Organisation for European Economic
Co-operation initiated negotiations to establish a free trade area in
Europe. Its objective was to establish a region within which there would
be no tariff barriers or other restrictions to trade, although the EEC
and each of the other countries within the proposed trading bloc would
maintain protective defences against the rest of the world. As a member

of the OEEC since 1948, Ireland participated in the negotiations during 1957 and 1958. Two points were of particular importance to the Irish: the future of tariffs on agricultural products, and the proposals to give special treatment to underdeveloped countries (later known as 'countries in course of economic development') by extending the period in which tariffs might be eliminated and by providing financial assistance if required.[2] The Irish Government hoped to be included in this category, which also included Greece and Turkey.

Yet the prospect of a European free trade area embracing the member countries of the OEEC was viewed with grim scepticism by some Irish policy-makers, given that the dismantling of protection was seen as a serious threat to Irish industry. Furthermore, the removal of barriers to imports into Britain would eliminate Ireland's preferential position in that market vis-à-vis other OEEC countries.[3] Yet the weakness and instability of the Irish economy after a generation of self-Government, and the evident failure of traditional policies, led many to seek effective alternatives. As Garret FitzGerald pointed out at the time:

> The emergence of the Free Trade Area Plan, and its presentation to the Irish public, could scarcely have been more opportune ... and the interest, even excitement which this proposal has aroused throughout the country provides remarkable evidence of the existence of this new and receptive climate of opinion.[4]

Three working parties were set up by the council of the OEEC in March 1957: Working Party 21, which would deal with the general constitution of the proposed free trade area; Working Party 22, dealing with the special position of agriculture; and Working Party 23 to deal with the position of 'countries in course of economic development'. It was to the latter working party that the Irish Government turned its attention. At a meeting on 9 October 1956, the second Inter-Party Government decided that, acting under the direction of the Taoiseach, the secretaries of External Affairs, Industry and Commerce, Agriculture, Finance and the Department of the Taoiseach should examine the probable effects on Ireland's interests of an association between the proposed Customs and Economic Union and the other member countries of the OEEC in a free trade area.[5]

This was the genesis of the four-secretaries group that was to play the key role in moving Irish economic policy from a protectionist framework to one where interdependence with other European economies was assumed. Seven meetings were held before a memorandum was issued on 18 January 1957. The report pointed out that in considering the question of Ireland's participation in a free trade area, the Government had to take into account not only the economic considerations but also more general matters of national policy regarding Ireland's participation in a movement towards closer association of the countries of Western Europe. As T.K. Whitaker pointed out:

> It was taken as granted by Irish policy makers from an early stage that economics and politics were mixed in a European context. We realised that serious issues had to be faced on both fronts when we first debated entering EFTA.[6]

For the Government, economic considerations were still paramount, and formed the bulk of the memorandum. While acknowledging that the establishment of the free trade area was intended to secure the economic benefits of a unified market of 250 million people – providing the opportunity for specialisation, lower-cost production, more productive investment, constant growth in the output of goods and services, and rising real incomes – the memorandum noted that this of itself would not ensure that individual countries would share proportionately in the expected benefits. It was also uncertain as to whether investment and adaptation funds would be made available to any member country that would otherwise struggle to fulfil the obligations of membership.

Whether Ireland joined or not, the formation of a free trade area and the emergence of an integrated Western European market of 250 million people were developments that would have profound implications for the Irish economy, necessitating a fundamental reappraisal of economic plans and policies. The Government was therefore compelled to consider both the immediate economic impact of joining a free trade area, and the question of whether participation in such an area would best promote the expansion of the economy in the future. Among the specific considerations the Government was concerned with were the effects of assuming an obligation to progressively remove existing protection over a period of years, and of foregoing the right to impose further protection against countries within the area. It mooted the possibility of including in the agreement escape clauses related, for example, to balance-of-payments difficulties, of which Ireland faced plenty in 1956, and special arrangements modifying the obligations in favour of member countries, like Ireland, whose economies were not fully developed.

Not surprisingly, Industry and Commerce was the most fearful regarding Ireland's position. It came to the following conclusion:

> As regards a large section of existing industries, the Department of Industry and Commerce can see no prospect of their survival, even as suppliers of the home market, except with permanent protection. The Department of Industry and Commerce can see no prospect of a significant expansion of industrial exports from Ireland to the continental part of the Free trade Area even if we were members of the Area and could thus enter this market without any tariff barriers.[7]

The Department of Agriculture viewed events in much the same light, and due to the overwhelming reliance on the British market for Irish exports saw:

> … little prospect of a significant expansion of agriculture exports from Ireland to the continental part of the free trade area even if we were members of the area and agricultural products were freely traded by all members other than Britain.[8]

There is a grim fatalism to Industry and Commerce's view of engagement with the free trade area:

> Ireland has reason not merely to be worried about the setting up of a free trade area, but about her future economic and political prospects generally. It is obvious that we can avoid economic stagnation and continuous loss of population only by making the most strenuous and urgent efforts to raise the efficiency and volume of production both in agriculture and in industry. If a free trade area is established and we had to accept from the start the full obligations of membership, those existing industries which need permanent protection (and therefore could not adjust themselves over the transitional period) would go to the wall. Few new industries could be established in the absence of a protective shield and a guaranteed home market.[9]

Whilst this report has retrospectively been subjected to justifiable criticism for its negativity and paucity of thinking – considering that it offered no positive recommendations but a continuation of protectionism – it nevertheless illustrates the important point that Irish policy-makers were actually engaged in a debate about Europe.[10] The negative tone is not unusual, and nor should it be read as so. Industry and Commerce felt a loyalty to those industries that had survived and even prospered under protection, whilst Agriculture was obviously very wary of any continental trading bloc that would have the potential to interfere with Ireland's special trading position with Britain. It was the question of a period of adjustment that was crucial to any proposed Irish application. In any event, despite the dire warnings about Ireland's future, one avenue that was going to be explored was the European option.

Having considered the report, the Government adopted a sit-on-the-fence approach, contending that no commitment to join the proposed area should be entered into until every possibility had been explored for securing adequate safeguards for a country in the process of economic development. No initiatives were to be taken until the concession of special arrangements enabling Ireland to enter the area became part of the equation. J.C. Nagle defended the position taken by Agriculture as 'the only one practicable at the time. We were in a very difficult situation. Britain was our predominant market and we had to consider all aspects of policy with that in mind.'[11] This was the position the Irish delegation was to adopt at the meeting of the council of the OEEC fixed for 12 February 1957. At a Cabinet meeting four days earlier, it was agreed to issue a formal statement voicing general approval of the idea of a free trade area:

In accordance with her general attitude to movements by European countries towards closer economic association, Ireland welcomes the proposal to form a European Free Trade Area. While her attitude to the question of participating in an area will, as in the case of other countries, be determined in the light of consideration of her own national interests, Ireland views with sympathy this latest movement towards closer association among European countries and wishes the proposal every success.[12]

J.J. McElligott – by then governor of the Central Bank – supported a more active approach to Europe; in early 1957, on behalf of the board of the Central Bank, he went on record in favour of Ireland joining EFTA:

> Taking the long view the board was of the opinion that it would not be in the best interests of this country to remain aloof from the main stream of European economic development and that the disadvantages which would result from failure to join the proposed free trade area were likely to outweigh the temporary adjustments necessary in our economy consequent on a decision to join.[13]

It is significant that at this stage even McElligott was of the opinion that the country could not operate economically in isolation. He had overseen the dominance of protection in his role as secretary of the Department of Finance between 1927 and 1953 but was now effectively renouncing it. Seán Cromien notes that McElligott's support for EFTA can in many ways be linked to the fact that:

> He was a sponsor of Whitaker and he was open to ideas like EFTA as philosophically he would have seen it as a classic free trade idea. I think also he had reached the conclusion that protectionism had had its day and a new economic philosophy had to be put into place.[14]

Whitaker also emphasised the need for closer association with some larger economic unit, arguing:

> It would be a sad commentary on our industrial and agricultural policy over the last thirty years if we could now choose only between two alternatives of (a) continuing to fall behind other countries in material progress, with an unabated outflow of emigrants, or (b) economic reintegration with the United Kingdom. Whatever difficulties it may involve, the European

free trade area offers us a better prospect than either of those alternatives and we should hesitate long before we would decide to stay out. At the moment it is obviously the right policy to try to secure the most favourable terms of membership.[15]

At the first meeting of Working Party 23, held on 18 March 1957 – less than two weeks after Fianna Fáil had won a resounding victory in the general election – the Government indicated that it would be submitting a claim for special treatment: this was to be based on the belief that the aim of EFTA should be to establish conditions that would enable every member of the OEEC to enter EFTA without fear of serious damage to its economy. Ireland would be unable to join unless special treatment in this regard was agreed. In the meantime, a vigorous debate was going on within the principal departments about the route to be taken.

## COMPETE WITH THE BEST IN EUROPE

Fianna Fáil's general election victory saw Lemass appointed once again as Minister for Industry and Commerce; in this capacity, he chaired the committee of ministers to which the four-secretaries group reported. He immediately took a keen interest in the development of the EFTA proposals. A week after the general election, the secretary of Industry and Commerce, J.C.B. MacCarthy, had advanced the view:

> [We] might agree that we could offer to submit ourselves for examination (say in three years' time and at successive three year intervals) and to accept the results of such examinations. It was also possible that in the last resort we might be able to agree to make an initial reduction of say 10 per cent in our tariffs, subject to exemption for certain sensitive industries, provided the choice was left to us.[16]

Although MacCarthy's tone was hesitant – and he was to bitterly argue with Whitaker about protectionism a number of years later – he realised that association with some sort of trading bloc might have benefits for Irish industry.

In April the Government decided to submit a memorandum to Working Party 23 that would include:

> … an intimation to the effect that Ireland is willing to submit herself to independent examination, at suitable intervals, by the appropriate institutions of the Free Trade Area and to assume obligations of membership when it has been established, as a result of such examination, that her economy has attained a better relationship with the economies of those member countries of the area which are at present more highly industrialised than Ireland.[17]

The Irish ambassador in Paris, William Fay – who was chairman of Working Party 23 – urged the Government to present its submission in a more 'optimistic' fashion. He suggested the application should note that Ireland welcomed the idea of the creation of a large, free market that might at last provide a solid basis for the development of Irish industry through exports. He argued that the submission should declare that such development was 'up to now frustrated by the limits of the small home market' but that the creation of a free trade area would enable the Government 'to compete with the best in Europe and thus make a substantial contribution to the success of the free trade area'.[18]

The eventual memorandum to the working party – submitted in May – stated that Ireland could not hope to share in the benefits of a free trade area unless the obligations of membership were modified so as not to deprive the country of its freedom to protect its industries over an extended transitional period.[19] The Government made it clear that it was 'most anxious to avail of external capital for the financing of national development', and confirmed its interests in any proposals that would be formulated for the creation of finance institutions in the free trade area.[20] The London financial magazine, *The Statist*, summed up the dilemma some months later, when negotiations were still ongoing: 'there is no doubt that entry into a free trade area on a basis of equal responsibility with partners vastly better developed industrially would strike a death blow to the Irish economy'.[21] While Whitaker undoubtedly realised this, he wanted to see a situation develop where Ireland would one day be able to compete with these partners. It was with this in mind that he had issued in March 1957 a memorandum on the state of the economy in which he declared that something would have to be done economically or the achievement of national independence would prove to have been a futility:

> In the political field the primary national objective is the re-unification of the country. Until that is achieved, however, and no doubt after it has been achieved, the principal economic problem of the Irish Government will continue to be the safeguarding of political independence by ensuring economic vitality. Without a sound and progressive economy, political independence would be a crumbling facade.[22]

It was with this memorandum in mind that the official application to EFTA was drafted. In essence, it was an analysis of the Irish economy: it began by outlining the late start Ireland had made in the industrial field, 'as prior to independence no autonomous policy for the development of Irish industry existed', and added that a lack of industrial tradition, managerial skill, adequate risk capital and native raw materials, coupled with the country's proximity to such a heavily industrialised country as Britain, and Ireland's insular position, made the new state's task of establishing Irish industries particularly difficult.[23] As an example of economic 'poor-mouthism', this would be pretty hard to beat. In the memorandum, the Government recognised the urgent need to develop an industrial sector comparable to that of other Western European countries. There was a lack of balance between agriculture and industry, with only 15.3 per cent of the labour force engaged in manufacturing industry. Furthermore, a high level of unemployment – aggravated by the degree of underemployment on the land – and the scale of emigration, which was higher than the natural increase in the population, highlighted the importance of Ireland securing industrial economic growth. The Government put forward the following vision:

> If the home market could be preserved by the maintenance of protective measures, Irish enterprises would become more attractive as an investment proposition to our people at home and to the investor from abroad. According as capital was forthcoming through the growth of the habit of investment among our people, and through the attraction of money, technical skill and enterprise from outside, development could be expected to proceed on the pattern of other European countries and in a measurable time to reach a point when the assumption of the obligations of membership of the Free Trade Area would become a practical proposition.[24]

The 'measurable time' the Government had in mind was twenty-five years, within which Ireland would be prepared to submit to independent examination its economic position at suitable intervals. Once Ireland's economy had attained a satisfactory relationship with the economies of other member countries, the Government would assume obligations of membership to the extent justified by such an improvement.

The presentation of the Irish case for special treatment is noteworthy in two respects: primarily, it marks some softening of the hard-line attitude previously adopted by Industry and Commerce in that it was accepted that there must be a time limit to protection; secondly, the proposal was silent on the treatment of agriculture in the free trade area.[25] The Government was prepared to accept the Department of Agriculture's view that the best option for Irish agriculture lay in exploiting bilateral arrangements with Britain. In April 1957, as we have seen, Agriculture had maintained that as Britain would continue to be the predominant market for Irish agriculture generally, the policy with regard to the free trade area and any common market should be co-ordinated with a policy of ensuring that any special advantage Ireland had in the British market should be preserved and developed, and that any trading difficulties should be alleviated.[26]

The Irish case was considered at a meeting of the working party in Paris on 28 May 1957, at which supplementary information in support of the submission was presented orally by J.C.B. MacCarthy. The majority of the various delegations of OEEC countries took a sympathetic attitude to Ireland's submission, although some nations felt that the Irish case was unduly pessimistic.[27] Accepting that the Irish presentation was very much an outline one, the working party sent a delegation to Dublin in June. Its principal objective was to gain further information on the issues of tariffs, agriculture and capital. In the first instance, the delegation wanted to know whether tariffs would be taken off during the twenty-five-year period mentioned in the Irish memorandum, and, if so, would this be on a global or a selective basis.

Before the Government formally replied, MacCarthy had informed Fay, the ambassador, that Ireland could not guarantee in advance to have removed all quotas after a twenty-five-year period, although that was its aim:

I did not say that the Government would undertake not to reduce existing quotas. What I did say was that they would not impose new quotas ... I do not want you to think from what I have said that in practice we will reduce existing quotas.[28]

While this made MacCarthy's position clear, the report of a meeting of the committee of secretaries on 12 June noted:

The Government would wish that the discussions with the working party delegation and negotiations generally with the OEEC should proceed on the assumption that Ireland will go into the Free Trade Area if at all possible.

It was with this approach in mind that the response dealt comprehensively with the tariff question, where it argued that Ireland should be exempt from any obligation to effect automatic tariff reductions, and advanced several supplementary proposals.[29] The Government concluded its case for special treatment with an assurance that more than adequate measures were being taken to obtain increased investment. Included with this communication was an extract from James Ryan's budget speech of 8 May 1957, which spelled out the economic objectives of the Government and its commitment to attaining them:

The examination of our affairs which we have been pursuing in connection with the European Free Trade Area (EFTA) proposals will undoubtedly show up defects in our economy and should guide us in making the improvements so urgently needed. The direction and rate of our future advance will depend on the decisions we take now. There are no easy expedients by which our difficulties can be solved.[30]

This speech also claimed that the Government had full confidence in the inherent soundness of the economy and its ability to provide higher living standards for an expanding population on the firm basis of an increase in production and exports. Ryan – who had considerable business experience in his native Wexford – believed that the relaxation of restrictions and the assurance of new reliefs, together with the maintenance of the state capital programme at a high level and the prospects of a continuing improvement in exports, would strengthen business confidence and stimulate production. He asserted that the resultant growth of opportunities for work should effect a marked improvement in the unemployment situation, and check the outflow of people from the country.[31] In reality, 60,000 more people emigrated in 1957.

## 'A FAIR-MINDED, UNPREJUDICED MAN'

This was a crucial time for Lemass, who recognised that existing investment and output were not sufficient to maintain the level of demand he considered necessary to attaining full employment. He believed that the promotion of industrial exports was the best way to achieve export-led growth. The evidence available to him suggested that indigenous industry could not fulfil this objective; he therefore proposed to amend the Control of Manufactures Acts, and use other institutional devices to attract foreign investment to Ireland, noting that export-led growth could only be achieved if foreign investment contributed capital, technology and experience to Irish industry. The Control of Manufactures Acts of 1932 and 1934 were subsequently amended, and a series of proposals was initiated with a view to attracting outside investors to Ireland. As Tom Garvin has pointed out, many local manufacturers would have opposed such a move reflexively. Thus, Lemass – aware that many of these manufacturers had been in operation since protectionism was introduced in 1932 – rescinded in 1958 only the acts for industries that exported the bulk of their produce. He then changed the title of the new act from a 'Repeal of the Control of Manufactures Act' to an 'Act for the encouragement of exports'. Those selling on a small scale to the local market would not be concerned, and would remain quiescent.[32] In many ways, this summed up Lemass' problem. He was trying to reorient economic policy but could not afford to leave his political base behind. As Tadhg Ó Cearbhaill has pointed out of Lemass:

> He was a fair-minded, unprejudiced man. I mean that if you could show that schemes brought up were useful, or that old schemes and ideas were redundant, he would go with the new. To some extent that was the case with the Control of Manufactures Acts.[33]

Lemass was careful to point out, however, that the key fulcrum for change would remain indigenous industry.[34] This may well have been to satisfy those within Fianna Fáil who viewed the attraction of foreign investment as a betrayal of the policy of self-sufficiency that the party had fostered in the 1930s. How Lemass proposed to resolve this conundrum between indigenous industry and foreign investment is unclear. Indigenous Irish industry was – as the Government itself had made clear – extremely weak and suffered from both a lack of entrepreneurship and adequate risk capital. Furthermore, protectionism had given industrialists a particular mindset that was proving extremely difficult to change. Colm Barnes, one of the more dynamic industrialists of the period, has talked of the difficulties Lemass experienced with industry:

> Looking at it from the vantage point of our company, Glen Abbey, for example, we had predictable, secure markets. Sometimes we were even short of workers at particular times. What Lemass was trying to change in many ways was that state of mind of being comfortable. Companies had great security and quite acceptable profit. But it wasn't a large enough economy ... and Lemass knew that well.[35]

Thus, while Industry and Commerce in mid-1957 was advocating strong protection for Irish industry and a bleak future, Lemass – once more minister – was contemplating new strategies, with Europe to the forefront. He was prepared to remove all restrictions on inward investment if companies exported most of their production. Yet most companies were not thinking along the same lines. Theoretically, Lemass might have wanted to bring industry with him in his efforts to attract outside industry and encourage indigenous industry to export; in practice, it was an undertaking of colossal proportions as, in effect, it was an attempt to completely overhaul industrial policy in place since the beginning of the state.

Fine Gael, now in opposition, also had strong views on EFTA, and circulated a private memorandum on Ireland's prospects within any European trading bloc.[36] This noted that the creation of a common customs barrier would profoundly affect the whole pattern of Irish external trade. Like other commentators, it foresaw the transition from a highly protected industrial framework to an open one as having a considerable effect on Irish industrial production and employment. While the immediate danger to Irish industry could not be exaggerated, Fine Gael estimated that any drop in employment in one sector could be compensated for by increases in others. The effects of thirty years of protection had been to increase the numbers employed in manufacturing industry by less than 60,000. Furthermore, this figure included industries not affected by protectionism, such as grain milling, baking, construction engineering, electrical construction and newspaper production. Thus, the labour increases in industries manufacturing some protected goods could be put at no more that 50,000 – 4 per cent of the working population. Fine Gael interpreted this as evidence that the advent of free trade would certainly not lead to large-scale unemployment in the country. It was necessary, however, to have a free period in which protected industries could prepare themselves to meet fair competition from abroad. It had been conclusively proved, the party argued, that the way to full employment was not to be found in protectionism, as it was increasingly recognised that the small size of the Irish market had hindered Irish manufacturers from obtaining the benefits of the economies of large-scale production. Expansion of productivity and employment could be obtained only if a larger market was secured. Such a market would be available in a free trade area, which should prove a means of expansion for many Irish industries:

> The onus of proof must be on those who argue that we should not join EFTA or be associated in some way with the EEC. With chronic unemployment, large-scale emigration and a sluggish rate of industrial and agricultural expansion, nobody can be satisfied with the present framework of our economy. The prospect of increased exports bringing with them higher agricultural earnings and production and greater supplies of foreign exchange to help finance domestic development is one not lightly to be turned down. The Free Trade Area may not contain a magic formula to heal all her economic ills. But for a country so economically sick as Ireland is, it may easily point the way to a remedy, and should certainly not make our situation any worse.[37]

It is doubtful if all in Fine Gael approved of such a policy, which in essence mirrored the policy of Lemass. But it demonstrates that Fianna Fáil did not have a monopoly in pursuing the European option.

At a meeting with the British in November 1957, Lemass noted that as far as industry was concerned, the Government realised that 'in the Free Trade Area protection would ultimately have to go'.[38] The Government was hopeful that improved standards of living in Europe would in time lead to an expansion of demand for manufactured goods, which would be a stimulus to economic activity 'even in fringe countries like Ireland'. He intimated that such a 'spill-over' process would not materialise until the more highly developed centres in Europe 'where activity was already concentrated were further developed to the point at which factors like labour shortages made it necessary for industrial promoters to consider outlying areas'. It was with this in mind that the Government was asking for time to consolidate existing home industry before asking it to stand up to tariff cuts. Basically, the Government was looking to achieve a number of objectives in its negotiations with the British. Its principal position was:

> The British should be asked to support, in the negotiations concerning the Free Trade Area, the proposition that there should be a recognition of a special economic relationship between this country and Britain – particularly as far as trade in agricultural products – that such relationships must continue in the Free Trade Area and that any bilateral arrangements made by virtue of it should not be regarded as being incompatible with the rules of the Area.[39]

The result of these negotiations with the British was a visit to Dublin in January 1958 by British Paymaster General and Minister without Portfolio, Reginald Maudling, to whom the Government spelled out the above objective. Of paramount importance was winning the support of Britain – as yet not forthcoming – for Ireland's case for special treatment as a country in the process of economic development.[40]

## PUT YOUR BACKS INTO IT

On the industrial front, a substantial proportion of capital formation in Ireland had consisted of basic infrastructure, and this seemed likely to continue for the immediate future. The Government's argument was that the availability of external funds for infrastructural projects would release funds for the financing of competitive industries, thus providing further and wider opportunities for employment. These proposals were underwritten by a Government strategy to attract investment into the country. The IDA had embarked on an active campaign to secure the establishment in Ireland of factories based on external financial and technical participation. A delegation had been sent to the US and to a number of European countries, and the Government spoke of its taxation and other incentives towards industrial expansion that had been recently introduced and which were available to foreign industrialists who established industries in Ireland. Thus, the Government strongly supported the Greek proposal that facilities and incentives should be provided in the advanced countries for the purpose of positively encouraging business enterprises towards countries in the process of development.

Some officials involved in the OEEC had doubts about the wisdom of Ireland categorising itself with Greece and Turkey. J.F. Cahan, secretary-general of the OEEC, told an audience at UCD in May 1958 that Ireland was not underdeveloped in the sense that Greece and Turkey were. He went on to castigate the pessimistic mindset that prevailed in Ireland:

> I have heard a certain amount of rather pessimistic comment since I arrived. People who say that Ireland can never develop; that there is no hope. I think that it is desirable, from time to time, that one should sit down and count one's blessings before abandoning oneself to this kind of black despair.[41]

For Cahan, the free trade area offered a challenge to the less developed countries. Ireland, he argued was not underdeveloped but less developed. He contended that Ireland should draw up a programme 'of what it is that you think you ought to achieve in the way of development, in the next five or next ten years'. Cahan explicitly proclaimed that

Irish policy-makers should attempt to foresee progress, set themselves targets, judge as time advanced how near these targets were to being achieved, and not leave it to the 'Good God or the whim of the moment' in deciding how development was to take place. He went on to argue that the Irish Government should look to Europe in its search for economic progress, within which the OEEC would do all in its power to help. This help, however, would have to be linked with indigenous growth:

> You will get nowhere if you merely rely upon the help of others. The foundation of your development must be produced here by you, yourselves. We, who are outsiders, can give you help, but it will be useless unless you put your own backs into it as well.[42]

Moreover, some British policy-makers were asking if it was worth including such underdeveloped countries as Ireland at all, with R.W. Clarke – later, Sir Otto Clarke – of the Treasury maintaining that they 'would be more trouble than they were worth'.[43] Indeed, the placing of Ireland, Greece and Turkey into a single working party could well be taken as a sign that the OEEC considered them of little importance.

Irish ambitions to enter such the free trade area received a knock from a different source when, in late 1958, events took a dramatic turn as the negotiations for a free trade area were suspended following a French veto. Almost immediately, seven members of the OEEC commenced secret negotiations to form a free trade area among themselves. In June 1959 these talks came into the open, and six months later the Stockholm Convention establishing EFTA was ready for signing. The Irish Government was not invited to the preliminary discussions in February 1959 probably because the seven nations did not want to be encumbered with the kind of problems identified with Ireland during the OEEC negotiations.

In Ireland, the prospect of isolation gave cause for concern in some official circles, particularly within Finance. *Economic Development* had proclaimed in its first chapter that 'Sooner or later, protection will have to go and the challenge of free trade be accepted. There is really no other choice for a country wishing to keep pace materially with the rest of Europe.'[44] Now the European offer upon which, in many respects, free trade hinged seemed less attainable than ever. Nonetheless, for Lemass, the European dimension to economic policy remained at the hub of Government thinking. This was noted by the US embassy in Dublin in August 1959:

> Although Ireland has demonstrated in the UN that it has a wide interest in foreign affairs that do not directly affect the interests of Ireland, the country has failed to show a realistic interest in foreign affairs that do have a direct bearing on its progress. In this regard the opposition … have been most critical of the Taoiseach's failure to cope with Ireland's interest in European markets … it appears that the necessity of foreign co-operation is being brought home to Lemass and that he now realises that he must deviate from his Government's policy of indifferent isolation and take an active role in establishing a place for Ireland in the European trade pattern.[45]

This was also true at an administrative level. Finance's emphasis was on the dismantling of protection and the evolution of an external economic policy that would be export-led; thus, the notion of being outside any of the major European trading blocs was anathema to the department.

At this junction, the Irish Government had two alternatives in its quest to protect its interests: one was to seek participation in EFTA, and thus secure a seat at subsequent negotiations; the other course was to work for closer economic relations with Britain. The second was adopted in recognition of the preponderant place occupied by Britain in Ireland's external trading relations. As Whitaker has maintained: 'at that stage considering so much of our exports went to Britain, it was really the only substantive option we could take'.[46] The Government decided that since three-quarters of Irish exports were going to Britain and Northern Ireland, it should seek to explore the possibility of building on the preferential arrangements of 1938 and 1948 before turning to Europe in its efforts to expand Irish exports and develop the economy.

In spring 1959 the committee of secretaries undertook an in-depth review of economic relations with Britain so as to examine how those relations might be changed in order to gain the maximum benefit for the future development not simply of the economy but of the state itself. It attempted to give future economic relations with Britain a new angle, and recommended that any review of the Anglo-Irish trade agreements should not be confined to seeking concessions within the frameworks of existing agreements merely to compensate for losses arising out of whatever new trading relations Britain might build up with Europe. It argued that what was needed was a different and wider approach that would have as its objective a substantial and significant improvement in general economic relations with Britain. It called for an improvement in such relations, claiming:

> It is necessary for further economic expansion if we are to retain the market outlets we already enjoy, secure the improved outlets necessary for further economic expansion and avoid being squeezed between the emergent trading blocs in Europe.[47]

As freer trade developed within Europe, the Irish were afraid that there would be a weakening of the special trading relationship with Britain as other European countries – primarily in EFTA but possibly in a wider trading association – gradually achieved parity with Ireland by the attainment of free entry into the British market.

At a meeting in June 1959 of the Foreign Trade Committee, of which Lemass was chairman, he succinctly summed up the problems of Ireland's weak bargaining position in relation to EFTA: 'because of the liberal Irish import regime there is virtually nothing to offer to the other side'.[48] Industry and Commerce then prepared a preliminary study on this matter, which was circulated to Agriculture, External Affairs and Finance. In the meantime, and with this in mind, representatives of the British and Irish Governments met on 13 July 1959, with Lemass and Maudling heading the negotiating teams. The British were reluctant to embark on talks along the lines suggested by the Irish representatives, pointing to the difficulty of according to Ireland more favourable treatment than that granted to the Commonwealth. For the British, any new Anglo-Irish trading relationship would have to take cognisance of their obligations to the Commonwealth.

Over the ensuing months, various documents were exchanged between the two sides. The Irish Government's ultimate position was that it would be prepared, on a sector-by-sector analysis, to negotiate such progressive reductions in the prevailing rates of duty on British products as would give British suppliers full opportunity of reasonable competition while affording Irish industries such protection as might be necessary for their progress. This measure represented a substantial concession that would virtually guarantee to British goods an increasing share of the Irish market. Following this meeting, the Department of Agriculture maintained that 'we cannot afford to stay outside a regional grouping and that in particular we should strengthen and develop our relations with our most important trade customer Britain'.[49] This attitude was supported by the other departments, and was the strategy henceforth pursued by Lemass in his dealings with the British. Early in 1960 Whitaker made it clear in a memorandum on Ireland's position in relation to free trade in Europe that the Government's 'immediate concern is to redress and improve the balance in her trade relations with Britain'.[50]

At a meeting on 12 February 1960 between Lemass and Maudling – at this stage president of the Board of Trade after his promotion following the October 1959 British general election – the British made it clear that they would not be able to take any positive steps to steer investment into Irish industry. With regard to agriculture, it was decided that further negotiations should take place in order to conclude a trade agreement. This agreement was produced on 13 April 1960, and saw the British Government state that it would not reduce or eliminate any preferential margins on Irish agricultural produce without consultation with the Irish Government. The Irish Government undertook to initiate another review of protective duties and other import restrictions on British goods. The Government retained the power, subject to consultation, to impose additional duties or other import restrictions where it was satisfied that, following a review, a reduction of protection was in danger of causing material injury to an established Irish industry. Finally, provision was made for further yearly meetings to discuss trading relations and views on agricultural policies.[51]

The Anglo-Irish trade agreement was the result of a concerted effort by the Irish Government to inaugurate a movement towards closer economic ties and some sort of free trade initiative with the British. While the resultant outcome was modest enough, Finance considered it a significant first step in the direction it wanted the Government to take with regard to its economic policies. Tadhg Ó Cearbhaill has maintained that the Anglo-Irish free trade agreement was 'seen as a half-way house by the Government and was very much a preparation for entry to the Common Market'. In this context, the agreement can be seen as another step on a winding road to some form of economic association with Europe.[52]

As the details of Anglo-Irish trade were being discussed, Lemass wanted to formulate an Irish position on EFTA. He had four questions on the free trade area; primarily, he wanted to know the short and long-term implications of joining EFTA on the Portuguese terms: Portugal had obtained terms that allowed tariff reductions to be spread over twenty years, and had secured the right to introduce new tariffs up to 1972 as long as they were removed by 1980. Secondly, there was the minimum agricultural concessions required from Britain for entry. Thirdly, he wondered would it be more advantageous to seek a free trade area with Britain alone. Finally, there was the question of the compatibility of an Anglo-Irish free trade area with Britain's obligations to EFTA.[53]

Finance, Industry and Commerce, Agriculture and External Affairs coalesced to present a memorandum to the Taoiseach on 8 February 1960 outlining a response to these questions.[54] Opposing views were taken by Finance and Industry and Commerce regarding protectionism. Industry and Commerce considered it essential to have some arrangement under which the Government would be free to maintain protection and to take whatever steps would be necessary to promote industrial development and exports. Only when Irish industry in general had reached a point where tariff reductions and quota dismantlement could be adopted without too much risk to Irish industry could some sort of free trade development be adopted. Thus, the principle of a free-trading period during which tariffs would be maintained was crucial to Industry and Commerce. Entering a free trade area would in effect be a betrayal of indigenous Irish industry. It had earlier suggested that as many as 100,000 of the 150,000 or so manufacturing jobs of that time could be lost if trade was liberalised across all of Western Europe, and noted that these conclusions were broadly valid with respect to EFTA membership. Depending on the precise nature of the terms to be agreed with Portugal,

Industry and Commerce suggested that between 20 and 40 per cent of manufacturing employment could be threatened. As Frank Barry has pointed out, 'in this, the department is clearly equating competition with ruin'.[55] He also notes that the view of Industry and Commerce is very similar to the Irish Farmers' Association reaction to what appeared to be a likely World Trade Organisation deal in the summer of 2008, when the IFA claimed that such a deal would result in 50,000 jobs being lost in the food industry and services, and a further 50,000 farmers losing their livelihoods with farm output being halved. This again goes to show that in Ireland, protecting the interests of one's own patch seems to be an overriding principle for at least some economic interests.

The Department of Finance argued that economic expansion depended on greater industrial efficiency, reflected in lower costs and better quality. Failure to achieve this would jeopardise the future of Irish industry and its associated employment whether Ireland participated in a free trade area or not. It opposed the necessity of obtaining a period of freedom from the obligation to reduce protection. Finance, furthermore, maintained that participation in some form of free trade arrangement was the most advantageous context in which to effect a gradual reduction in tariffs that would be necessary to ensure progress in industrial efficiency; thus, it favoured entry on the Portuguese terms, but did not want a free-trading period, which, it believed, would be a psychological as well as an economic mistake. In a European setting, an external commitment, provided it was not too severe, would be more effective and beneficial than a system operated entirely at the discretion of the domestic Government. External Affairs supported Finance's view. Agriculture, however, saw little benefit in joining EFTA unless it would be possible to secure agricultural arrangements with Britain that would be substantially better than those operating between Britain and the other members of the seven.

The joint-departmental memorandum addressed the question of whether it would be more in Ireland's interest to seek 'free trade' arrangements with Britain alone than with EFTA as a whole. Agriculture gave a positive response. Finance and External Affairs agreed that it could be possible to gain substantially better agricultural advantages from a free trade agreement with Britain alone. Both departments, however, were still anxious for Ireland in the long term to associate itself with EFTA. Industry and Commerce was consistent in its opposition in that it maintained that much the same industrial risks would be present in a free trade area with Britain alone as would be present in EFTA. This was standard Industry and Commerce fare. Tadhg Ó Cearbhaill maintains:

> Industry and Commerce regarded itself as the protector of Irish industry. In a way it was like a lawyer with a brief and their brief was to protect Irish employment. That was the strongest aspect in their thinking. If foreign goods were to flood the market as they feared, then Irish jobs were at risk. They felt it was their job to draw attention to this scenario and they did so in strong language. This was in order to discourage the Department of Finance from advising the Government on taking what Industry and Commerce would have regarded as precipitous steps.[56]

In essence, between 1958 and 1960 Ireland's external trading position had changed greatly. The creation of the two trading blocs in Europe and the rapid progress towards freer trade had forced the Government and the policy-making community in general to reconsider the economic future of the country. It was within this context that the Irish Government entered into trade talks with the British in 1959. Ireland, as *The Statist* pointed out, faced a two-fold task in the light of such new trading conditions in Europe:

She must first produce food at increasingly competitive prices if she is to retain her position in the British market. Secondly, she must seek markets outside Britain on the European continent and elsewhere for the increasing surplus of foodstuffs she must produce if she is to attain economic prosperity.[57]

Whether Ireland joined EFTA or not, the Government still had to expect that Ireland would suffer a certain weakening of its preferential position in the British market due to the reduction of British tariffs vis-à-vis other EFTA members. Yet by joining EFTA, Ireland would not necessarily be in a position where rapid dismantling of its own tariff barriers would be called for. Portugal had been accepted for membership of EFTA on quite indulgent terms, and Irish policy-makers could expect to secure membership on equally favourable grounds. Moreover, the British perspective on EFTA was that it had been set up 'essentially as a bridge-building step between itself and the EEC'.[58] If an alignment between the two could be secured, Ireland's interests would best be served by being present at the conference table. As Desmond Fisher, in *The Statist*, put it:

If the process of linking the Six and Seven achieved success – and even the most pessimistic would hope for some progress eventually – it is a safe guess that a bit of further give-and-take not only in the industrial but in the agricultural field will be necessary. In this regard it is vital for Ireland to be in at the start. Otherwise undertakings to the other European food exporting countries may be such as to leave very little scope for entry by Ireland into continental markets.[59]

Looking at the development of Europe from this perspective, it did seem quite logical for Ireland to be a member of EFTA. At this stage, it appeared undesirable for Ireland to be isolated from European developments. Any country that was not in either of the two trading blocs would find itself out in the cold when decisions concerning the relationship between EFTA and the EEC were being discussed.

## 'WE WERE NOT THAT ENTHUSIASTIC'

The main consequence of Ireland joining EFTA would be the necessity of a methodical reduction in tariff barriers. Most of Ireland's industries set up since the 1930s had failed to develop any export capacity, and it was questionable whether some of them would be able to justify their existence in a free trade environment. Yet whether Ireland joined EFTA or not, it had become abundantly clear to most of the policy community that some step towards dismantling, or at least reducing, tariff barriers was essential. Lemass had pointed this out many times since becoming Taoiseach. A unilateral tariff reduction would, however, bring with it strong internal political tensions; thus, some were arguing that it would be more palatable to undertake the exercise within the context of a formal undertaking inside a European grouping, where there would be some compensating advantages, and Ireland would be able to exert at least nominal influence on decision making. If Ireland did not join a trading bloc, its tariff reductions and quota increases would have to be unilateral. If Ireland joined EFTA, however, the effect upon Irish industries of the removal of trade barriers would be partially offset by the new markets opened up for Irish products. In the view of Garret FitzGerald, at this stage, chairman of the executive committee of the Irish Council of the European Movement:

> While the potential markets for our goods in the continental Little Free Trade Area countries may not be of first importance they are certainly better than nothing – and may indeed prove a good deal more valuable than is at present supposed. Current estimates of the value of these markets to us

tend to be based on the assumption that the efficiency of our industries, and the vigour of our export drive will be no greater in the future than they are today whereas current trends in Irish industry, if reinforced by the spur of the gradual removal of protection, may before long transform the scene, and greatly enhance the value to us of free access to new foreign markets.[60]

Moreover, the Irish European Movement argued, if Ireland did not become a member of EFTA, the Government could find it difficult to put across a programme of unilateral tariff reductions. This failure to move ahead with the dismantling of protective tariff barriers at a time when public opinion had to an extent been prepared for such a development – said the Irish European Movement – could well have adverse consequences for the economy: 'increased pressure on industry to improve efficiency and to become even more "export-conscious" will be needed if we are not to fall behind in the very early stages of the European economic race'.[61]

Irish membership of EFTA would entail the removal of tariff and quota restrictions on imports from all the members of EFTA, including the UK, though it was likely that the Government would be able to secure a gradual phasing-out of such restrictions – probably up to twenty years, as in the case of Portugal.

Whether Ireland joined EFTA or not, it seemed quite clear that its prosperity still depended on the agricultural economy. Membership of EFTA – though it would subject Irish manufacturers to unfettered competition – would provide new markets for farmers to sell their produce, although, as we have seen, their prime target was the EEC. Faced with the options of embarking on a process of accession to EFTA or of negotiating free trade agreements with Britain alone, the Government came down in favour of the latter when it turned its attention to the possibility of acceding to GATT. Lemass, in May 1961, explained why EFTA negotiations were not pursued. Besides Britain, he remarked:

The other six members of the EFTA have not been important markets for us in the past and, while we must not of course neglect any market, it is doubtful whether the advantages we could hope to reap in those countries would satisfy acceptance of the Stockholm Convention, particularly as agriculture is expressly excluded from its provisions.[62]

Irish interest in the free trade area, set up by the convention signed in Stockholm on 4 January 1960, had naturally stemmed from the prospect of greatly expanded agricultural exports that might have been opened up by Irish participation. The Government had informed the council of the OEEC early in 1960 that its trade returns showed:

Our trade balance with non-sterling member countries is extremely unfavourable – in roughly the proportions of three to one. This position has recently become more serious by reason of the emergence among our partners in this Organisation of two trading groups, EFTA and the EEC.[63]

When agriculture was not going to be included in the EFTA context, Irish policy-makers felt they had no option but to revert to the old formula of negotiating independent trade agreements with Britain. Yet in many ways, the negotiations had taken down one of the great psychological barriers impeding developmental progress. By these negotiations – in the words of Terence Brown:

An Ireland that had sought to define its identity since independence principally in terms of social patterns rooted in the country's past was to seek to adapt itself to the prevailing capitalist values of the developed world.[64]

Tadhg Ó Cearbhaill – assistant secretary in the Department of the

Taoiseach at the time and intimately involved in the EFTA negotiations
– noted:

> In the end we were not that enthusiastic as there was a feeling within
> Government at the time that the whole concept of Europe would come
> right in the end and it was within a larger unified EEC that we wanted
> to be associated. Lemass was very much of that view. Policy was directed
> with that in mind.[65]

Thus, the Government suspended deliberations on EFTA and explored
new avenues in its quest for economic development. Its immediate aim
was to seek membership of the EEC. Within a month of Lemass'
speech on rejecting the EFTA option, the Government published a
White Paper on membership of the EEC, to prepare public opinion
for the official application the following month. There were still many
in the administrative framework who doubted the wisdom of fully
entering a European trading bloc. Con Cremin – by this time secretary
of External Affairs – outlined in June 1960 Ireland's relationship with
both European trading groups when suggesting a Dáil reply to the
deputy secretary of Industry and Commerce regarding Ireland's refusal
to join EFTA:

> It is probable that in our circumstances association would be the most
> appropriate formula having regard particularly to the fact that we could
> not accept the full obligations of either instrument nor accord that
> degree of reciprocity which would be required for full membership. The
> terms of association on our part with either group would have to safe-
> guard the special trading relationship between this country and Britain
> which is provided for in the Anglo-Irish trade agreements. Such associa-
> tion would be considered primarily as a means of enabling us to share
> in the benefits of a general European settlement of trade and economic

relations on terms which would take account of our own economic circumstances.[66]

The premise that Ireland seek initially association rather than full membership of an economic group suggested that the EEC negotiations would also be tortuous.


## IRELAND IS READY TO ASSUME ALL OBLIGATIONS

The prospect of Irish involvement in European economic integration was not an explicit feature of either *Economic Development* or the *First Programme for Economic Expansion*. Yet both documents did recognise that the country would have to engage substantially more with Western Europe, at least in trade terms, if it was to prosper economically. Most policy-makers – though somewhat committed to change – continued to believe that, for the immediate future, the country's economic prospects rested on access to British markets. Nor did the accession of Lemass to Taoiseach in 1959 precipitate a completely radical departure in this respect. A distinction was drawn between the movement to free trade and a decision to join any multilateral organisation. The former policy was adopted towards the end of the 1950s, but the latter was avoided until July 1961. Throughout 1960 and into 1961, Lemass reiterated the view that it was not to Ireland's advantage to join either the EEC or EFTA. While examining the options, the conclusion drawn was that Ireland's economic development would not be significantly improved by membership of any multilateral group.[67] In essence, the Government's – and, indeed, the civil service's – reluctance to embark on the European option can be traced to the belief that international organisations such as GATT and the OEEC 'were not likely to succeed in liberalising agricultural trade'.[68] Yet there was a growing belief in some sections of the policy community that there was a wider perspective to policy-making in the 1950s, and that wider events in Western Europe could not simply be ignored by the Irish body politic.[69] As Whitaker pointed out:

> It was painfully obvious there was a lack of any meaningful future in our over-reliance on the British market. Thus there was no complacency within the civil service. How could there be? Our independence was threatened. There was a restless discontent as we tried to get out of the dark night of the soul.[70]

There can be little doubt, however, that there was many industrialists – including some in the FII – who would have been quite content to carry on trading in the rather stultifying atmosphere of the protectionist shelter.[71]

In theory, the more interventionist-minded but free trade-led Department of Finance was all in favour of joining a trading bloc, but would only do so on terms favourable to Ireland. Thus, prior to July 1961, policy development had continued to move in a bilateral direction on the grounds that this would provide the greatest advantage for Ireland. Many within the policy community were deeply worried by the prospect of Irish entry into the EEC without a simultaneous British entry. For Industry and Commerce, entry into the EEC would result in:

> [The] withdrawal of preferential treatment given by Ireland to United Kingdom goods, but by requiring Ireland to adopt a common external tariff which would have to be applied to British goods, would put Britain at a disadvantage in the Irish market as compared with EEC countries. It would be foolhardy to expect the United Kingdom would continue to give trade advantages, agricultural or industrial, to this country in those circumstances.[72]

Industry and Commerce further argued that all measures of industrial protection would have to be eliminated, with wages and conditions of competition equated with those obtaining in the highly developed countries of the EEC: 'it should be noted that the principle of adequate protection for Irish industry, including special consideration for industries not fully established, is enshrined in the existing trade agreement with the United Kingdom'.[73] This attitude reflects and reasserts the traditional gloomy outlook of Industry and Commerce towards economic development within Ireland. It was unwilling to look beyond habitual arrangements with Britain to expand either Irish industry or agriculture. The position of the British was crucial to Irish attitudes towards membership of the EEC, as Ireland was clearly in no position to join unless Britain did so as well.

An informal Irish delegation to the European Commission in April 1961 was informed of the difficulties an Irish application would meet, and told that association rather than full membership could well be the best method for developing Ireland's relationship with the Community, with full membership following in due course.[74] The reason given was that Ireland was considered to be an underdeveloped economy and would require special consideration prior to full membership. This could best be described as an 'unfortunate' outcome of the EFTA negotiations, where it was well known throughout the Community that the Irish Government had considered entry on the basis that the country was underdeveloped economically. The delegation drew up a memorandum for the Government, within which it made two observations: the first was that it believed the official position of the Commission was that Ireland should apply for associate membership rather than full membership at this stage, and that the Government should be careful before it decided to apply for full membership; the second was that Ireland might pursue a high-risk strategy of applying for full membership in the hope that the Commission would offer concessions to make association more attractive. It concluded that full membership carried considerable disadvantages for Ireland, especially for its industrial economy and the special relationship with Britain, but that association also carried the risk that Ireland would neither benefit from Commission programmes nor be in a position to influence the future development of the EEC itself.[75]

A White Paper on membership of the EEC was published in June 1961 prior to the official application. This flurry of activity can be attributed to the decision of Britain to apply. Once the Government became aware of the British decision, it quickly prepared its own application and forwarded it to Brussels to anticipate the British application. As Dermot Keogh has shown, this was for public consumption in order to claim that the Irish decision was not a consequence of British pressure or example.[76] While such behaviour might be considered somewhat bizarre, the application itself made sense because Ireland could not afford to be outside the Community if Britain was in it. Lemass admitted that the application was inevitable once Britain had decided to apply. He told the *Economist* in February 1962:

> It was Britain's decision to apply for membership that opened the way for our own application. The predominant position of British trade on our economy, as a market for our exports, and the special character of the trading arrangements between the two countries, made it difficult to contemplate membership unless Britain were also to become a member.[77]

The decision to apply for membership was quickly seen as historic. It was described by William Tyler, the US assistant secretary of state for European affairs, as the first move by the Irish Government towards participation in international affairs, and particularly in the economic affairs of Western Europe. Maintaining that Ireland was shedding its 'narrow provincialism', Tyler proclaimed:

> The decision to apply for membership of the EEC is most significant. Though obviously motivated to a large extent by a feeling that Ireland would be excluded from the British market the decision is not merely a reaction to this prospect. There is evidence that Irish leaders weighed their decision carefully and concluded that Ireland must become a member of the Common Market. This is further borne out by the Prime Minister's declaration that Ireland is ready to assume all obligations, political as well as economic, of membership of the EEC.[78]

The EEC suggested to the Irish Government in October 1961 that it should present its case in Brussels the following January. While Lemass was primarily concerned about the economic implications of membership, he realised there were political ramifications, too. He told the secretary of his department that he considered it 'essential to the success of Ireland's application to include in the draft statement a declaration of Ireland's attitude to the political aims of the Community'.[79] This related to the setting-up of an inter-Governmental working party to reconcile the continued refusal to join NATO (North Atlantic Treaty Alliance) with Irish support for the ideal of European unity. Con Cremin, departmental secretary at External Affairs, had initially procrastinated only to be bluntly told by Lemass to come up with a formula.[80] The formula reached within two days in the week coming up to Christmas ingeniously stated that the reason Ireland was not a member of NATO was not because of any lack of sympathy with its basic objectives but due to the fact that membership would place the state under an obligation to not only respect but defend the territorial integration of the countries party to the treaty, including of course Britain, whereas it was a fundamental aspiration of the Irish people to see the unity of the country restored: 'Our non-participation in NATO is thus not an expression of any principle of neutrality, nor does it weaken in any way our positive attitude towards the ideal of European unity'.[81] While Lemass noted correctly that membership of NATO was not a prerequisite for membership of the EEC, he voiced reasonable fears:

> Some countries or interests … may be opposed, or at least indifferent, to our entry to the EEC, it would be prudent not to imply, by anything said prior to being accepted as a member that joining NATO (even with a reservation) is something we could not face in any circumstances. To do so might merely supply them with a test of membership which, as they might hope, would transfer from them to ourselves the responsibility of negativing our application.[82]

This, in turn, related to the Government's discovery in November 1961 that a very senior member of the Kennedy administration – the under-secretary for economic affairs, George Ball – was hostile to the idea of Ireland's full membership of the EEC. Ireland's refusal to join NATO and its policy of neutrality at the UN did not sit well with Ball for one, who was arguing in Washington that no neutrals should be allowed join the EEC.[83]

## 'WE FULLY REALISE WHAT THE COMMUNITY IS'

Lemass' reasoning on NATO was further reinforced by a memorandum written the previous day by Ireland's ambassador to the Community, Frank Biggar. He reported that the British approach – as outlined by Edward Heath to the Community – had been received positively, and while the British would encounter serious technical problems in pursuing their application, Ireland could not expect to have any lesser difficulty in this process; indeed, Ireland – because it was a small, neutral state – could expect more serious problems compared to Britain. Biggar added that the draft memorandum for the January meeting could well be seen as suspect by the existing EEC members in that Ireland might be viewed as indifferent in its application, and that the Government would have to demonstrate it was applying without reservations of any kind if it were to make its application convincing. He urged the Government to redraft in a positive vein, warning that the existing draft suffered:

> From a failure to emphasise sufficiently at the outset our appreciation of the fact that the EEC despite its title, is first and foremost a political concept and not merely an economic organisation with a few political ideas as an afterthought.[84]

This was something Industry and Commerce had also warned about – though with its traditional gloomy economic mindset – when it argued:

> It must be remembered that the final objective of the six is political integration. What we need in this country is a combination of reasonable long term price stability in agriculture, together with a very substantial expansion in activity.[85]

Implicit in this statement was that Industry and Commerce saw the political developments of the EEC impinging on Ireland's economic development and its capacity to make independent policy – namely, sustaining protectionism.

Biggar's memorandum stressed the means by which the official application should proceed:

We fully realise what the community is and what it is seeking to achieve. This would involve a general expression of our belief in the vital and unique importance of Western Europe for the future of humanity and the conviction that it can only play its proper role if politically strong and economically prosperous, conditions for which political and economic unity are the essential prerequisites.[86]

Biggar's memorandum did not find favour with all in the civil service. Nicholas Ó Nuailláin, secretary of the Department of the Taoiseach, wrote to Whitaker a number of days later:

We do not agree with all of his comment. In particular we here do not agree that it is essential that we 'inflate' the sections concerning our acceptance of the political objectives. Any judgement on this point is, of course, largely subjective but it is our feeling that the sincerity of our professions in this regard will not be assessed by the six by reference to the length of what we say but rather by our making it clear that we know what we are talking about and do so in a direct and unambiguous fashion. Above all, we here would be somewhat nervous about appearing to 'protest too much'. I don't think that the six generally and, in particular some of them (such as the French), would be impressed by what they might describe as 'literature'.[87]

In between Biggar's memorandum and Ó Nuailláin's rebuttal, a revised draft of the application statement was circulated on 1 January 1962, and it contained a brief reference to political aspects. The statement was careful to place Ireland's application in the context of its Christian heritage and its commitment to Christian values in a European context:

Indeed for some centuries after the break up of the Roman Empire, Ireland was a haven of spiritual and intellectual life in which the essence of the European tradition was preserved and from which it was brought back again to many continental lands.

The statement insisted that Ireland had favourably viewed the various movements towards European union, but noted that while Ireland had actively participated in the OEEC and the Council of Europe, it had not been able to join NATO:

> The fact that we did not accede to the North Atlantic Treaty, despite our agreement with its aims, was due to special circumstances and is not an expression of any principle of neutrality nor does it qualify in any way our positive attitude towards the ideal of European unity.[88]

Cremin – not withstanding his Christmas 1961 formula explaining the NATO/European-unity conundrum – still had doubts over the whole question, and suggested two lines could still be taken: the first involved withdrawing the application if NATO membership proved to be a prerequisite for entry, the second was to insist that special circumstances were involved, and that Ireland would join the organisation if partition was ended.[89] Moreover, Hugh McCann – ambassador in London – had reported to Cremin that 'Britain is not keen that EEC membership should be coterminous with NATO', which might explain External Affairs' attitude of attempting to avoid the NATO question entirely.[90] According to External Affairs, the Taoiseach was in favour of the second approach; this led Finance to take a vigorous line on the application, with the result that Cremin and External Affairs were in the main ignored. External Affairs had, to an extent, been fudging on the application since late December 1961, with the result that Finance grabbed the initiative and moved the application forward. Thus, Finance took the lead in promoting the Irish application, with Whitaker playing a central role in the background discussions in Dublin and subsequently in Brussels. As Whitaker stated:

> What was at stake was the economic independence of the country, thus we, in Finance, felt that we had to give the lead and take the strongest line possible in arguing for entry to the community. I felt really that it was the only way we could advance in an economic sense.[91]

Finance, then, was insisting that joining the Community was imperative if Ireland was to survive economically. It had shrugged off its previous reticence regarding the economic benefits of entry. With the British committed to entry, Finance now saw the EEC as the only place to be. It was not open to Ireland to pick or choose the circumstances under which it would join. Once the country had decided on full membership, it would be incumbent on the Government to proceed with the application without any reservations. Whitaker insisted that it would be 'extremely unfortunate' if the application was to be withdrawn on the issue of NATO membership. Early in January, he wrote a long memorandum to his minister, James Ryan, outlining the NATO problem in relation to the EEC:

> Nobody has yet told us that this is a condition of a membership of the EEC. On the other hand, nobody so loves us as to want us in the EEC on our own terms. The Community has difficulties enough without adding those introduced by a 'contrary' new member who will bring the Community no particular benefits but will inflict on it additional problems including (as they might well view it) this tiresome forty year old problem with Britain ... It is well to remind ourselves that it is our own propaganda which has given such an artificial significance to NATO in relation to partition. There is, in fact, no necessary incompatibility between joining NATO and maintaining our stand on partition ... We

say we agree with the aims of the North Atlantic Treaty and are not ideologically neutral. But are these not in danger of being regarded as empty professions when effect is deliberately not given to them because of preoccupation with a national problem which we have lived with for forty years? To others it may seem that we are treating a narrow national interest as being more important than unity and co-operation in the defence of Western civilisation.[92]

Whitaker also argued that the Government should not press its neutral status in terms of the Swiss or the Swedes, who were ideological neutrals and whose neutrality, as such, ruled them out of membership of the EEC even in an associate capacity. Notwithstanding this critical approach, Whitaker advised Ryan that the Government should adopt a wait-and-see approach to the question of NATO, while insisting that it should not ignore the real political and defence requirements that would in time come with membership.

The fact that much of the diplomatic wrangling about political issues went through Whitaker is significant in that it shows the crucial role of Finance with regard to membership of the EEC. While External Affairs had played key roles in relation to Marshall Aid and other European commitments, Finance had taken the lead when it came to decisions regarding Europe, despite these matters not being formally economic. External Affairs – which had harboured some doubts about the EEC – was effectively sidelined as Lemass took control of the debate and interacted more with Whitaker and Finance on the issues of the EEC and NATO.[93] Ultimately, for Whitaker, the economic and political roles of membership were intertwined. He bluntly told his minister:

If we want to safeguard our economic future – and on this, basically, our independence and influence in the world rests – we should not ourselves raise obstacles to being admitted as members of the EEC. To say that we would withdraw our application if membership of NATO were insisted upon would be extremely unfortunate.[94]

The NATO question had, to an extent, dogged the application, and Lemass accepted that he would have to reassure the Community on this question. On 5 February the Minister for Lands, Michael Moran, addressed the Chamber of Commerce in his native Castlebar on the application issue. He pointed out that it would be unrealistic to ignore the fact that all members of the EEC were in NATO, and that neutrality in the context of East-West divisions was something that had not been envisaged by the Irish people. He famously went on to argue that between communism and the free world:

> Neutrality ... is not a policy to which we would even wish to appear committed ... I mention this to emphasise that we are entering negotiations for membership of the EEC without any pre-committed attitude, political or otherwise. Our whole history and cultural tradition and outlook have been bound up with that of Europe for past ages. We have, I believe, a full part to play in this day and age in the integration and development of a United States of Europe, and towards this end it may be necessary for us to share any political decisions for the common good.[95]

This speech caused quite an uproar within both Fianna Fáil and in the country at large. While there is no substantive evidence to show Lemass was well informed as to what Moran would say, as a known Cabinet disciplinarian it seems inconceivable that Lemass would not have known and approved of Moran's speech, hinting as it did at a fundamental change in Irish foreign policy.[96] At a parliamentary party meeting nine days later, Lemass 'gave a lengthy explanation to the party' of Moran's speech.[97] While the minutes of this meeting are no clearer than that, it does appear that

Lemass was able to convince his colleagues that the economic benefits of membership of the Community were paramount, and, in any event, there was no stipulation that entry into NATO was a prerequisite to joining the EEC. This was something the US embassy picked up on:

> It is much to be doubted that the Government wished to prepare the people of Ireland for admission into NATO ... Rather it would seem that the Government felt that the time had come for the public at large to start thinking about what is inevitable if Ireland becomes a member of the EEC, namely a marked change in its present neutral status and complete independence of action ... By raising the subject of NATO, the Government was sure of stirring the public into awareness that there were significant political implications in the application for membership in the EEC.[98]

In the October 1961 general election campaign, Lemass had vowed that a Fianna Fáil Government would bring Ireland into the EEC. It was the tangible benefits of economic expansion that brought about this vow, and Lemass was not about to let the NATO question interfere with that. The point about political integration was also addressed within the civil service. At a meeting of department secretaries in March 1962, J.C. Nagle of Agriculture wondered whether the emphasis placed on NATO in some preliminary discussions was intended to convey the message that some countries were opposed to Irish entry into the EEC on grounds other than economic.[99] Adding to this, Frank Biggar claimed: 'I would not indeed think it impossible that, if we fail to convince on the political side, our economic difficulties might be used as a device to block our membership application'.[100] Politically, Lemass recognised the extent to which the EEC required assurances on a number of issues. In the area of foreign policy Lemass stated that the Government accepted its obligation in this field fully:

Economic integration is not regarded as an end in itself but as a step towards political union, and is, of course, in itself a political develop-ment of major significance. Indeed the removal of all causes of economic conflict between the member states is a very great political achievement.[101]

What worried the Government, and Finance in particular, was the possibility that political questions would impede Ireland's entry and subsequently stifle its economic development.

## THE TERRIBLE COST

At a more basic level, the official application also pointed out that an understanding of the Community's character and aims was not confined to the Government but had come to be shared by the Irish people generally through debates in Parliament, widespread press comment and a great deal of discussion by trade unions, employers' organisations, farmers' groups and similar bodies.[102] Indeed, there was a remarkable sense of homogeneity about the application. During the 1961 general election, the three major parties openly supported entry into the EEC, leaving it to independent socialists Noël Browne and Jack McQuillan to be lone voices in the Dáil in opposing the application.[103] Speeches by all Fine Gael's important figures – such as James Dillon, Gerard Sweetman, Richard Mulcahy, Liam Cosgrave, T.F. O'Higgins, Gerry L'Estrange and Seán MacEoin – emphasised in the campaign the need to develop policies conducive to benefiting from membership of the EEC, and placed great emphasis on the need to prepare sufficiently to meet the new challenges that membership would bring. Cosgrave explained to an audience in Dalkey what he considered to be the key issue of the campaign: 'this country is facing a new era and that with developments in Europe conditions in the future will be quite different'.[104] Labour's 4,000-word manifesto did not mention the EEC once. While its new leader, Brendan Corish, argued that strong Labour representation in the Dáil was necessary as drastic changes would come about with membership, Niamh Puirséil perceptively points out that voters could be forgiven for wondering what the point was in having strong Labour representation when it did not have a strong policy on Ireland's role in Europe.[105] In fact, Labour's position was largely due to the influence of former party leader, William Norton, who regarded the Common Market as a 'bulwark against communism'.[106]

At a wider level, the major newspapers and interest groups were all notionally pro-European in outlook. Nicholas Harman of the *Economist* noted such unanimity in an interview with Lemass: 'Ireland's application to the Common Market is a revolutionary step in Irish history, yet it seems that Irishmen, irrespective of their political party, are almost solidly behind the Government.'[107]

For the most part, the academic economic community was also in favour of Ireland joining the EEC. There was, however, one significant opponent: David O'Mahony was a college lecturer who later succeeded John Busteed as professor of economics in University College, Cork, and who published in the same year, 1964, the first textbook on the Irish economy by a professional economist; he opposed entry on the grounds that Ireland would be as well off in GATT following free trade policies from within that organisation. He argued that there was nothing to stop Ireland staying out if Britain entered, as in that case the British-Irish labour market would be broken up into two markets that would enable the country to stand a good chance of being able to turn improvements in productive efficiency into lower prices. This would also happen if Ireland entered and the British stayed out. In the latter case, Irish products would not enjoy free entry into the Common Market, which would include Britain. But if Ireland pursued a free trade policy, there would be no obstacle to it becoming a member of GATT:

It should then be comparatively easy for us to make an agreement with the EEC within the framework of GATT providing for the free entry which its products would enjoy into this country by virtue of its free trade policy. Ultimately indeed such a course might perhaps be the most desirable one for this country to follow. It would probably be regarded in a very favourable light by the community which quite evidently is not over anxious to dilute its membership with the fringe countries of Europe.[108]

Others were worried by the approach taken by Lemass. A commentator in *Hibernia* in late 1962 wondered whether there were alternatives to full entry, claiming that, though Lemass maintained Ireland could undertake the responsibilities of full membership:

No man in Ireland is more painfully aware of the limitations of Irish industry – limitations of size, of management, of capital and of enterprise ... Lemass may well be right in saying that Ireland can bear full membership but has he really counted the terrible cost?[109]

Strangely, this writer declared that the majority of people in the country were leaderless, and that a great opportunity existed for the Labour Party to fight and win the next election by running on an anti-EEC platform. He accused Fianna Fáil of playing politics with the Common Market issue:

Nothing could be more harmful to a democratic community than that a major segment of opinion, and perhaps even a majority of the electorate should be unable to find political expression for their hopes and fears on an issue of such magnitude ... It would be a poor state of affairs if our people were to escape great and unnecessary hardship because the Europeans more conscientiously assessed our situation and our well-being than our leaders to whom we had entrusted our affairs.[110]

It would appear, however, that this was a voice in the wilderness. The Labour Party was not ideologically opposed to entry at this stage (although it did oppose the later successful application in 1972). Furthermore, the Catholic church offered no significant opposition to the application, though some of its members did warn of the dangers if the country joined. One contributor to the January 1962 edition of *Christus Rex* sounded a note of caution:

> Before we decide finally to enter the EEC we should fully consider its very far reaching obligations which entail a surrender of so much control over our own 'household' and of independence of action in economic, social, and perhaps political fields. Also entering EEC will be like swimming out into the open sea from the former shelter of a bathing pool: unless our various branches of agriculture and industry can keep pace with those in other countries they will certainly be submerged without any hole of 'protection'. Assuredly the Common Market is no 'gift on the silver salver' but only an opportunity to be grasped with resolute energy – if at all.[111]

Nevertheless, there was no resistance on the part of the church to EEC membership, as the hierarchy had no collective stance on the issue. While one or two of the bishops had been outspoken on economic issues – most notably Bishop Cornelius Lucey of Cork, who was a strong defender of small farmers, and Bishop William Philbin of Clonfert, who wrote substantially on social issues – as a group the hierarchy do not seem to have commented on the EEC. Philbin was of the view that it was Ireland itself that was largely responsible for its classification as an underdeveloped country, and, as Diarmaid Ferriter points out, 'for the loss of many of its more adventurous citizens, who would look for the rewards that more advanced economies could offer'.[112] Philbin – along with other clerical sociologists of the 1950s and early 1960s – saw it as his duty to point out the failures of rural self-sufficiency, which had been a key feature of Irish revolutionary rhetoric.[113] Indeed, Lemass and Cardinal William Conway both stressed in separate interviews in 1969 the limited role the church had in influencing Government policy in the economic sphere.[114]

The Catholic journals did offer some critical comment on the application, with *Studies* and *Christus Rex* opening their pages for commentary. It was William Philbin who offered the most cogent analysis of the application from the clergy, in an address entitled 'The Irish and the New Europe', which was reprinted in *Studies*. For Philbin, the challenge of the Common Market was 'above everything else a moral challenge'. He noted that while it seemed to be commonly accepted that Ireland would receive a trade advantage from membership, the benefits of such would not just be confined to the field of international trade:

> Our admission to the Common Market might well provide the stimulus we need, nationally and personally, to use our talents and resources generally to better account. The material factor might react favourably on the spiritual, making a two-way traffic as the body serves the soul. Enrichment in the field of human character is a better justification of the risks we are taking than any prospects of enhanced prosperity, because our personal qualities are, ultimately, the only possessions we need care about. Indeed personal improvement is the only adequate reason, in the last reckoning, for any corporate enterprise.[115]

In essence, the Common Market – as perceived by Philbin – had formalised a pattern that was already implicit in the economic pattern of modern society. He therefore called on the whole population to interest themselves in the industrial concerns of the country:

Unless Irish people in our present circumstances of combined opportunity and peril shoulder the responsibilities that modern social organisation is imposing among us, unless we are prepared to be a nation in the twentieth-century sense, we had better forget our European ambitions and settle for something much more primitive, and forget too our hopes of staunching the flow of our life-blood in emigration … And an essential condition for advance is that we should think and act as a nation in the economic field, regarding lesser loyalties as subsidiary to our general duty of citizenship. If individuals or groups that hold strong economic positions of one kind or another press their advantage to the detriment of the public good, they will make even the most enlightened national planning and even the most elaborate material provision quite futile.[116]

As we have seen, the farmers, unions and employers were all pressing their claims with Government when it seemed that entry into the EEC was at hand. Ultimately, Philbin declared that membership of the EEC was a good thing for Ireland, but that sectional interests would have to take a back seat for the overall good of society:

Leadership or planning will not be enough. We shall all be to blame if we fail or only half-succeed … Let us then, in the midst of all our detailed and technical preparation for the Common Market, not neglect to persuade ourselves about what it entails in terms of ordinary human character, of moral stamina. We are meeting in the current phase a moment of truth. Let us see and accept that a challenge faces us, simply as men and women, to prove what we are made of.[117]

Philbin's lecture – originally entitled 'The moral challenge of the Common Market' – is the only substantive statement from a member of the hierarchy on the question of membership. Other clergy writing on the application followed Philbin's lead and urged the economic interest groups to play a larger role in the policy process and to not leave everything to the state. James Kavanagh of UCD, writing in *Christus Rex*, declared that 'looking to the state is a national disease. Our industrialists – many of them – have been feather-bedded for too long and only a few of them are aware that management is expected to be enterprising'.[118] Those few Catholic writers who did write on economic issues were basically advocating a quasi-corporatist approach to the economy, and calling on Government and interest groups to work together.

Whilst domestic discussion developed, a meeting was held in Brussels on 18 January 1962 to explore some of the questions raised by the Irish application. The *Irish Press* reported that Lemass was 'optimistic' that full membership of the Common Market could be obtained.[119] The European Commission was not convinced at first that Ireland could fulfil the obligations of membership, noting that Ireland had special problems in respect of membership, and that these had to be given serious consideration even prior to the opening of formal negotiations. Indeed, the Irish Government was worried that the Council of Ministers might separate the Irish application from those of Denmark and Britain, both of whom has been advised that agreement had been reached on the opening of negotiations.[120]

Lemass was told that in view of the existing commercial relations between Ireland and Britain, it would be difficult to begin negotiations with the Irish Government until at least some progress had been made towards a Community agreement with Britain. Lemass maintained after this meeting that he was 'satisfied with the results of his first contact with the commission', and that the Government would be pressing on with its application for full membership.[121] A more ominous note was sounded by the *Guardian* in Britain when it declared: 'although the Irish application has been officially welcomed, there is no doubt that individuals, among the French delegation especially, have severe reservations about the application'.[122] This probably related to worries the French had about any special concessions the Irish would seek. Yet some members of the European Commission saw merit in the Irish application. J.C.B. MacCarthy noted the reaction of the Belgian commissioner, Jean Rey, who saw:

> ... [the] clear principal danger lying in the field of agriculture. As regards industry there appeared to be no problem since we had accepted that protection must go by the end of the transitional period. While there was difficulty over the question of a common external tariff ... he was very pleased that the Taoiseach had given such emphasis to political considerations.[123]

MacCarthy also commented on the positive reaction of Signor Rosso, Parliamentary Secretary to the Italian Minister for Finance, who 'saw no difficulty in our becoming a full member'. The Dutch were also favourable to the Irish application, reporting that Lemass' speech was 'generally well received'.[124]

The memorandum prepared for Lemass prior to his departure for his key meeting in Brussels maintained that the fundamental economic emphasis for Ireland remained agriculture, despite the recent commitment to industrial development:

> ... for Ireland agriculture will always be of major importance. We are, naturally, anxious that, through membership of the European Economic Community, Ireland should be able to look forward to a balanced development of agriculture and industry.[125]

Irish officials were aware of the consequence of entry for Irish agriculture. It was assumed that Britain would remain the focus for agricultural exports, though it was recognised that the special relationship would be eroded, if not terminated, by the Common Agricultural Policy. The farming community, as we have seen, had no doubts that after the disappointment of the Anglo-Irish trade agreement, Irish agriculture would boom within the framework of the EEC.

In terms of industrial policy, the Irish aim was to negotiate a protocol or special agreement under which Irish tariffs would be dismantled over an agreed period of time, while some recognition would be obtained for the difficulties that some exposed industries might encounter. Industry and Commerce remained pessimistic about Ireland's industrial future without long-term support, suggesting that protection should be maintained beyond the proposed 1970 transition date: 'the protocol should provide for maintaining protection after the end of the transitional period for any industries which might find it too difficult to comply with the general rhythm [of tariff reduction]'.[126] Industry and Commerce reiterated its customary position that around 100,000 jobs could be threatened unless some form of protection remained in place. This view – while undoubtedly pessimistic – had a basis in reality as the initial CIO reports began to show that Irish industry was ill prepared for competition. As one industrialist commented:

> When those reports came out first there was not a great deal of surprise among businessmen. Originally we were not conscious of any sort of competition and once it became known that the Government was serious about pursuing the EEC option we realised that we were hope-lessly ill equipped to cope with this new state of affairs.[127]

The CIO reports opened the eyes of many industrialists, as a professional economist worked closely with the survey teams. According to another industrialist, this 'was a complete new experience for us in the FII. We quickly got the message that we had to adapt or else go under'.[128] The CIO had found that, with a few exceptions, Irish industry was ill prepared for such a change in approach. The majority of firms in Ireland were heavily protected and had no experience of international trading conditions. Furthermore, a majority of those employed in the industrial sector were in these protected areas. The Government was working on the assumption that Ireland would enter the EEC early in 1963, and that all the transitional agreements would be completed by 1970. Technical decisions concerning the method by which tariffs might be reduced gave some scope for Ireland and Irish industry, but this in itself would be limited. This meant that Irish industry would have to meet the full force of competition by this latter date. It was in recognition of this threat that the Government had established the CIO to assess the potential of Irish industry in a free trade environment.[129]

The CIO had a dual function: one was to provide an assessment of Ireland's likely trading position in a free trade environment, and the other involved incorporating the industrial interest groups into Government structures. This strategy was successful in drawing the trade unions closer to the Government. Lemass urged trade unionists to accept that changes were already underway regarding Ireland's relationship with the wider world, and that existing preferences with Britain were consequently already weakening. He implied, but did not state directly, that even in the absence of EEC membership, considerable changes in the Irish economy would be necessary. As Donal Nevin points out:

> It had become pretty clear to the union movement that we would have an important role to play in the development of the economy, whether we were in a European body or not. Our thinking on the European issue was along the lines of if it was good for workers, Congress would not oppose it.[130]

Lemass believed that 'we can avoid the prejudicial effects of having to face a tariff on entry into Britain by ourselves joining the EEC'.[131] Ironically, he conceded that the negotiating strategy that had previously been adopted in respect of EFTA – insisting that Ireland was underdeveloped, and identifying with Greece and Turkey – could now work to Ireland's disadvantage. The most significant difference between EFTA and EEC entry was that in the former, agriculture was not in question for Ireland, and it had therefore been Government policy to pursue the effective protection of existing Irish industry. Considering the importance of agriculture within the EEC context, the implication here undoubtedly, even for Lemass, was that the main concern of Irish Government policy was agriculture, with industry being a distant, if increasingly important, second.

The concern expressed about industry should not obscure the main objective for Irish policy-makers and for the Government, which was to obtain favourable entry terms to the Community and to secure, if possible, continuing access to the British market for agricultural exports. The decision by Britain to apply for membership was the most important stimulus to Ireland's application. In addition, the decision to apply for full membership was inevitable, as the loss of Britain's markets for Irish exports was threatened if the British entered and Ireland did not.

## OUR PHILOSOPHY AND NATIONAL BACKGROUND

Shortly before he went to Brussels, Lemass addressed the Fianna Fáil *ard-fheis*. He had a number of objectives. The first was to assure the party membership of the significance and value of what the Government was trying to achieve. This was important because one of the main effects of entry would be the dismantling of the entire economic nationalist superstructure that had been established over the previous thirty years, since Fianna Fáil first took office in 1932. It was necessary to frame entry in a 'nationalist' or patriotic fashion. Some Fianna Fáil supporters were worried about the application on the grounds of sovereignty. As Aodogan O'Rahilly pointed out:

> There were some of us, close to Lemass, who had our doubts about the approach he was taking. I was totally opposed. I did not believe that any EEC was going to help Ireland economically or otherwise and I told him that straight up.[132]

Lemass, however, was determined to push on and bring 'nationalist' Fianna Fáil with him. He wished to assure foreign observers of the conference that the Government was fully committed to entry. Finally, he used the opportunity to develop a momentum of support for entry. The commitment to the Community was overt, and the statement in favour of entry was as clearly composed as was possible under the circumstances:

> Membership of the Common Market is open to those nations which accept the political aims which inspired it. A movement to political confederation in some form, is indeed a natural and logical development of economic integration. Henceforth our national aims must conform to the emergence, in a political as well as in an economic sense, of a union of Western European states, not as a vague prospect of the distant future but as a living reality of our own times.[133]

As part of this reality, Lemass maintained that the multilateral arrangements within the EEC would be more to the advantage of Ireland than existing bilateral arrangements. In addition, he reflected on the possibility that economic integration would remove the basis for the partition of the country. This argument was based on the theory that co-operation at transnational level would bring about the objective previously sought by economic nationalism; namely that an independent united Ireland co-existing in the EEC with the British would be able to provide a healthy future for all the citizens on the island, thus nullifying any economic arguments relating to partition. This can be seen as an attempt to appeal to nationalist sentiment, and a way of bringing the national aim of unification into line with European integration. Lemass also used the opportunity effectively to dismantle the ideological commitment to economic nationalism. The end of protectionism could also be presented in nationalist terms; economic efficiency could thus be presented in terms of patriotic endeavour: 'in the economic sphere, the task before the country can be defined simply as that of becoming fully competitive in every respect. It is a condition essential to our national survival.'[134] O'Rahilly was not convinced:

> The way I saw it the Europeans wanted us in to get control of our fishing and other stuff. How wrong can you be? While I was very strongly in favour of bringing in foreign capital I just could not picture us getting anything out of it. As for partition I was of the opinion that we would be losing more control of our own actions if we joined. If anything I saw entry putting the national question back.[135]

While Lemass had not been able to convert every one of his colleagues to the idea of entry, he went to Brussels with the *ard-fheis* and the majority of his party united behind him. A motion passed recording the 'approval of the manner in which the Government is handling the negotiations for Ireland's entry into the EEC and on its approach to international affairs in general' summed up the mood of the Fianna Fáil party.[136] Not all commentators were convinced. The *Sunday Independent* reported the following month that there was a 'Cabinet split on Common Market issues'.[137] Lemass, however, was quick to deny any such division, maintaining: 'The person who invented that should be able to make a fortune writing fairy tales. I advise him to take it up. Hans Christian Andersen would only be trotting after him.'[138]

Lemass' visit to Brussels and his presentation to the EEC went off well as far as the Irish delegation was concerned. Some commentators did not agree. An article by Jock Bruce-Gardyne in *The Statist*, entitled 'The unwanted suitor', claimed that the Irish application had received a 'frigid reception', and was being treated like a 'cold douche for a keen convert'.[139] The Government was appalled by the slant Bruce-Gardyne – a notorious cynic regarding the EEC – had taken, and considered the article important enough to lodge a protest with the publication. There had been a number of inter-journal conflicts between Bruce-Gardyne and Desmond Fisher, who had written enthusiastically about Ireland's place in Europe. In essence, it seemed that Bruce-Gardyne was echoing French Government sources, who continued to be dubious about the Irish application.[140] For them, as for pretty much everyone else, the Irish application was inextricably tied up with the British one. The US was as convinced about this as the Europeans. John R. Burke, State Department officer in charge of Irish affairs at the bureau of British Commonwealth and Northern European Affairs, wrote to Edward Prince, first secretary at the embassy in Dublin, to this effect in April 1962:

For the moment, Departmental attention is riveted, as you can appreciate, on the UK negotiations with the six at Brussels. Like a Cape Hatteras barometer the prognosis for the negotiation seems to shift daily from fair to stormy and though everyone continues to maintain that ultimate membership is the only possible result, there are those who consciously cross their fingers and touch wood as they say it ... The Department has not yet felt called upon to take a firm position on the Irish application.

This is due to two factors: (1) the aforementioned preoccupation with the progress of the UK bid and (2) the many statements indicating that the Irish application was tied with that of the UK, and that it would probably be withdrawn should the UK negotiation fail.[141]

The following month, a meeting was held in Brussels between the permanent representatives of the member states and a delegation from the Irish Government. Questions concerning agriculture, horticulture, industry and tariffs were raised and discussed. While Ireland gave a commitment to abolish all quantitative and tariff restrictions, it also made the case that some sectors would warrant special attention but that these would not conflict with European regulations. In addition, a full commitment to dismantling all tariffs on industrial goods within the time span agreed by negotiation was given. In this area, the only exception requested was for those industries that encountered difficulties during the transition, particularly in manufacturing, but had the capability to compete and whose difficulties were of a temporary nature. Ireland also sought assurances on dumping in the light of the small Irish market and the damage that such action could do if the response was not quick enough.[142]

While this meeting was largely of a technical nature, the Irish delegation believed that it had made its economic case succinctly and effectively. By early July, it appeared that the permanent representatives would decide favourably for Ireland, allowing the Irish application to be discussed at the meeting scheduled for 23 July. This may go some way to explaining Lemass' most outspoken remarks on NATO, when in the same month he told the *New York Times*:

We recognise that a military commitment will be an inevitable consequence of our joining the Common Market and ultimately we would be prepared to yield even the technical label of neutrality. We are prepared to go into this integrated Europe without any reservations as to how far this will take us in the field of foreign policy and defence.[143]

Here was evidence that with the Government convinced it was making a reasonable economic case, Lemass needed to reassure the Community that membership of NATO was not a problem for Ireland. Yet by September, Whitaker was forced to admit that the 'status of our application is as yet undetermined'.[144] In the Dáil two months later, Lemass – under hostile questioning from James Dillon of Fine Gael and Brendan Corish of Labour regarding the status of the application – was putting on a brave face, insisting that 'our application presents no great difficulty'.[145] Lemass reaffirmed to the second Fianna Fáil *ard-fheis* of 1962 – in November – the importance of the application for both party and country. He was again careful to frame the application in terms of the history of Fianna Fáil and the country, maintaining that there was no contradiction between previous Fianna Fáil economic policy and entry into the Community:

> We were always keenly conscious of the fact that winning of political independence would not mean that we had acquired economic independence in the same degree. We saw in the EEC a door opening to new economic opportunities not previously available to us and the prospect of a much more secure foundation for our future prosperity. For a party with our philosophy and national background no other course was possible. The alternative course would condemn us in perpetuity to a position of economic inferiority, leave us a beggar amongst the nations, seeking to maintain a dying economy on the crumbs of charity from our wealthy neighbours ... Membership of the EEC is, however, something very much more than a condition necessary to maintain our present level of economic activity: it is an opportunity for expansion greater than we have heretofore enjoyed.[146]

For Lemass, entry into the EEC was but a natural progression of Fianna Fáil policy in both economic and national policies. For him – and, in essence, the party – the political consequences of the application were welcome because 'we saw in this prospect a new source of national strength, an extension of our freedom, and a better opportunity of fulfilling our cultural, economic and social aims'. To Lemass, the goals remained the same: he still wanted to see 'full employment', which also meant 'the elimination of all economic causes of emigration ... a realistic objective in the early future'.[147] The new generation of Fianna Fáil politicians were impressed with this policy. Patrick Hillery – who, as his official biographer, John Walsh, points out, had never displayed much sympathy for the traditional Sinn Féin virtues of protectionism and self-sufficiency – enthusiastically embraced the new orthodoxy of export-led investment, tariff reduction and preparation for EEC membership.[148] Another rising star of the party, George Colley, even went so far as to table a motion calling for the party to 'consider and, if possible, to decide on the question of our representatives joining one of the European Groups or parties represented in the Council of Europe and the European Parliament'. Lemass, however, intervened to say that it would probably be better not to take an early decision on this matter 'pending a decision on our application for membership of the EEC'.[149] While the motion was then unanimously withdrawn, it is still indicative of the support that Lemass had managed to garner within the party.

Ireland's application eventually failed not on any economic or political matter but because of the intransigence of Charles de Gaulle towards the British.[150] Once de Gaulle vetoed the British application on 14 January 1963, the Irish Government suspended its application. A Finance memorandum outlined the dangers the suspension might bring:

There is a danger that, in the conditions of uncertainty that may prevail in the months ahead, the momentum that has been achieved in the preparations for entry to the EEC will be lost. Preoccupation with external events or with the short term discomforts of adjustment must not cause us to lose sight of our principal objective, namely, the reshaping of the economy to enable us to hold our place in a world that is moving towards freer trade and to maintain the rate of economic growth achieved in recent years.[151]

At a political level, Lemass responded primarily by devoting a parliamentary party meeting of Fianna Fáil in late January 1963 to the suspension of the application, where he dealt 'at some length' with the implications for the Government and the country following the effective withdrawal.[152] Some days later, he made an important speech to the Dáil in which he stressed his determination not to let any complacency slip back into the Irish industrial psyche:

> The deadlock is, we hope, purely temporary ... our desire is that a way will be found before long to enable all European countries which share the aims expressed in the Treaty of Rome to participate fully in a wider Community. The forces making for European unity which received such an impetus after the last World War, will, I feel sure, be strengthened as time goes on and must in the end prevail. The suspensions of the British negotiations should be viewed as a temporary setback and not as a final breach.[153]

He maintained that, while for the present it was not practicable or desirable for the Government to pursue its application, 'this decision will not of itself make our position any worse than it has been for the last two years'.[154] He was of the opinion that the country had gained permanently from the measures taken to gear up the economy for greater competition, and maintained that these measures would have to be reinforced and accelerated. Ireland, he declared, had become a stronger economy due to the changes brought about since the late 1950s, and would have to strive to make the most rapid advances in the forthcoming years as this would increase its capacity to benefit from eventual participation in a wider EEC. In an important passage, he argued:

> The promotion of industrial efficiency by reduction of protection is not being initiated because of free trade principles, but because in the circumstances now prevailing in the world it is recognised to be necessary for economic and social progress. To remain efficient in only parts of the economy, with limited capacity to expand exports, is to condemn ourselves to inert dependence on the British market in which we may expect a progressive hardening of competitive conditions for our products.[155]

This was an important point, in that Fianna Fáil could claim that there was no contradiction in its moving from protectionism to free trade as the latter could be framed in terms of the patriotic endeavour of doing what was best for the country. Lemass was setting the broad context within which this new economic policy, incorporated in the shift to Europe, was being situated. The social and political advancement of the nation, according to Lemass, could best be achieved by new methods that in themselves would secure the independence of the country, which, to some degree, had been threatened by the country's economic malaise.[156] This *volte-face* was too much for some of the opposition. Dillon attacked Lemass in blistering fashion:

> One must plead for some measure of indulgence if one experiences consternation in listening to the leader of the Fianna Fáil Party speaking for an hour and a quarter on the subject of free trade and the vital importance of the British market to the Irish economy. If he had

advanced either thesis to any member of his party during the past 20 years, they would have gone as near to assassinating him as the law would allow, and I can assure him from my own position looking at the faces of his own backbenchers that it is a most stimulating experience. Whether it is the reaction to learning the truth or the discovery that they have been made fools of for so long I cannot quite delineate, but the general air of bewilderment that characterises them from the youngest to the most venerable is a stimulating experience for those of us on this side of the house ... I am glad that the Taoiseach at least, and the Fianna Fáil Party, I assume, have woken up to the fact of the vital importance to this country of the British market but they really ought to go for 40 days into the desert, fast and pray to purge themselves of their past history.[157]

While this can be seen as part of the normal cut and thrust of politics, there was in Dillon's castigation of Fianna Fáil a serious charge that it had to answer. Lemass' argument in favour of membership of the EEC was theoretically an anti-nationalist policy rooted firmly in free trade. But he had to frame it in nationalist terms of serving the country.

EEC entry was part of a developmental strategy. Since 1958 and the production of *Economic Development*, the Government and a civil service – whose prime economic department had changed dramatically – were searching for new avenues along which to lead the country into the promised land of economic prosperity. While the immediate application was in a sense an emergency response to external changes over which the Government had no control, this merely speeded up an evolutionary process the Government had embarked on. The decision to look for full membership – something that would have been considered lunacy only ten years earlier – was an act of faith in the Irish economy and its constituent parts, the sectional interest groups.[158] In essence, there was no reluctance about the application. The decision to apply focused policy-makers' attention on the need to restructure industry to meet the competitive challenge of Europe. Policy-makers had realised that Ireland could not develop as an autonomous economic unit if it wished to benefit from growth and trade expansion. The application finally confirmed the views of those within and outside the Government who had argued that in an uncertain economic world, it was better to be prepared for uncertainty by being aligned rather than by standing alone.

The collapse of the EEC negotiations in 1963 provided the Government with the motivation to move quickly to reduce tariffs and to prepare for a second application. Lemass' goal was to transform the state into a modern entity – one able to confidently take its place amongst a community of Western European nations. He told a US audience that 'although Ireland was an ancient nation, she is a young state. The limited size of the Irish market means of necessity that our growth target must be realised through export trade.'[159] As Whitaker told an OECD economic-policy-committee meeting: 'We inhabited the cellar … Although the cellar proves to have been quite a respectable club, we were not happy there and wanted to break out into a more invigorating atmosphere.'[160] It might have been an invigorating atmosphere but it was also a rarefied one. In the context of moving out of the safety net of protectionism and a reliance on the British market, the decision to apply for membership of the EEC was the most important psychological decision taken by any Government since the foundation of the state.

# CONCLUSION

Throughout late 2008 and early 2009 the Taoiseach, Brian Cowen, spoke of his belief that the best way out of the worst economic recession since the 1950s was through consensus and the process of social partnership. The failure of the talks between the Government and the social partners to initiate a series of substantial savings to the exchequer led the Government in February 2009 to forsake the partnership process in major macroeconomic policy for the first time since 1987. Even then, Cowen was insisting that social partnership was alive and well.

Fianna Fáil has been the party most associated with social partnership. During the general election of 2007, the party was perhaps somewhat surprisingly returned to office for the third election in a row precisely because enough voters believed that Fianna Fáil was the best party to guide the country during what looked an inevitable downturn in the economy.[1] Yet political success brings with it the potential for hubris, as longevity in power can lead to complacency and conservatism. This is exactly what happened to Fianna Fáil in 1948. Political success from 1932 had made the party much more conservative, and by the end of the Second World War, it had long since lost the radicalism that it promised when first elected.[2]

The ending of the war can be seen as the moment when Ireland significantly begins to fall behind the Western European norm, as it becomes poor in comparative terms. The question the Irish body politic faced was how the independent Irish state could improve the economic and social welfare of its population. Most Irish nationalists had assumed that political independence would significantly improve Ireland's economic position to the point where the state could provide enough employment opportunities for an increased population. By the time of the 1948 election, this had proven not to be the case. When Fianna Fáil sought another term in office, it did so having governed a state where the Irish economy was heavily subsidised and intensively protected. In addition, the strength of the economy was heavily dependent on privileged access to the British market and the success of British policy-making. This was a bitter pill for Fianna Fáil to swallow after sixteen years of Government, but the party offered little in the way of alternatives, and paid the price by losing power for the first time.

The crisis that Ireland faced in the 1950s led to the most fluid political situation since the establishment of the state. Political instability due mainly to voter disenchantment with the economy-plagued successive Governments throughout the period, as voters inevitably blamed the party in Government for the stagnating economy. Mass emigration – which returned after the end of the Second World War – increased steadily throughout the 1950s. The crisis of emigration, unemployment and the widening gap between the standard of living between Ireland and Britain, and – most sensitively – with Northern Ireland, could not be ignored by Ireland's political elite. For the vanishing Irish of the 1950s, *Economic Development*, the *Programme for Economic Expansion*, Seán Lemass and T.K. Whitaker did not feature prominently in their first-hand accounts of leaving Ireland and the process of adjustment to life in Britain.[3] Yet for Lemass, who had a strong vision of a practical as distinct from idealised nationalism, such emigration hurt deeply. He more than any other politician of the period recognised that conditions in Ireland were driving young men and women out of the country, and his various policy suggestions during the 1940s and 1950s attempted to explicitly address this. While Lemass remained a nationalist, in contrast to de Valera his nationalism was promoted as an active commitment to change and development. De Valera seems to have had little interest in the economy or in the conditions under which Irish people had to live. His call to Irish emigrants in Britain to return home – as their living conditions in British cities were often poor – demonstrated a worrying lack of understanding about the underlying state of Ireland. What can be seen in the 1950s is Lemass developing a set of ideas that challenged the certainties of de Valera and the Fianna Fáil of Seán MacEntee, amongst others. As Patrick Hillery noted:

> It was exciting with Lemass. He was through all the politics of Fianna Fáil, his brother was murdered, but he was stepping away from the bitterness, you know; he never went in for shouting or downing the other people [the opposition]. He had a kind of politics that I could go along with.[4]

More fundamentally, Lemass appreciated that the world outside had changed, that it did not owe Ireland a living, and that Ireland had to change to meet the challenge of this new environment.[5] That was the nationalism that led him – the apostle of protectionism in the 1930s – to tear down that particular house and build another on the foundations of free trade and – more slowly – entry into the EEC. Yet he was not clear how free trade and the benefits it would bring could be achieved without widespread disruption of the Irish economy, and nor was he sure whether the Irish economy could survive in a European trading bloc.

It is against this background that one should consider Lemass' court-ship of the various economic interest groups in the period. It was his view that the development of the country in economic terms necessarily revolved around a corporatist-style arrangement, with the Government leading these groups in a new economic partnership. For that to happen, Lemass realised that Government in its political form would have to be the hegemonic player in the policy-making system. Of even more importance was that he be at the head of such a system, and for that to happen he would have to devise a long-term economic strategy that would return Fianna Fáil to Government. While he bemoaned the fact that civil servants did not do enough independent thinking, he was firmly of the belief that it was political Government that should lead. This was the context within which the evolution of the formulation of public policy towards a more conscious and overt corporatist set of arrangements occurred. Within these parameters, the political interests – particularly in the form of Lemass – would lead, but it was intrinsic on individual interest groups – farmers, employers and trade unions – to play a full and active role in a modernising coalition of sorts. But of course, Lemass had to be in power to enact any significant policy change.

It is something of a caricature to portray Lemass as the saviour of modern Ireland. The second Inter-Party Government – while it undoubtedly made significant mistakes, perhaps principally in 1956 by prolonging the fiscal crisis – was not without its own ideas regarding Ireland's future.[6] The package of grants, reliefs and other incentives to industry and agriculture to encourage expansion of production – which were to become the hallmark of the new system of foreign-led indus-trialisation under free trade – was first mooted by this Government in September 1956. This Government also initiated the Irish application for membership of the International Monetary Fund and the World Bank. Implementing policy is, however, about being in Government, and politics is about winning elections. In that context, the second

Inter-Party Government had too much of the aura of bad news about it, and its defeat in the 1957 general election left Fianna Fáil and Lemass to push the modernisation drive.

In the aftermath of the 1957 general election, Lemass was determined that his modernising coalition be brought together to bring Ireland into the promised land of economic development, where it could share in the prosperity apparent in Western Europe. Once Lemass became Taoiseach in 1959, he used the power of that office to promote an active expansion of the economy. Furthermore, he and the Fianna Fáil party accepted that Ireland had to be reintegrated into the global economy if it were to benefit from the worldwide expansion then under way. The key to this was entry into a trading bloc. The British decision to apply for membership of the EEC in 1961 was hugely important in this regard: it both forced Ireland to apply but also made it very dependent on Britain, because without British goodwill, Ireland could not hope to gain any type of entry. More fundamentally, it oriented policy in a much more external way than had previously been the case, as Irish entry into the EEC became the overriding aim of Government economic policy.

The decision to apply for entry into the EEC copper-fastened the commitment to free trade and signalled the death knell for the narrowly protectionist policies dictated by de Valera's commitment to economic nationalism and isolationism. Writing fifty years after Lemass came to power as Taoiseach, it is worth restating that this commitment to multilateralism has been maintained ever since, and open markets have been a keystone of Irish economic policy, leading to a situation where Ireland was ranked in the early twenty-first century as one of the most open economies in the world. This was a startling departure from previous Fianna Fáil policies. Indeed, the very man who introduced the original economic policies of protectionism removed them from the statute book.

The road to the EEC application led to a different economic policy – one that integrated Ireland into the wider world economically and, increasingly, politically. Lemass clearly would have been willing to give up Irish neutrality if that had been necessary to join the European Community, though that did not prove to be the case. The EEC application was a classic case of Fianna Fáil *étatisme*. Critics of Fianna Fáil have long since complained of the party's tendency to treat itself as one with the state it should theoretically serve.[7] In adopting free trade and leading Ireland's entry into the EEC, Fianna Fáil actually did the state some service by performing a somersault with regard to its dearly held mantras of self-sufficiency and protectionism. By doing what was good for Ireland in abandoning both, Fianna Fáil was also doing something good for itself. If nothing else, the immediate post-war period showed Fianna Fáil that the Irish people would not give it *carte blanche* at every election if it could not satisfy their economic needs. When considering Ireland's search for the promised land of economic prosperity in the post-war period, Tom Garvin's comments in 1982 are worth reflecting on:

> The penetration of Fianna Fáil into the bureaucracy appears to be very great, and is due mainly to the fact that the party has had a near monopoly on public office for almost fifty years and has, by its own success, generated social categories created in its own image.[8]

No matter how deep this penetration, the scale of the economic crisis in the 1950s, and its concomitant electoral fluidity, persuaded the party that it was not guaranteed electoral success in perpetuity. The attempt by Fianna Fáil to change the electoral system to a first-past-the-post system would seem to be further evidence that Ireland's largest political party felt its secure hold on Government was under threat, and it is clear that this was not simply due to the vagaries of proportional representation via the single transferable vote.

The search for the promised land in post-war Ireland took place in an atmosphere of unprecedented political uncertainty. Political matters and political success did motivate Lemass, but they were not his only concerns in an Ireland that had lost 300,000 people to other lands through emigration since Fianna Fáil first took power in 1932. Political concerns did not motivate Whitaker or, for that matter, those on the other side of the free trade fence, such as J.C.B. MacCarthy. Their concerns were of a more nationalist bent: nationalist in terms of loyalty to the state and attempting to get the state out of the economic mire it was stuck in. Somewhat paradoxically, the population as a whole did not seem to view the EEC as a panacea to Ireland's ills, as the levels of ignorance surrounding that organisation in the early 1960s were truly staggering. When, in 1961, the *Irish Press* asked 943 people if they had *heard* of the Common Market, 36 per cent of those polled said they had a 'vague idea' of it, while the same percentage said they had 'never heard of it'.[9] Given those figures, it is appropriate to ask whether anyone outside the political elite was actually listening to the leaders of the Irish state in relation to EEC membership. Yet what is important to note here is that it is the job of politicians to lead. In the case of both the movement to free trade and entry into the EEC, that is what Seán Lemass more than any other politician of this era did.

The lesson for current policy-makers dealing with certainly the gravest economic crisis since the 1950s is that leadership and political decision-making matters. Even when the general populace seems to be unmoved by, or even unaware of, major policy initiatives, it is the responsibility of political leaders to argue for them and drive them through. Politics might be about power, but it also leads to apathy amongst a significant section of all electorates. That apathy can only be overcome through engaged citizenship, but such engaged citizenship must be spurred on by political leadership. The rejection of the Lisbon Treaty in the June 2008 referendum was, in the main, due to an anaemic campaign by the proponents of the 'yes' vote. The referendum showed that the public has to be convinced of the merits of European integration much more so than in the past, and it was therefore the task of the Fianna Fáil/Green Party/Progressive Democrats coalition Government to show much more substantive leadership in that campaign than it actually did. Politicians and policy-makers in the post-war period did not get everything right – and, in fact, got much wrong – but what they were able to do was show leadership and thus begin a process by which Ireland would be able to take its place in the world as a mature interdependent state able to provide a future for its citizens.

# Notes & References

Abbreviations

AG – Attorney General
CAB – Cabinet
DCU – Dublin City University
DO – Dominions Office
DT – Department of the Taoiseach
EC – European Community
EFTA – European Free Trade Area
GATT – General Agreement on Tariffs and Trade
ICTU – Irish Congress of Trade Unions
ILSHA – Irish Labour History Society Archive
ITUC – Irish Trade Union Congress
NAI – National Archives of Ireland
NAI DFA – National Archives of Ireland Department of Foreign Affairs
NAI DT – National Archives of Ireland Department of the Taoiseach
NARA RG – National Archives and Records Administration Record Group
NLI – National Library of Ireland
PUTUO – Provisional United Trade Union Organisation
TID – Trade and Industry Division
UCDA – University College Dublin Archives

## Introduction: The Promised Land?

1    http://www.budget.gov.ie/2009/financialstatement.html
2    See 'A.T. Kearney/Foreign Policy Globalisation Index', measuring globalisation: the global top twenty for the years 2002–05 at www.atkearney.com
3    http://www.heritage.org/index/Country/Ireland
4    http://www.taoiseach.gov.ie/attached_files/Pdf%20files/Towards2016 PartnershipAgreement.pdf
5    http://www.taoiseach.gov.ie/index.asp?locID=582&docID=4148
6    Address by the Minister for Finance to IPA conference, '*Economic Development* 50 Years On', 19 Sept. 2008, http://www.finance.gov.ie/viewdoc. asp?DocID=5465&CatID=54&StartDate=1+January+2009&m=p
7    http://www.irishtimes.com/newspaper/breaking/2008/0620/breaking60. html
8    Tom Garvin, *Preventing the Future: Why Was Ireland so Poor for so Long?* (Dublin, 2004), p. 4.

## Chapter 1: The War was Over, but the Emergency was Not

1   Patrick Lynch, 'The Irish economy since the war, 1946–51' in Kevin B. Nowlan and T. Desmond Williams (eds), *Ireland in the War Years and After* (Dublin, 1969), p. 185.
2   Enda Delaney, *Demography, State and Society: Irish Migration to Britain, 1921–1971* (Liverpool, 2000), p. 113.
3   *Ibid.*
4   *Ibid.*, p. 125; this includes Northern Ireland.
5   *Ibid.*, p. 130.
6   *Ibid.*, p. 122; see also Lynch, 'Irish economy', p. 185.
7   Bryan Fanning, *The Quest for Modern Ireland: The Battle for Ideas, 1912–1986* (Dublin, 2008), pp. 194–5.
8   John Horgan, *Seán Lemass: The Enigmatic Patriot* (Dublin, 1997), p. 110.
9   See *Journal of Social and Statistical Inquiry Society*, 1942–47, volume xvii, sessions 96–100, pp. 438–59.
10  *Ibid.*, pp. 439–40.
11  *Ibid.*, p. 442.
12  *Ibid.*, p. 459.
13  Arnold Marsh, *Full Employment in Ireland* (Dublin, 1945), p. vii.
14  Paul Bew and Henry Patterson, *Seán Lemass and the Making of Modern Ireland 1945–66* (Dublin, 1982), pp. 19–20; John Horgan, *Lemass*, p. 129.
15  Clair Wills, *That Neutral Island: A Cultural History of Ireland During the Second World War* (London, 2007), p. 424.
16  Eunan O'Halpin, *Defending Ireland: The Irish State and its Enemies Since 1922* (Oxford, 1999), pp. 254–5.
17  Lynch, 'Irish economy', p. 189.
18  *Ibid.*, p. 188.
19  Department of External Affairs, memorandum on emigration, cited in Enda Delaney, 'Emigration, political cultures and the evolution of post-war Irish society' in Brian Girvin and Gary Murphy (eds), *The Lemass Era: Politics and Society in the Ireland of Seán Lemass* (Dublin, 2005), pp. 53–4.
20  See David McCullagh, *A Makeshift Majority: The First Inter-party Government, 1948–51* (Dublin, 1998), p. 142.
21  J.J. Lee, *Ireland 1912–1985: Politics and Society* (Cambridge, 1989), p. 289.
22  Lynch, 'Irish economy', p. 186.
23  UCDA, Costello papers, P190/713 (17), policy suggestions from the AG [nd, *c.* Sept. 1956].
24  Dáil Debates, vol. 9, col. 562, 30 Oct. 1924.
25  Kieran A. Kennedy and Brendan R. Dowling, *Economic Growth in Ireland: The Experience Since 1947* (Dublin, 1975), p. 201.
26  Author's interview with Domhnall McCullough.
27  David Jacobson, 'Theorising Irish industrialisation: The case of the motor industry', *Science and Society*, vol. 53, no. 2 (summer 1989), p. 167.
28  NLI, Brennan papers, MS 26, 359, J.J. McElligott to Minister for Finance, 11 Feb. 1948.
29  NLI, Brennan papers, MS 26, 383, Dillon to Glenavy, n.d., but by context late

Dec. 1949.

30  *Ibid.*

31  *Ibid.*, Glenavy to Dillon, 30 Dec. 1949.

32  Author's interview with Patrick Lynch. Lynch credited his appointment to his friendship with Alexis Fitzgerald, son-in-law of Costello, but it is also clear that Costello had a recommendation from McElligott regarding Lynch.

33  MacBride is quoted in the *Sunday Independent*, 25 Sept. 1949.

34  Maurice Moynihan, *Currency and Central Banking in Ireland 1922–60* (Dublin, 1975), p. 354. See also Ronan Fanning, *The Irish Department of Finance 1922–58* (Dublin, 1978), pp. 442–55 for a vivid description and analysis of the devaluation crisis.

35  *Sunday Independent*, 6 Mar. 1950.

36  NLI, Brennan papers, MS 26 428, memorandum for the Government, financial policy, 16 Oct. 1951.

37  *Ibid.*

38  Author's interview with Seán Cromien.

39  Kennedy and Dowling, *Economic Growth in Ireland*, p. 202.

40  See Denis O'Hearn, 'The road from import-substituting to export-led industrialisation in Ireland', *Politics and Society*, vol. 18, no. 1 (1990), pp. 14–15; also Lars Mjoset, *The Irish Economy in a Comparative Institutional Perspective* (Dublin, 1992), p. 268.

41  Even in the dark days of 1957, Gerard Sweetman, Minister for Finance in the second Inter-Party Government, echoed the predominant economic view when telling the Fine Gael *ard fheis*: 'it is quite useless to talk of a long-term economic plan in a free private-enterprise economy': NAI, DT, S.16066A, speech by Sweetman at Fine Gael *ard fheis*, 6 Feb. 1957.

42  Richard Dunphy, *The Making of Fianna Fáil Power in Ireland 1923–1948* (Oxford, 1995), pp. 249–50.

43  NAI, DT, S.13814A, Industry and Commerce memorandum on the control of prices and promotion of industrial efficiency, 26 Feb. 1946.

44  *Ibid.* See also O'Hearn, 'Road from import-substituting', p. 14.

45  Author's interview with Tadhg Ó Cearbhaill.

46  NAI, DT, S.13814B, Department of Finance memorandum: comments on proposed legislation to establish an Industrial Efficiency Bureau, 4 Mar. 1946.

47  Quoted in O'Hearn, 'Road from import-substituting', p. 14.

48  Author's interview with Colm Barnes.

49  Emmet O'Connor, *A Labour History of Ireland, 1824–1960* (Dublin, 1992), p. 132.

50  See Niamh Puirséil, *The Irish Labour Party, 1922–73* (Dublin, 2007), pp. 102–3.

51  Stefan Berger and Hugh Compston, *Policy Concertation and Social Partnership in Western Europe* (Oxford, 2002) p. 158.

52  O'Connor, *Labour History*, p. 160.

53  *Ibid.*, p. 161.

54  Puirséil, *Irish Labour Party*, p. 119.

55  *Ibid.*, pp. 130–1; Niamh Puirséil, 'Political and party competition in post-war Ireland' in Girvin and Murphy, *Lemass Era*, p. 14.

56  O'Brien had retired from the ITGWU, although he retained his well-remunerated position as a director of the Central Bank. Larkin died in January 1947.
57  O'Connor, *Labour History*, p. 155.
58  Plunkett is quoted in John L. Pratschke, 'Business and labour in Irish society, 1945–70' in J.J. Lee (ed.), *Ireland 1945–70* (Dublin, 1979), p. 39.
59  Author's interview with Donal Nevin.
60  Brian Girvin, 'Trade Unions and Economic Development' in Donal Nevin (ed.), *Trade Union Century* (Cork & Dublin, 1994), p. 123.
61  An account of Lemass' success in originally defeating MacEntee in responding to Labour, the unions and the working class can be found in UCDA, MacEntee papers, P67/362–66.
62  Brian Farrell, *Seán Lemass* (Dublin, 1983), p. 82.
63  Bew and Patterson, *Seán Lemass*, p. 12.
64  Ó Cearbhaill interview.
65  NAI, DT, S.11752A, interim report of the Industrial Development Authority regarding industrial exports, 27 Sept. 1949.
66  UCDA, McGilligan papers, P35B/55, note for Minister for Finance, 18 Oct. 1949.
67  *Ibid.*, P35B/69, Finance memorandum on proposed Industrial Development Board, 1949.
68  *Ibid.*, P35B/47, memorandum on proposed Industrial Development Board, n.d., *c.* 1949.
69  Barnes interview. McGilligan's comment can be found in UCDA, McGilligan papers, P35B/47.
70  O'Hearn, 'Road from import substituting', p. 16.
71  *Irish Independent*, 21 Feb. 1949.
72  See Brian Girvin, *Between Two Worlds: Politics and Economy in Independent Ireland* (Dublin, 1989), pp. 173–4.
73  Lynch interview. Lynch was a member of the Dollar Export Advisory Committee and the Foreign Trade Committee at this time.
74  Interviews with Dr Aodogan O'Rahilly, Joseph McCullough, Domhnall McCullough and Colm Barnes.
75  Dáil Debates, vol. 119, col. 1585, 9 Mar. 1950.
76  Lemass to Dwyer, quoted in Michael O'Sullivan, *Seán Lemass: A Biography* (Dublin, 1994), p. 118.
77  Joseph McCullough interview.
78  Girvin, *Between Two Worlds*, p. 176. See also Mary E. Daly, *Social and Economic History of Ireland Since 1800* (Dublin, 1981), pp. 164–5.
79  Ó Cearbhaill interview.
80  NAI, DT, S.11987, establishment of Industry: Underdeveloped Areas (Amendment Act), 1957.
81  NLI, Brennan papers, MS 26 248, memorandum for the Government, financial policy, 16 Oct. 1951.
82  For a useful account of the different historiographical interpretations of Irish involvement in the Marshall Plan, see Till Geiger, 'The enthusiastic response of a reluctant supporter: Ireland and the Committee for European Economic Co-operation in the summer of 1947' in Michael Kennedy and Joseph Morrison

Skelly (eds), *Irish Foreign Policy 1919–1966: From Independence to Internationalism* (Dublin, 2000), pp. 222–3, 244–6.

83  Whitaker is quoted in Ronan Fanning, *Department of Finance*, p. 406.

84  In a number of interviews with the author, Whitaker insisted that Marshall Aid was in no way a development programme of any kind, but simply a mechanism by which the US gave funds to the Irish Government.

85  Author's interview with Charles Murray.

86  Murray and Boland are quoted in Bernadette Whelan, 'Ireland and the Marshall Plan', *Irish Economic and Social History*, no. xix (1992), p. 54.

87  For a comprehensive account of the background to the original conference, see Bernadette Whelan, 'Integration or isolation? Ireland and the invitation to join the Marshall Plan' in Kennedy and Skelly, *Irish Foreign Policy 1919–1966*, pp. 203–21. See also her thorough study, *Ireland and the Marshall Plan, 1947–57* (Dublin 2000), for a further elucidation of this theme.

88  This comment is in a source entitled 'Reminiscence of an Irish diplomat: Frederick H. Boland, ambassador to London, permanent representative at the United Nations and president of the General Assembly 1960'. It was compiled by Boland's daughter, Mella Boland (Crowley), and is based on a series of extended conversations between the two during the latter stages of his life. Copy in possession of the author.

89  Michael Kennedy and Eunan O'Halpin, *Ireland and the Council of Europe* (Strasbourg, 2000), pp. 23–32.

90  NAI, DFA, 305/57/I, European Economic Co-operation Conference, EECC/9, speech by Lemass, 14 July 1947.

91  *Ibid.*

92  NAI, DFA, 305/57/I, report from Boland to Taoiseach, 30 Aug. 1947.

93  De Valera is quoted in D.J. Maher, *The Tortuous Path: The Course of Ireland's Entry into the EEC 1948–1973* (Dublin, 1986), pp. 23–4.

94  NAI, DFA, 305/57/1A, Boland to Ó Broin, Leydon and McElligott, 8 Mar. 1948.

95  UCDA, P176, Fianna Fáil parliamentary-party minutes, 441/A, 30 June 1948.

96  NAI, DFA, 305/57/III, Ireland's relation to ERP, 29 June 1948.

97  *Ibid.*

98  NAI, DFA, 305/57I, general considerations on Ireland's position in relation to ERP, n.d., but by context mid-1948. This document – although untitled and undated – was probably written by Whitaker, and contains much of the same arguments as the document 'Ireland's Relation to ERP'. The arguments, however, are stated in much bolder and more forceful terms.

99  NAI, DT, S.16877X/62, statement to ministers of the Government of the member states of the European Economic Community, revised 1 Jan. 1962. This document – though written some eighteen years later – also bears Whitaker's imprint. He was the official most involved with the EEC application.

100  NAI, DFA, 305/57I, general considerations on Ireland's position in relation to ERP.

101  *Ibid.*

102  *Ibid.*

103  McCullagh, *Makeshift Majority*, p. 153.

104 NAI, DFA, 305/57/1A, Nunan to Boland, 28 Apr. 1948.
105 NLI, Brennan papers, MS 26 414, Boland to McElligott, n.d., but by context early Mar. 1948.
106 NAI, DFA, 305/57/3, speech of Frank Coffey to Jersey City Lions club, 16 Mar. 1948.
107 *Ibid.*
108 *Ibid.*, External Affairs to Washington, 18 Mar. 1948.
109 *Ibid.*, Washington to External Affairs, 18 Mar. 1948.
110 *Ibid.*, 305/57/3, Washington to secretary, 1 Apr. 1948.
111 *Ibid.*, 305/57/3, speech of Frank Coffey.
112 *Ibid.*, External Affairs to Washington.
113 The full text of this speech is in NAI, DT, S.17246A/62, 5 Feb. 1962, and came in the context of Ireland's application to join the European Economic Community in 1961.
114 Diarmaid Ferriter, *The Transformation of Ireland, 1900–2000* (London, 2005), p. 467.
115 NAI, DFA, 305/57/1A, memorandum of meeting in McElligott's room, 1 June 1948.
116 *Irish Press*, 2 June 1948.
117 NAI, DFA, 305/57/1A, comment by Department of External Affairs.
118 McCullagh, *Makeshift Majority*, p. 153.
119 NAI, DFA, 305/57/1A, Brennan to Boland, 15 June 1948.
120 Alan Milward, *The Reconstruction of Western Europe 1945–51* (London, 1992), pp. 183–4.
121 Dáil Debates, vol. 110, cols. 332–3, 10 Mar. 1948. Both Brennan and MacBride are quoted in NAI, DFA, 305/57/1A.
122 NLI, Brennan papers, MS 26 413, Department of External Affairs, submission to Government concerning interdepartmental and staff organisation for administration for the European Recovery Programme, 28 Apr. 1948.
123 *Ibid.*
124 McElligott is quoted in Fanning, *Department of Finance*, p. 411.
125 NLI, Brennan papers, MS 26 413, McElligott to Boland, 30 Apr. 1948.
126 Lynch interview.
127 Cromien interview.
128 *Ibid.*
129 Boland, *Reminiscences*.
130 UCDA, P35C/2, McElligott to McGilligan, 17 Dec. 1948.
131 UCDA, P35C/47, Department of Finance memorandum, financial policy, 26 Nov. 1949.
132 Whitaker interview.
133 NLI, Brennan papers, MS 26 428, George Duncan, 'The budget of 1950' to Dublin Chamber of Commerce, 24 May 1950.
134 Brian Girvin, 'Did Ireland benefit from the Marshall Plan? Choice, strategy and the national interest in a comparative perspective' in Till Geiger and Michael Kennedy, *Ireland, Europe and the Marshall Plan* (Dublin, 2004), p. 207.
135 Donal Ó Drisceoil, *Peadar O'Donnell* (Cork, 2001), p. 113; *The Bell*, vol. 16, no. 6 (Mar. 1951).

136  Geiger, 'The enthusiastic response of a reluctant supporter', p. 244.
137  Girvin, 'Did Ireland benefit from the Marshall Plan?', p. 207.


## CHAPTER 2: THIS DARK AND DISMAL LAND

1   Dáil Debates, vol. 120, col. 1629, 3 May 1950.
2   Lynch interview.
3   Lynch interview. Keynes' Finlay lecture is reprinted as John Maynard Keynes, 'National self-sufficiency', *Studies*, vol. xxii, no. 86 (June 1933), pp. 177–93.
4   Fanning, *Department of Finance*, pp. 457–8; also Lynch interview.
5   Lynch, 'Irish economy', p. 187.
6   NLI, Brennan papers, MS 26 383, McGilligan to Brennan, n.d., but by context *c.* mid-1950.
7   J.J. Lee, *Ireland 1912–1985,* pp. 312–13.
8   NLI, Brennan papers, MS 26 240, annual report of the Central Bank, 1949–50.
9   NLI, Brennan papers, MS 26 240, annual report of the Central Bank, 1950–51.
10  For a vivid account of both views, see Moynihan, *Currency and Central Banking*, pp. 374–85.
11  *Irish Press*, 24 Oct. 1951.
12  NLI, Brennan papers, MS 26 240, trend of external trade and payments 1951, 23 Oct. 1951. MacEntee maintained that the Government paper showed the correctness of the Central Bank's position.
13  Dáil Debates, vol. 127, col. 300, 7 Nov. 1951.
14  MacBride went public with his protest, writing to the *Irish Independent* on the folly of the Government's position; see his letter of 25 Oct. 1951.
15  Dillon is quoted in the *Sunday Independent*, 28 Oct. 1951.
16  The ITUC's response is given in Moynihan, *Currency and Central Banking in Ireland*, pp. 379–80.
17  NLI, Brennan papers, MS 26 241, McElligott to McGilligan, 17 Feb. 1951.
18  *Ibid.*
19  *Ibid.*, memorandum for the Government, third report of the OEEC, 15 Mar. 1951.
20  Noël Browne, *Against the Tide* (Dublin, 1986), p. 200.
21  Cromien interview.
22  Browne, *Against the Tide*, p. 200.
23  John Horgan, *Noël Browne: Passionate Outsider* (Dublin, 2000), p. 285.
24  T.K. Whitaker, quoted in Fanning, *Department of Finance*, p. 458.
25  *Ibid.*, p. 459.
26  NLI, Brennan papers, MS 26 241, memorandum for the Government, financial policy, 16 Oct. 1951.
27  Moynihan, *Currency and Central Banking in Ireland,* p. 390. Moynihan was a director of the Central Bank from 1953 to 1960, and governor from 1961 to 1969. From 1937 to 1960 he was secretary to the Government, and is historically regarded as a fiscal and social conservative.
28  Dáil Debates, vol. 130, col. 1123, 2 Apr. 1952.

29  Seanad Debates, vol. 40, col. 1648, 19 June 1952.
30  Tom Feeney, *Seán MacEntee: A Political Life* (Dublin, 2009), p. 186; Dáil Debates, vol. 130, col. 1155, 2 Apr. 1952.
31  http://www.budget.gov.ie/2009/en/financialstatement.html
32  Interdepartmental committee on food subsidies to Minister for Industry and Commerce, n.d., but by context early 1952, NLI, Brennan papers, MS 26 428. This committee consisted of chairman J. Williams (Industry and Commerce), T.J. Barrington (Local Government), P.J. Keady (Social Welfare), M.D. McCarthy (Central Statistics Office), J.C. Nagle (Agriculture), T.K. Whitaker (Finance) and secretary to the committee, M. Morton.
33  NLI, Brennan papers, MS 26 428, memorandum for the Government, food subsidies, 1952–53, 31 Dec. 1951.
34  *Ibid.*, MS 26 040(1), untitled file dated 3 Mar. 1952.
35  UCDA, MacEntee papers, P67/227, Whitaker to MacEntee, 2 June 1954.
36  Feeney, *MacEntee*, pp. 179–80.
37  *Ibid.*, p. 180.
38  *The Leader*, 12 Apr. 1952.
39  *The Leader*, 2 Aug. 1952.
40  *The Statist*, 19 Apr. 1952.
41  Seanad Debates, vol. 40, col. 1628, 19 June 1952.
42  Dáil Debates, vol. 130, col. 1315, 3 Apr. 1952.
43  *Ibid.*
44  NAI, Irish Congress of Trade Unions Archive, box 33 (part 1) 7222, statement on budget issued by National Executive, 21 Apr. 1952.
45  *Ibid.*
46  Quoted in Fanning, *Department of Finance*, p. 485.
47  NLI, Brennan papers, MS 26 435, annual report of the Central Bank, 1951–52.
48  *The Standard*, 28 Nov. 1952.
49  *Cork Examiner*, 3 Apr. 1953.
50  *The Leader*, 5 July 1952.
51  NLI, Brennan papers, MS 26 435, annual report of the Central Bank, 1951–52.
52  *Cork Examiner*, 20 Nov. 1952; *Evening Herald*, 20 Nov. 1952.
53  Eamon de Valera, 'An election broadcast' (14 May 1954) in Maurice Moynihan (ed.), *Speeches and Statements of Eamon de Valera* (Dublin, 1980), p. 567.
54  NLI, Brennan papers, MS 26 041, Brennan to Fussell, 22 Mar. 1953.
55  *Ibid.*, Meenan to Brennan, 21 Apr. 1953.
56  *Ibid.*, MacEntee to Brennan, 6 Jan. 1953.
57  *Ibid.*, Glenavy to Brennan, 7 Jan. 1953.
58  UCDA, MacEntee papers, P67/224, McElligott to MacEntee, 11 Mar. 1954.
59  See his speech to the Dáil on the report: Dáil Debates, vol. 127, cols. 298–316, 7 Nov. 1951.
60  Dáil Debates, vol. 130, cols. 241–2, 21 Mar. 1952.
61  NLI, Brennan papers, MS 26 040 (2), MacEntee to Lemass, 27 Sept. 1952. Feeney, *MacEntee*, p. 191 states that the Stacy May reported was submitted to the Government in 1952, but judging by this letter in late September, there is

the possibility that the Government may have seen some sight of it earlier than that.

62  IBEC Technical Services Corporation, *An Appraisal of Ireland's Industrial Potential* (Dublin and New York, 1952).

63  Confidential source.

64  *Economist*, 6 Dec. 1952.

65  NAI, DT, S.15389, Finance to Industry and Commerce, 27 Oct. 1952.

66  De Valera is quoted in Diarmaid Ferriter, *Judging Dev: A Reassessment of the Life and Legacy of Eamon de Valera* (Dublin, 2007), p. 285.

67  UCDA, MacEntee papers, P67/221, Department of Finance observations on establishment of a National Development Fund, 25 Aug. 1953.

68  UCDA, MacEntee papers P67/221(3), observations of Central Bank on National Development Fund, 24 Aug. 1953.

69  *Ibid.*

70  UCDA, P167, Fianna Fáil parliamentary-party minutes, 441/A, 26 Nov. 1952.

71  *Ibid.*, 14 Jan. 1953.

72  *Ibid.*, 22 July 1953.

73  *Ibid.*, 27 Jan. 1954.

74  NAI, DT, S.13101C/1, report of meeting between ITUC, the Labour Party and the Taoiseach and Tanaiste, 4 July 1953.

75  O'Rahilly interview.

76  The TID 2600 file series of the department shows manufacturers of a wide range of products inundating the department with applications for increases in tariffs on imported opposition. The TID 1207 'Control of Manufactures Acts' files has in its index over sixty pages of files on questions from various manufacturers on how any removal of duties would affect their businesses.

77  Girvin, *Between Two Worlds*, p. 180.

78  The Control of Manufactures Acts, 1932–34 attempted to ensure that companies established behind the increasing tariff barriers of the 1930s and the numerous quota and licensing restrictions would remain under Irish control by requiring that more than half the equity of new firms should be Irish-owned. For a detailed analysis of the Acts, see Mary Daly, 'An Irish Ireland for business? The Control of Manufactures Acts, 1932 and 1934', *Irish Historical Studies*, vol. xxiv, no. 94, Nov. 1984.

79  Cromien interview.

80  E.A. McGuire, 'Private enterprise or socialism?', *Irish Monthly*, Oct. 1951, pp. 424–5.

## CHAPTER 3: OPENING OUT

1  Horgan, *Lemass*, p. 354.

2  Girvin, *Between Two Worlds*, p. 180.

3  O'Rahilly interview.

4  T. Desmond Williams, 'The politics of Irish economics', *The Statist*, special issue on Ireland, 24 Oct. 1953, p. 24.

5  Lynch interview.

6  Michael Gallagher, *The Irish Labour Party in Transition, 1957–82* (Dublin, 1982),

pp. 179, 293 n. 79.

7    UCDA, Costello papers, P190/551, copies of memorandum outlining the principal objects of the Government's policy, nd, 1954.

8    Boland, *Reminiscences*.

9    *Round Table*, vol. 40 (1956), p. 375.

10   ILHSA, Norton papers, box 6 (103), Department of Industry and Commerce, memorandum on setting up of state-owned pulp and paper industry, 15 Oct. 1956.

11   Bew and Patterson, *Seán Lemass*, p. 82.

12   ILHSA, Norton papers, box 3 (59), speech by Beddy on investment possibilities in Ireland, 22 Mar. 1955.

13   William Norton, 'Ways to prosperity', *The Irish Times Review and Annual*, 1957, p. 4.

14   O'Rahilly interview.

15   UCDA, McGilligan papers, P35C/117, Department of Finance notes on speech by Taoiseach, 5 Oct. 1956.

16   UCDA, McGilligan papers, P35C/117, O'Donovan to Sweetman, n.d., Jan. 1956.

17   UCDA, Costello papers, P190/713 (17), policy suggestions from the attorney general, nd, but by context Sept. 1956.

18   This paper is reprinted in T.K. Whitaker, 'Ireland's development experience' in T.K. Whitaker, *Interests* (Dublin, 1983), pp. 19-54.

19   *Ibid.*, p.9.

20   UCDA, McGilligan papers P35/117. Costello's speech was to an inter-party meeting in Dublin; it was entitled 'The policy for production', and formed the basis for Fine Gael's manifesto in the 1957 general election.

21   John F. McCarthy, 'Ireland's turnaround' in John F. McCarthy (ed.), *Planning Ireland's Future: The Legacy of T.K. Whitaker* (Sandycove, 1990), p. 68 n. 36.

22   UCDA, MacEntee papers, P67/391, Sweetman address to electors of Kildare, nd, but by context Mar. 1957.

23   *Ibid.*, P67/391, speech by de Valera in Cork, 31 July 1956.

24   *Ibid.*, P67/392(6), speech by MacEntee at Naas, 3 Mar. 1957.

25   *Ibid.*

26   *Ibid.*, P67/392(6), speech by MacEntee at Dún Laoghaire, nd, but by context early Mar. 1957.

27   *Ibid.*

28   Horgan, *Seán Lemass*, p. 158.

29   This memorandum can be found in UCDA, MacEntee papers, P67/53(1), with criticisms by MacEntee marked in pencil in the margins.

30   UCDA, Fianna Fáil party papers, P176, party committee meeting, FF48, 7 Sept. 1955.

31   UCDA, Costello papers, P190/741 (21), memorandum on Deputy Lemass' Full Employment Policy, nd.

32   UCDA, Fianna Fáil party papers, P176, party committee meeting, FF48, 17 Nov. 1954.

33   MacEntee's reaction is quoted in Ronan Fanning, 'The genesis of Economic Development' in McCarthy (ed.), *Planning Ireland's Future*, p. 95. The exact

quote can be found in UCDA, MacEntee papers, P67/815, where it is termed 'note of meeting with Dev'. MacEntee rarely mentioned political events in his diary, and does not offer any explanation for de Valera's decision.

34  See for example Fianna Fáil parliamentary-party minutes, FF441/A, 26 Feb. 15 Apr., 26 May 1948.
35  Whitaker is quoted in McCarthy, 'Ireland's turnaround', p. 52.
36  Ferriter, *Judging Dev*, p. 285.
37  UCDA, Andrews papers, P91/136(1), notes for 1957 lecture entitled 'Is emigration inevitable in Ireland?' The speech is undated.
38  For an analysis on the comparative success of protectionism in the 1950s, see Girvin, *Between Two Worlds*, pp. 199–200.
39  UCDA, Fianna Fáil parliamentary-party minutes, FF441/A, 15 Jan. 1957.
40  Dáil Debates, vol. 16, col. 958, 8 May 1957.
41  Whitaker is quoted in Fanning, *Department of Finance*, p. 507.
42  Whitaker, 'Ireland's development experience', pp. 8–9.
43  UCDA, Andrews papers, P91/136(1), notes for 1957 lecture entitled 'Is emigration inevitable in Ireland?'
44  *Studies*, vol. xliv, no. 173 (spring 1955), p. 1; the editor was Ronald Burke Savage, SJ.
45  Ó Drisceoil, *Peadar O'Donnell*, pp. 110–115.
46  C.S. Andrews, *Man of No Property: An Autobiography* (Dublin, 1982), pp. 298–300.
47  Author's interview with Dr Tom Barrington.
48  Garret FitzGerald, 'Four decades of *Administration*' in *Administration: Cumulative Index, Volumes 1–40 (1953–1992)* (Dublin, 1994), p. ix.
49  Barrington interview.
50  UCDA, Andrews papers, P91/136(1), notes for 1957 lecture entitled 'Is emigration inevitable in Ireland?'
51  Andrews, *Man of No Property*, p. 297.
52  Ruth Barrington, *Health, Medicine and Politics in Ireland 1900–1970* (Dublin, 1987), p. 252.
53  Bishop William Philbin, 'Patriotism', *Christus Rex*, vol. xii, no. 2 (Apr. 1958), p. 86.
54  Whitaker interview.
55  Philbin, 'Patriotism', p. 87.
56  Fr Terence Cosgrove, 'Retrospective of thirty years of Irish freedom', *Christus Rex*, vol. xiii, no. 4 (Oct. 1959), pp. 267–8.
57  Notes and comments, *Christus Rex*, vol. xiii, no. 3 (July 1959), p. 119.
58  William Conway, 'The church and state control', *Christus Rex*, vol. vi, no. 2 (Apr. 1952), p. 119.
59  *Ibid.*, pp. 113, 126.
60  Fanning, 'The genesis of Economic Development', p. 104.
61  Labhras O Nuailláin, 'Potentialities of the Irish economy', *Christus Rex*, vol. xii, no. 2 (Apr. 1958), pp. 127–8.
62  *Ibid.*, p. 136.
63  Gary Murphy, 'Towards a corporate state: Seán Lemass and the realignment of interest groups in the policy process, 1948–1964', *Administration*, vol. 47, no. 1 (1999), pp. 86–102.

64  UCDA, Andrews papers, P91/136(1), notes for 1957 lecture entitled 'Is emigration inevitable in Ireland?'

65  Fianna Fáil parliamentary-party minutes, FF441/A, 13 Nov. 1952.

66  Garret FitzGerald, 'Grey, white and blue: A review of three recent economic publications' in Basil Chubb and Patrick Lynch, *Economic Development and Planning* (Dublin, 1969), p. 118.

67  Garret FitzGerald, *Planning in Ireland* (Dublin, 1968), p. 26.

68  Lee, *Ireland 1912–1985*, p. 344.

69  *Economic Development* (Dublin, 1958), p. 218.

70  David O'Mahony, 'Economic expansion in Ireland', *Studies*, vol. xlviii, no. 190 (summer 1959), p. 134.

71  UCDA, Andrews papers, P91/136(1), notes for 1957 lecture entitled 'Is emigration inevitable in Ireland?'

72  Garret FitzGerald, 'Mr Whitaker and industry', *Studies*, vol. xlviii, no. 190 (summer 1959), p. 149.

73  T.K. Whitaker, 'Financial turning points' in Whitaker, *Interests*, p. 91.

74  Richard Aldous and Niamh Puirséil, *We Declare: Landmark Documents in Ireland's History* (London, 2008), p. 172.

75  Fanning, *The Quest for Modern Ireland*, p. 197.

76  Fianna Fáil parliamentary-party minutes, FF441/B, 11 Dec. 1958.

77  Fianna Fáil parliamentary-party minutes, FF441/B, 28 Jan. 1959.

78  Fianna Fáil parliamentary-party minutes, FF441/B, 4 Mar., 11 Mar., 29 Apr. 1959.

79  NAI, DT, S.15281D, effects on industry of the formation of the Free Trade Area, 2. Feb. 1957.

80  Ó Cearbhaill interview.

81  This correspondence is reproduced in full in T.K. Whitaker, *Protection or Free Trade – The Final Battle* (Dublin, 2006). I first came across the correspondence when researching in the files of the Department of Finance a number of years ago; hence, the notes on this section refer to these files; DF, F.121/15/59, reasons for reducing protection, 14 Dec. 1959.

82  Barnes interview.

83  DF, F.121/15/59, reasons for reducing protection, 14 Dec. 1959.

84  *Ibid.*

85  DF, 121/15/59, MacCarthy to Whitaker, 22 Dec. 1959.

86  *Ibid.*

87  DF, F.121/15/59, Whitaker to MacCarthy, 23 Dec. 1959.

88  DF, F.121/15/59, MacCarthy to Whitaker, 24 Dec. 1959.

89  *Ibid.*

90  Andrews quotes Kavanagh in his notes for 1957 lecture entitled 'Is emigration inevitable in Ireland?': UCDA, Andrews papers, P91/136(1).

91  DF, F.121/15/59, Whitaker to MacCarthy, 31 Dec. 1959.

92  DF, F.121/15/59, MacCarthy to Whitaker, 5 Jan. 1960. Whitaker's original point about the narrow protectionist plateau is in DF, F.121/15/59, Whitaker to Cremin, 22 Dec. 1959.

93  Horgan, *Seán Lemass*, p. 216.

94  DF, F.121/15/59, Cremin to Whitaker, 21 Dec. 1959.

95    DF, F.121/15/59, Whitaker to Cremin, 22 Dec. 1959.
96    DF, F.121/15/59, Whitaker to MacCarthy, 7 Jan. 1960.
97    Confidential source.
98    *Ibid.*
99    DF, 121/15/59, MacCarthy to Whitaker, 9 Jan. 1960. EFTA was founded as the European Free Trade Association in 1960, but documentation and discussions about forming such an association usually referred to EFTA as the European Free Trade Area.
100   DF, 121/15/59, Whitaker to MacCarthy, 11 Jan. 1960.
101   Ó Cearbhaill interview. The four-secretaries committee refers to a committee on free trade consisting of Cremin (External Affairs), MacCarthy (Industry and Commerce), J.C. Nagle (Agriculture) and Whitaker (Finance).
102   NAI, DT, S2850 F/64, Lemass to Margaret Greenan, 18 July 1959.
103   Bruce Arnold, *Jack Lynch: Hero in Crisis* (Dublin, 2001), p. 54.
104   Dermot Keogh, *Jack Lynch: A Biography* (Dublin, 2008), pp. 70–1.
105   Frank Barry and Stephen Weir, 'The politics and process of trade liberalisation in three small peripheral European economies', paper presented to GlobalEuroNet workshop: 'Economic convergence of small peripheral countries in the post-Second World War. Examples of Finland, Ireland and Portugal', Department of Social Science History, University of Helsinki, Finland , p. 9. I am grateful to Frank Barry for providing me with a copy of this paper and for discussing these issues with me.

## CHAPTER 4: A NATIONAL GOVERNMENT FOR IRELAND?

1     *The Irish Times*, 24 Jan. 2009.
2     *The Irish Times*, 25 May 1944.
3     See Puirséil, 'Political and party competition' p. 14; Fianna Fáil, *The Story of Fianna Fáil: First Phase* (Dublin, 1960).
4     Puirséil, 'Political and party competition', p. 14. Farrell, *Seán Lemass*, p. 84; Horgan, *Lemass*, p. 144; Michael B. Yeats, *Cast A Cold Eye. Memories of a Poet's Son and Politician* (Dublin, 1998), p. 49.
5     Lord Longford and Thomas P. O'Neill, *Eamon de Valera* (London, 1970), p. 439. See also Farrell, *Seán Lemass*, p. 85. Farrell's evidence is based on an interview with Lemass.
6     See Farrell, *Seán Lemass*, p. 53.
7     UCDA, MacEntee papers, P67/338(5), speech at Rathmines, nd, but by context mid-May 1954.
8     NAI, DT, S.13240, MacBride to de Valera, 23 May 1954.
9     *Ibid.*
10    *Ibid.*
11    *Ibid.*, See also Elizabeth Keane, *Seán MacBride: A Life* (Dublin, 2007), p. 210; Kevin Rafter, *The Clann: The Story of Clann na Poblachta* (Cork, 1996), p. 165.
12    UCDA, de Valera papers, P150/3063, Kavanagh to de Valera, 20 May 1954.
13    *Ibid.*, de Valera to Kavanagh, 28 May 1954.
14    *Ibid.*, Slattery to de Valera, 20 May 1954.
15    *Ibid.*, Humphries to de Valera, 20 May 1954.

16  *Ibid.*, de Valera to Humphries, 28 May 1954.

17  *Ibid.*, McCauley to de Valera, 25 May 1954.

18  *Ibid.*, McCauley to de Valera, 1 June 1954.

19  Bew and Patterson, *Seán Lemass and the Making of Modern Ireland*, p. 76.

20  *The Irish Times*, 25 July 1953.

21  *The Leader*, 12 Apr. 1952.

22  NARA, record group 59, box 3168, 740A/00/2–1857, Dublin embassy to State Department, 18 Feb. 1957.

23  UCDA, Fine Gael papers, P39/GE62, Alex Bolster to Richard Mulcahy, nd, but by context early Feb. 1957.

24  Fine Gael papers, 'Ireland 1957 – A new deal: Task for national Government'.

25  UCDA, MacEntee papers P67/815(4). I am grateful to MacEntee's biographer, Dr Tom Feeney, for discussing this issue with me.

26  Interview of John F. McCarthy with Seán Lemass, 14 Aug. 1969, copy in possession of the author.

27  Mackenzie King diaries, 9 Sept. 1948, http:www.collectionscanada.gc.ca/databases/king/index-e.html

28  *Irish Independent*, 24 May 1951.

29  *Ibid.*, 26 May 1951.

30  *Ibid.*, 6 June 1951.

31  *Ibid.*, 17 May 1954.

32  *Ibid.*, editorials, 17 May 1954, 27 Feb. 1957, 4 Mar. 1957.

33  *Ibid.*, 8 Mar. 1957.

34  *Ibid.*, 2 Sept. 1961.

35  I am grateful to my former DCU colleague, Professor John Horgan, for discussing this issue with me.

36  *Irish Independent*, 3 Oct. 1961.

37  *Ibid.*, 7 Oct. 1961.

38  *The Irish Times*, 8 Mar 1957. See also Mark O'Brien, *The Irish Times: A History* (Dublin, 2008), p. 154; I am grateful to Dr O'Brien for discussing this issue with me.

39  UCDA, de Valera papers, P150/3063, de Valera speech in Mallow, 20 Feb. 1957.

40  National Archives, London, DO 35/5195, Clutterbuck to Lord Home, 23 Mar. 1957.

41  NARA, record group 59, box 3168, 740A/00/8–857, Dublin embassy to State Department, 8 Aug. 1957.

42  Farrell, *Lemass*, p. 95.

43  *Ibid.*

44  Lee, *Ireland 1912–1985*, p. 341.

45  See for example Fianna Fáil parliamentary-party minutes, FF441/A, 26 Feb., 15 Apr., 26 May 1948.

46  Feeney, *Seán MacEntee*, p. 201.

47  National Archives, London, 35/790, G. Kimber, Dublin, to G.W. Chadwick, Commonwealth Relations Office, 3 Dec. 1958.

48  Lynch to John Skehan, quoted in the RTÉ documentary, *Any Other Business*, Jan. 1999.

49    Horgan, *Seán Lemass*, p. 180.
50    *Ibid.*, p. 186; O'Sullivan, *Seán Lemass*, p. 146.
51    John F. McCarthy interview with Seán Lemass, 14 Aug. 1969.


CHAPTER 5: OWNERS, WORKERS AND FARMERS: THE INTEREST-GROUP
        EXPERIENCE

1    Nevin interview.
2    This figure is given in NAI, DT, S.16474A, criticism of *Economic Development* by
     Departments of Health and Industry and Commerce, with details of disparity
     between Ireland and Britain, 4 July 1958.
3    See Milward, *The Reconstruction of Western Europe;* Peter Katzenstein, *Small States
     in World Markets* (Ithaca, N.Y., 1985).
4    Girvin, 'Trade Unions and Economic Development', p. 124.
5    For a detailed analysis of the split in the trade union movement, see Charles
     McCarthy, *Trade Unions in Ireland, 1894–1960* (Dublin, 1977), p. 229–80; see
     also Donal Nevin, 'Decades of dissension and divisions, 1923–1959' in Nevin
     (ed.), *Trade Union Century*, pp. 94–6.
6    NAI, ICTU Archive, box 41 (part 1) 7331, 'Attitude of the trade unions towards
     the European Free Trade Area', n.d., but by context mid-1957.
7    NAI, ICTU Archive, box 41 (part 1) 7331, 'Report on European industrial
     conference', London 19–21 Feb. 1958.
8    NAI, ICTU Archive, box 41 (part 1) 7331, 'Ireland and the Free Trade Area',
     16 July 1957.
9    *Ibid.*
10   *Ibid.*
11   *Ibid.*
12   NAI, ICTU Archive, box 41 (part 1) 7331, 'Statement by Laurence Hudson,
     president of PUTUO, at Jury's under auspices of Chartered Institute of
     Secretaries', 21 Mar. 1957.
13   See Francis Devine, '"A dangerous agitator": John Swift, 1896–1990, social-
     ist, trade unionist, secularist, internationalist, labour historian', *Saothar*, no. 15
     (1990), pp. 7–19; see also John P. Swift, *John Swift: An Irish Dissident* (Dublin,
     1991).
14   NAI, ICTU Archive, box 41 (part 1) 7331, John Swift to secretary of PUTUO,
     12 Aug. 1957.
15   *Ibid.*
16   *Ibid.* See also Swift's memorandum to the secretary of PUTUO on 'Proposed
     Free Trade Area in Europe', 7 Mar. 1957.
17   Nevin, 'Decades of dissension and divisions', p. 96.
18   McCarthy, *Decade of Upheaval*, p. 24.
19   NAI, ICTU Archive, box 42 (part 2), meeting with the Taoiseach 1959, 3 Sept.
     1959.
20   Girvin, 'Trade Unions and Economic Development', p. 125.
21   NAI, ICTU Archive, box 42 (part 2), ICTU proposed meeting with Taoiseach
     – meeting of Resident Committee, 24 Aug. 1959.
22   Address by Pádraic O'Halpin entitled 'An authority for the mechanical

engineering industry', 3 Apr. 1959. I would like to thank Joseph McCullough for supplying me with a copy of this paper. It can also be found in NAI, ICTU Archive, box 43 (part 2), economic committee, 4005/B.

23   NAI, ICTU Archive, box 42 (part 2), meeting with the Taoiseach, 1959, 3 Sept. 1959.
24   Whitaker interview.
25   Girvin, 'Trade Unions and Economic Development', p. 126.
26   NAI, ICTU Archive, box 42 (part 2), speech by Lemass at Inchicore on state development activities, 4 July 1959.
27   Whitaker interview; Murray interview.
28   NAI, ICTU Archive, box 41 (part 2) 3810, meeting between representatives of Congress and FII, 10 May 1956.
29   NAI, ICTU Archive, box 41 (part 2) 3810, J.J. Stacey, director-general of the FII to Ruaidhrí Roberts, joint-secretary of ICTU, 14 Mar. 1960. The comment 'not acceptable' is written in the margin of the letter in the file.
30   The report of this conference was published in *Irish Industry*, the journal of the FIM, vol. 25 (Mar. 1957). The anti-free trade speaker was James Boylan. Domhnall McCullough was the other speaker.
31   *Irish Industry*, vol. 25, no. 3 (Mar. 1957), p. 25.
32   *Irish Industry*, vol. 25, no. 2 (Feb. 1957), p. 3.
33   Barnes interview.
34   J.I. Fitzpatrick, 'Ireland and the Free Trade Area', *Christus Rex*, vol. xii, no. 3 (July 1958), pp. 200–1.
35   Federation of Irish Industries, annual report, 1959, quoted in NAI, DT, S.15279B/1.
36   Tonge is quoted in the *Irish Press*, 27 Jan. 1960.
37   J.C. Tonge, 'Irish industry in the EFTA era', *The Statist*, 19 Mar. 1960, p. 19.
38   Barnes interview.
39   Tonge, 'Irish industry in the EFTA era'.
40   *Ibid.*
41   Barnes interview.
42   NAI, DT, S.2805F/64, R.C. Owens, Carley's Bridge Potteries, Wexford to An Taoiseach, 29 Jan. 1960.
43   NAI, DT, S.17046A, Taoiseach's address to the Federation of Irish Industries' national export conference, 16 Jan. 1961.
44   Federation of Irish Industries, *European free trade and the prospects for Irish industry*, Sept. 1959.
45   NAI, ICTU Archive, box 41 (part 1) 7331, meeting between Department of Industry and Commerce and Provisional United Trade Union Organisation, 8 Jan. 1958.
46   Garret FitzGerald, *All in a Life: An Autobiography* (Dublin, 1991), p. 59.
47   FitzGerald is quoted in C. Brock, 'The CIO Industrial Survey', *Journal of the Statistical and Social Inquiry Society of Ireland*, vol. 21 (1963–64), p. 176.
48   *The Irish Times*, 6 July 1961.
49   O'Rahilly interview.
50   Fitzpatrick is quoted in *Hibernia*, Mar. 1962.
51   *Industrial Review: The Journal of the Federation of Irish Industries*, vol. 18, no. 5

(Sept.–Oct. 1961).

52  Seán Hutton, 'Labour in the post-independence Irish state: An overview' in Seán Hutton and Paul Stewart (eds), *Ireland's Histories: Aspects of State, Society and Ideology* (London, 1991), p. 63; Gary Murphy, 'Towards a corporate state? Seán Lemass and the realignment of interest groups in the policy process, 1948–1964', *Administration*, vol. 47, no. 1 (spring 1999), pp. 92–3.

53  NARA, RG59, box 1652, 740/00(W)/5–2562, Dublin embassy to State Department, 25 May 1962.

54  Lynch interview; see also Patrick Lynch, '1894–1994: An overview' in Nevin (ed.), *Trade Union Century*, p. 169.

55  Nevin interview.

56  NAI, ICTU Archive, box 44 (part 2) 4011, ICTU Economic Committee, memorandum on the application for entry to the EEC, July 1961.

57  Nevin interview.

58  Barnes interview.

59  NAI, DT, S.16877Y/62, meeting between the Taoiseach, the Minister for Industry and Commerce and the Federation of Irish Industry, 8 Jan. 1962.

60  Confidential source.

61  Joseph McCullough interview.

62  Domhnall McCullough interview.

63  NAI, DT, S.17120A/62, meeting between the Taoiseach, the Minister for Industry and Commerce and the Irish Congress of Trade Unions, 11 Jan. 1962.

64  *Hibernia*, Jan. 1962.

65  ICTU, Congress Archive, annual conference, Cork, July 1961, p. 256; ICTU, Congress Archive, annual conference, Galway, July 1962, p. 227.

66  ICTU, Congress Archive, annual conference, Galway, July 1962, p. 227.

67  NAI, ICTU Archive, box 44 (part 2) 4011, 'ICTU policy statement on entry to the EEC', July 1962.

68  ICTU, Congress Archive, annual conference, Galway, July 1962, p. 235.

69  ICTU, Congress Archive, annual conference, Cork, July 1961, p. 269.

70  ICTU, Congress Archive, annual conference, Killarney, 1963, p. 278.

71  NAI, ICTU archive, box 43 (part 2), consultative conference – 'Free trade and industrial reorganisation', 4011/A, 22 Mar. 1963.

72  ICTU, Congress Archive, annual conference, Killarney, 1963, p. 278.

73  NAI, ICTU archive, box 43 (part 2), consultative conference – 'Free trade and industrial reorganisation', 4011/A, 22 Mar. 1963. Lemass is quoted as speaking on 25 Feb. 1963. No place is given.

74  NAI, ICTU archive, box 43 (part 2), consultative conference – 'Free trade and industrial reorganisation', 4011/A, 22 Mar. 1963.

75  Committee on Industrial Organisation, final report (Dublin, 1965).

76  Conroy is quoted in the *Irish Press*, 10 July 1963.

77  Gary Murphy, 'Fostering a spurious progeny?' The trade union movement and Europe, 1957–1964, *Saothar*, vol. 21 (1996), p. 69.

78  For an authoritative account of Clann na Talmhan, see Tony Varley, 'Farmers against nationalists: The rise and fall of Clann na Talmhan in Galway' in Gerard Moran and Raymond Gillespie (eds), *Galway: History & Society* (Dublin, 1996), pp. 589–622.

79   Lee, *Ireland 1912–1985,* pp. 72–73.
80   Maurice Manning, 'The farmers' in J.J. Lee (ed.), *Ireland 1945–1970* (Dublin, 1979), p. 48.
81   John P. Gibbons, 'The origins and influence of the Irish Farmers' Association', PhD thesis, University of Manchester, 1990, p. 113.
82   Manning, 'The farmers', p. 53.
83   Louis P.F. Smith and Seán Healy, *Farm Organisations in Ireland: A Century of Progress* (Dublin, 1996), p. 52.
84   NAI, DT, S.16405, speech by Greene to NFA members in Kildare, n.d., but by context Feb. 1958.
85   John Horgan, *Seán Lemass,* p. 235.
86   NAI, DT, S.16405, Greene to de Valera, 1 Mar. 1958.
87   NAI, DT, S.16405, speech by Ryan to Fianna Fáil cumann in Wexford, 28 Feb. 1958.
88   *The Irish Times,* 1 Mar. 1958.
89   Interview with Louis Smith.
90   NAI, DT, S.16405, Greene to Smith, 17 Sept. 1959.
91   Nagle to the author, 28 Feb. 1995. I interviewed J.C. Nagle in his house on Winton Avenue a number of times before his death, and we corresponded about this period.
92   This description is cited in Mary E. Daly, *The First Department: A History of the Department of Agriculture* (Dublin, 2002), p. 343.
93   *NFA Quarterly Supplement,* Sept. 1959.
94   *Ibid.*
95   *Ibid.*
96   Nagle interview.
97   *NFA Quarterly Supplement,* Sept. 1959.
98   NAI, DT, S.16405, Smith to Greene, 25 Sept. 1959.
99   Nagle interview.
100  NAI, DT, S.16405, Smith to Greene, 25 Sept. 1959.
101  Nagle to the author, 28 Feb. 1995.
102  NAI, DT, S.16405, Smith to Greene, 25 Sept. 1959. The *Farmers' Journal* had a two-page slot for NFA news in every edition. This consisted mostly of addresses and comments made by NFA officers. These speeches were routinely critical of the Department of Agriculture and general Government policy with regard to the agricultural industry, and Paddy Smith complained of the 'almost constant abuse and misrepresentation' emanating from it. A further problem for Smith and his officials was that many farmers believed that the *Farmers' Journal* was an official organ of the NFA, an idea from which, Smith argued, it never seemed to dissociate itself.
103  Louis Smith interview.
104  NAI, DT, S.16405, Smith to Greene, 25 Sept. 1959.
105  *Ibid.*
106  Seán Moylan was briefly Minister for Agriculture between March and November 1957. Dermot Keogh has speculated that just hours before his untimely death, he had resigned over a major policy issue. This was never made public, and I have uncovered no other evidence to substantiate this claim. See Dermot

Keogh, *Twentieth Century Ireland: Revolution and State Building* (Dublin, 2005), p. 240.

107  NAI, DT, S.16405, Smith to Greene, 25 Sept. 1959.

108  NAI, DT, S.16719, NFA memoranda to the Department of Agriculture to defray costs of attending conferences, various dates in 1959.

109  Louis Smith interview.

110  Whitaker interview, Nagle interview.

111  NAI, DT, S.16877Y/62, NFA statement on entry to the EEC, 20 July 1960.

112  D.J. Maher, *The Tortuous Path: The Course of Ireland's Entry into the EEC, 1948–73* (Dublin, 1986), p. 120.

113  Nagle interview.

114  NAI, DT, S.16877Y/62, Department of Agriculture memorandum, Ireland and the EEC, Aug. 1960. The six and seven referred to the economic blocs that existed in Western Europe. The six (EEC) consisted of Belgium, France, Italy, Luxembourg, the Netherlands and West Germany. The seven (EFTA) consisted of Austria, Britain, Denmark, Norway, Portugal, Sweden and Switzerland.

115  NAI, DT, S.16877G, memorandum on Ireland's trade relations: prospects for agricultural trade, 8 Nov. 1960.

116  *Ibid.*

117  Juan Greene, 'The next ten years in agriculture', quoted in Department of Finance, D.306/10/61.

118  NAI, DT, S.16877G, meeting between the Taoiseach, the Minister for Agriculture, the Minister for Industry and Commerce, and the NFA, 20 Dec. 1960.

119  *Ibid.*

120  NAI, DT, S.16877X/62, Whitaker to Minister for Finance, 5 Jan. 1962.

121  NAI, DT, S.16877W, memorandum for the Government: application for membership of the European Community, 8 Jan. 1962.

122  Dáil Debates, vol. 185, cols. 560–1, 1 Dec. 1960.

123  NAI, DT, S.16877X/62, Lemass statement to the Council of Ministers, 18 Jan. 1962.

124  Deasy is quoted in *The Irish Times,* 11 Jan. 1962.

125  *Farmers' Journal,* bimonthly supplement, 20 Jan. 1962.

126  Daly, *First Department,* p. 379.

127  DF, D.306/10/61, draft observations on NFA demand for larger share of national income for agriculture, 14 Dec. 1961.

128  DF, D.306/10/61, J. Horgan, Central Statistics Office, to C.H. Murray, Department of Finance, 5 Sept. 1961.

129  DF, D.306/10/61, Nagle to Whitaker, 16 Dec. 1961.

130  DF, D.306/10/61, Department of External Affairs, comment on NFA memorandum on farmers' incomes, 26 Nov. 1961.

131  NAI, DT, S.11563C/62, meeting between the Taoiseach and the NFA, 16 Mar. 1962.

132  *Ibid.*

133  *Irish Press,* 12 Jan. 1962.

134  Lemass is quoted in the *Irish Press,* 12 Jan. 1962.

135  *Irish Press* reported on 12 January 1962 – the day after the NFA annual convention

– that the farmers planned 'aggressive action' in their campaign for a balancing of incomes. See also Deasy's interview in *The Irish Times*, 10 Mar. 1962.

136 NAI, DT, S.11563C/62, Lemass to Smith, 2 Mar. 1962. The 'impractical totals' referred to the NFA's demand for an £83 million subsidy.

137 NAI, DT, S.17313A/62, speech by Taoiseach at Muintir na Tíre rural week, Scoil Ailbhe, Thurles, 14 Aug. 1962.

138 For an analysis of the Government's co-opting of industry into its political strategy for entry into the EEC, see Gary Murphy, 'Government, interest groups and the Irish move to Europe: 1957–1963', *Irish Studies in International Affairs*, vol. 8 (1997), pp. 57–68.

139 Healy is quoted in *The Irish Times*, 11 July 1962.

140 Both Deasy and Smith were given space in the April 1962 edition of *Hibernia* to put forward their views on the agricultural situation.

141 *Irish Independent*, 13 Apr. 1962.

142 NAI, DT, S.11563E/62, meeting between the Taoiseach and the NFA, 6 Apr. 1962.

143 *Irish Press,* 11 Apr. 1962.

144 *Connacht Tribune*, 18 Aug. 1962.

145 Alan Matthews, 'The state and Irish agriculture, 1950–1980' in P.J. Drudy (ed.), *Ireland: Land, Politics and People* (Cambridge, 1982), p. 244.

146 NAI, DT, S.17543A/63, Lemass to Smith, 5 Nov. 1963. Lemass was telling Smith of a meeting with Deasy at which he expressed these views.

147 Maurice Manning, *The Blueshirts* (Dublin, 1986, 2nd edn.), p. 57.

148 *Ibid.*, p. 30.

149 Dáil Debates, vol. 206, col. 1219, 12 Dec. 1963.

150 NAI, DT, S.17543A/63, Smith to Lemass, 20 Nov. 1963.

151 Lemass' memorandum is quoted in Gibbons, 'The origins and influence of the Irish Farmers' Association', pp. 156–57.

152 Joseph Robins, *Custom House People* (Dublin, 1993), pp. 151–2.

153 Smith's resignation letter is reproduced in Brian Farrell, *Chairman or Chief? The Role of Taoiseach in Irish Government* (Dublin, 1971), pp. 66–7.

154 NARA, RG59, box 2343, pol 2–1 Ire., Dublin embassy to State Department, 9 Oct. 1964.

155 *Ibid.*, box 2343, pol 15–1 Ire., Dublin embassy to State Department 16 Oct. 1964.

156 *The Irish Times*, 10 Oct., 15 Oct. 1964.

157 Horgan, *Seán Lemass*, p. 356.

158 Daly, *First Department*, p. 459.

159 M.A.G. Ó Tuathaigh, 'The land question, politics and Irish society, 1922–1960' in P.J. Drudy (ed.), *Ireland: Land, Politics and People*, pp. 186–7.

160 Andrews, *Man of No Property*, p. 242.

## CHAPTER 6: EXPLORING FARAWAY LANDS

1 NARA, RG59, box 3170, 740A/00 (W)/18–157, Dublin embassy to State Department, 18 Jan. 1957.

2 Meenan, *The Irish Economy Since 1922*, p. 81.

3    Maher, *The Tortuous Path*, p. 55.
4    Garret FitzGerald, 'Ireland and the free trade area', *Studies*, vol. xlv, no. 181 (spring 1957), p. 19.
5    NAI, DT, S.15281D, interim report of the committee of secretaries, 18 Jan. 1957.
6    Whitaker interview.
7    NAI, DT, S.15281D, interim report of the committee of secretaries, 18 Jan. 1957.
8    *Ibid.*
9    *Ibid.*, Appendix from the Department of Industry and Commerce.
10   Girvin, *Between Two Worlds*, pp. 191–2; J.J. Lee, '*Economic Development* in historical perspective' in McCarthy (ed.), *Planning Ireland's Future*, p. 121.
11   Nagle interview.
12   NAI, DT, CAB G.C. 7/183, 8 Feb. 1957.
13   Quoted in Moynihan, *Currency and Central Banking in Ireland*, pp. 438–9.
14   Cromien interview.
15   Quoted in Maher, *The Tortuous Path*, p. 67.
16   NAI, DT, S 15281F, committee of secretaries, ninth meeting, comments of J.C.B. MacCarthy, 12 Mar. 1957.
17   NAI, DT, CAB G.C. 8/5, European Free Trade Area, 9 Apr. 1957.
18   NAI, DT, S 15281G, Fay to secretary, Department of External Affairs, 15 Apr. 1957.
19   NAI, DT, S 15281J, memorandum of Government to OEEC Working Party 23, 11 May 1957.
20   NAI, DT, S 15281J, European Free Trade Area, 13 July 1957.
21   'Ireland and the European Free Trade Area', *The Statist*, 11 Jan. 1958, p. 44.
22   Whitaker's memorandum is quoted in Fanning, 'The genesis of *Economic Development*', p. 96.
23   NAI, DT S 15281J, memorandum of Government to OEEC Working Party 23, 11 May 1957.
24   *Ibid.*
25   Maher, *The Tortuous Path*, pp. 77–8.
26   NAI, DT, S.15281 F, Department of Agriculture policy with regard to the free trade area, 4 Apr. 1957.
27   NAI, DT, S.15281J, Working Party 23, consideration of the Irish case, 28 May 1957.
28   NAI, DT, S.15281I, MacCarthy to Fay, 6 June 1957.
29   NAI, DT, S.15281J, European Free Trade Area, 13 July 1957.
30   Extract from the budget speech of Minister for Finance, 8 May 1957. The speech can be found in Dáil Debates, vol. 161, cols. 933–62.
31   *Ibid.*, col. 961.
32   Garvin, *Preventing the Future*, p. 118.
33   Ó Cearbhaill interview.
34   Dáil Debates, vol. 165, cols. 531–81, 20 Feb. 1958.
35   Barnes interview.
36   NAI, ICTU Archive, box 41 (part 1), 7331, 'Fine Gael memorandum on EFTA', 23 Jan. 1958. The memorandum was not intended to indicate official Fine Gael

policy. It was prepared by a committee of experts on behalf of its research and information centre.

37  *Ibid.*
38  NAI, DT, S.15281N, discussions with British Government on implications for Anglo-Irish trading agreements, third meeting, 13 Nov. 1957.
39  NAI, DT, S.15281L, extract from Cabinet minutes, G.C. 8/55, 1 Nov. 1958.
40  NAI, DT, S.15281N, European Free Trade Area: visit of British paymaster general, Jan. 1958, 28 Dec. 1957. Maudling had specific responsibility for chairing the talks with the members of the EEC in relation to joining a free trade area with Britain.
41  Cahan's lecture is reprinted as 'Ireland's role in a free trade area', *Studies*, vol. xlvii, no. 186 (summer 1958), pp. 122–30.
42  *Ibid.*
43  Clarke is quoted in Richard Lamb, *The Macmillan Years: The Emerging Truth* (London, 1995), p. 113.
44  *Economic Development* (Dublin, 1958), p. 1.
45  NARA, record group 59 box 3170, 740A/00 (W)/8–659, Dublin embassy to State Department, 6 Aug. 1959.
46  Whitaker interview.
47  NAI, DT, S.15281R, report of the committee of secretaries, 8 July 1959.
48  NAI, DFA, 348/69/II, minutes of the Foreign Trade Committee, 12 June 1959.
49  NAI, DFA, 348/69/II, Department of Agriculture, external trade policies, Aug. 1960.
50  NAI, DT, S.15281V, Ireland's position in relation to free trade in Britain, 13 Jan. 1960.
51  NAI, DT, S.15281X, memorandum for the Government, Anglo-Irish Trade Agreement, 13 Apr. 1960.
52  Ó Cearbhaill interview.
53  Whitaker interview.
54  NAI, DT, S.15281V, memorandum presented to the Taoiseach, 8 Feb. 1960.
55  Frank Barry, 'Theoretical and pragmatic elements in the civil service debates on trade liberalisation', paper to IPA conference in honour of T.K. Whitaker, '*Economic Development* 50 Years On', Dublin Castle, 19 Sept. 2008. I am grateful to Professor Barry for providing me with a copy of his paper and for discussing this issue with me.
56  Ó Cearbhaill interview.
57  Desmond Fisher, 'Ireland in Europe: Advantages of joining the EFTA', *The Statist*, 19 Mar. 1960, p. 15.
58  Interview with Christopher Audland.
59  Fisher, 'Ireland in Europe', p. 16.
60  FitzGerald is quoted in the Irish Council of the European Movement newsletter, Mar. 1960.
61  *Ibid.*
62  Dáil Debates, vol. 189, col. 1297, 16 May 1961.
63  NAI, DFA, 348/69/II, statement by Irish representative at OEEC Council, 14 Jan. 1960.

64    Terence Brown, *Ireland: A Social and Cultural History, 1922 to the Present* (Ithaca, N.Y., 1985), p. 214.

65    Ó Cearbhaill interview.

66    NAI, DT, S.16877B, Cremin to St.J. Connolly, deputy secretary, Department of Industry and Commerce, 18 June 1960.

67    NAI, DT, S.15281R, discussions between the Tanaiste and Mr Maudling, London, 26 May 1959. Also S.15279B/1, Taoiseach's statement on Irish policy, 12 July 1960.

68    NAI, DT, S.16877G, memorandum on Ireland's trade relations: prospects for agricultural trade, 8 Nov. 1960; For Ireland's reluctance to join GATT, see S.15030B-D.

69    Gary Murphy, 'A wider perspective: Ireland's view of Western Europe in the 1950s' in Michael Kennedy and Joseph Skelly (eds), *From Independence to Internationalism: Irish Foreign Policy, 1916–1966*, pp. 247–64.

70    Whitaker interview.

71    Barnes interview, Joseph McCullough interview.

72    NAI, DT, 16877G, membership of (or association with) EEC, comments by Industry and Commerce, 19 Dec. 1960.

73    *Ibid.*

74    NAI, DT, S.16023C/61, Whitaker to Ó Nuailláin, 2 May 1961.

75    Brian Girvin, '*Economic Development* and the politics of EC entry, Ireland 1955–63', paper presented at conference, 'The First Attempt to Enlarge the European Community, 1961–63', European University Institute, Florence, Feb. 1994, pp. 17–18.

76    Dermot Keogh, *Ireland and Europe 1919–1989: A Diplomatic and Political History* (Cork, 1990), pp. 232–3. The background to the decision to apply can be followed in NAI, DT, S.16877K, European Free Trade Area.

77    *Economist*, 9 Feb. 1962.

78    NARA, record group 59, Office of British Commonwealth and Northern European Affairs, alpha-numeric files relating to Ireland, box 1, Tyler to S/P – Mr McGhee, 11 Aug. 1961.

78    NAI, DT, S.16877X/62, Lemass to Ó Nuailláin, secretary, Department of the Taoiseach, 1 Jan. 1962.

80    Ronan Fanning, '*Raison d'état* and the evolution of Irish foreign policy' in Kennedy and Skelly (eds), *From Independence to Internationalism*, p. 324.

81    Quoted in *Ibid.* p. 325.

82    NAI, DT, S.16877X/62, Lemass to Ó Nuailláin, secretary, Department of the Taoiseach, 1 Jan. 1962.

83    Dermot Keogh, 'Irish neutrality and the first application for membership of the EEC' in Kennedy and Skelly (eds), *From Independence to Internationalism*, pp. 272–3.

84    NAI, DT, S.16877X/62, Biggar to Sheila Murphy, Department of External Affairs, 30 Dec. 1961.

85    NAI, DT, 16877G, membership of (or association with) EEC, comments by Industry and Commerce, 19 Dec. 1960.

86    NAI, DT, S.16877X/62, Biggar to Murphy, Department of External Affairs, 30 Dec. 1961.

87   NAI, DT, S.16877X/62, Ó Nuailláin to Whitaker, 4 Jan. 1962.
88   NAI, DT, S.16877X/62, draft statement to ministers of the Governments of the member states of the European Economic Community revised, 1 Jan. 1962.
89   Girvin, '*Economic Development* and the politics of EC entry', p. 14.
90   NAI, DT, S.16877X/62, McCann to Cremin, 7 Feb. 1962.
91   Whitaker interview.
92   NAI, DT, S.16877X/62, Whitaker to Minister for Finance, 5 Jan. 1962.
93   It is interesting to note that the files on the application to the EEC in the National Archives (S.17246A/62 to W/62) reveal that Lemass' handwritten accounts were effectively the line followed.
94   NAI, DT, S.16877X/62, Whitaker to Minister for Finance, 5 Jan. 1962.
95   Moran's speech can be found in NAI, DT, S.17246A/62.
96   See Horgan, *Seán Lemass*, p. 223; Keogh, 'Irish neutrality and the first application for membership of the EEC', p. 277.
97   Fianna Fáil parliamentary-party minutes, FF441/B, 14 Feb. 1962.
98   NARA RG59, box 1651, 740a.00/2–962, Dublin embassy to State Department, 9 Feb. 1962.
99   NAI, DT, S. 17246D/62, meeting of secretaries, 1 Mar. 1962.
100  NAI, DT, S.16877Y/62, Biggar to Cremin, 9 Jan. 1962.
101  NAI, DT, S.17246D/62, transcript of interview with Taoiseach on Telefís Éireann', 15 Mar. 1962.
102  NAI, DT, S.16877X/62, draft statement to ministers of the Governments of the member states of the European Economic Community revised, 1 Jan. 1962.
103  Horgan, *Noël Browne*, p. 209.
104  UCDA, Fine Gael papers, P39/GE102, Cosgrave speech at Dalkey, 2 Oct. 1961.
105  Puirséil, *Irish Labour Party*, p. 221.
106  *Ibid.*, pp. 218–21 for a further elucidation of this view.
107  *Economist*, 9 Feb. 1962.
108  David O'Mahony, 'On not following Britain's lead', *Hibernia*, Oct. 1962.
109  Hugh Charlton, 'Government, people and Common Market', *Hibernia*, Nov. 1962.
110  *Ibid.*
111  E.J. Hegarty, 'Statistics: the Common Market', *Christus Rex*, vol. xvi, no. 1 (Jan. 1962), pp. 55–7.
112  Ferriter, *The Transformation of Ireland*, p. 497.
113  *Ibid.*, p. 498.
114  J.H. Whyte, *Church and State in Modern Ireland 1923–1979* (Dublin, 1980), p. 354–5.
115  William J. Philbin, 'The Irish and the new Europe', *Studies*, vol. li, no. 201 (spring 1962), p. 31.
116  *Ibid.*, p. 36.
117  *Ibid.*, p. 43.
118  James Kavanagh, 'The state and economic and social policy', *Christus Rex*, vol. xvi, no. 4 (Oct. 1962), p. 277.
119  *Irish Press*, 18 Jan. 1962.
120  The Irish view is contained in NAI, DT, S.16877W, memorandum for the

Government: application for membership of the European Economic Community, 8 Jan. 1962. See also S.16877K-M, which includes correspondence with the Council of Ministers.

121 *Irish Press*, 19 Jan. 1962.
122 *Guardian*, 19 Jan. 1962.
123 NAI, DT, S.16877Y/62, comments made to J.C.B. MacCarthy regarding Taoiseach's statement, 18 Jan. 1962.
124 *Ibid.*
125 NAI, DT, S.16877W, memorandum for the Government: application for membership of the European Economic Community, 8 Jan. 1962.
126 NAI, DT, S.16877X/62, Department of Industry and Commerce to Department of Taoiseach, 8 Jan. 1962.
127 McCullough interview.
128 Barnes interview.
129 For a contemporary analysis of the CIO, see Brock, 'The CIO Industrial Survey'; for an historical analysis, see Girvin, *Between Two Worlds*, pp. 203–5.
130 Nevin interview.
131 NAI, DT, S.17120A/62, meeting between the Taoiseach, the Minister for Industry and Commerce and the Irish Congress of Trade Unions, 11 Jan. 1962.
132 O'Rahilly interview.
133 Fianna Fáil, F/729, presidential address by An Taoiseach to Fianna Fáil *ard fheis*, 16 Jan. 1962.
134 *Ibid.*
135 O'Rahilly interview.
136 Fianna Fáil, F/729, report of Fianna Fáil *ard fheis*, 16 Jan. 1962.
137 *Sunday Independent*, 11 Feb. 1962.
138 *Irish Press*, 12 Feb. 1962.
139 *The Statist*, 26 Jan. 1962, pp. 261–268.
140 NAI, DT, S.17246A/62, report on the *Statist* article, 26 Jan. 1962; Donal O'Sullivan, Brussels to Department of External Affairs, 29 Jan. 1962.
141 NARA, RG59, Office of British Commonwealth and Northern European Affairs, alpha-numeric files relating to Ireland, box 1, Burke to Prince, 20 Apr. 1962.
142 NAI, DT, S.17246H/62, transcript of meeting between Irish delegation and Committee of the Member States of the EEC, 11 May 1962.
143 Lemass is quoted in Joseph T. Carroll, 'General de Gaulle and Ireland's EEC application' in Pierre Joannon (ed.), *De Gaulle and Ireland* (Dublin, 1991), p. 87.
144 NAI, DT, S.17246N/62, meeting of secretaries, 7 Sept. 1962.
145 Dáil Debates, vol. 298, col. 1688, 21 Nov. 1962.
146 Fianna Fáil, F/729, presidential address by An Taoiseach to Fianna Fáil *ard fheis*, 20 Nov. 1962. The address was entitled 'Ireland in the new Europe: The case for Irish membership of the European Economic Community'.
147 *Ibid.*
148 John Walsh, *Patrick Hillery: The Official Biography* (Dublin 2008), p. 130.
149 Fianna Fáil parliamentary-party minutes, FF441/B, 5 Dec. 1962.

150 For an analysis of de Gaulle's motives and its implications for Ireland, see Carroll, 'General De Gaulle and Ireland's EEC application', pp. 81–97; see also Keogh, *Twentieth Century Ireland*, p. 247.

151 DF, F.121/30/62, memorandum on consequences of breakdown in British/EEC negotiations and measures to be taken, 31 Jan. 1963.

152 Fianna Fáil parliamentary-party minutes, FF441/B, 30 Jan. 1963.

153 Dáil Debates, vol. 299, col. 924, 5 Feb. 1963.

154 *Ibid.*, col. 925.

155 *Ibid.*, col. 942.

156 For an analysis of the ideological importance of Fianna Fáil's switch from pro-tectionism to free trade, see Susan Baker, 'Nationalist ideology and the industrial policy of Fianna Fáil: The evidence of the *Irish Press* (1955–72)', *Irish Political Studies*, vol. 1 (1986), pp. 57–66.

157 Dáil Debates, vol. 299, cols. 946–948.

158 Miriam Hederman, *The Road to Europe: Irish Attitudes 1948–61* (Dublin, 1983), p. 65.

159 DF, F.121\37\63, Lemass speech at Advertising Club of Greater Boston, 18 Oct. 1963.

160 DF, F.121\16\62, Economic Policy Committee Meeting of OECD, Paris, 21–2 Feb. 1962.

## CONCLUSION

1 Michael Marsh, 'Explanations for party choice' in Michael Gallagher and Michael Marsh (eds), *How Ireland Voted 2007: The Full Story of Ireland's General Election* (Dublin, 2008), pp. 128–9.

2 Brian Girvin and Gary Murphy, 'Whose Ireland?' in Girvin and Murphy, *Lemass Era*, p. 3.

3 Enda Delaney, 'The vanishing Irish? The exodus from Ireland in the 1950s' in Dermot Keogh, Finbarr O'Shea and Carmel Quinlan (eds), *The Lost Decade: Ireland in the 1950s* (Cork, 2004), p. 86.

4 Hillery is quoted in Walsh, *Patrick Hillery*, p. 71.

5 Girvin and Murphy, 'Whose Ireland?', p. 5.

6 Patrick Honohan and Cormac O'Grada, 'The Irish macroeconomic crisis of 1955–56: How much was due to monetary policy?', *Irish Economic and Social History*, vol. xxv (1998); Barry, 'Theoretical and pragmatic elements in the civil service debates on trade liberalisation'.

7 See for example R.F. Foster, *Luck and the Irish: A Brief History of Change 1970–2000* (London, 2007), p. 17.

8 Tom Garvin, *The Evolution of Irish Nationalist Politics* (Dublin, 1981), p. 224.

9 Gary Murphy and Niamh Puirséil, '"Is it a new allowance?": Irish entry to the EEC and popular opinion', *Irish Political Studies*, vol. 23, no. 4, p. 536.

# Bibliography

## Primary Sources

National Archives of Ireland (NAI), Dublin
Department of the Taoiseach, S Files
Department of Finance, F Files
Department of Foreign Affairs, Foreign Trade Files
Department of Industry and Commerce, TID Files
Irish Congress of Trade Unions, Congress Archives
Department of Finance, Dublin, D Files, F Files
National Archives, London
Dominions Office
National Archives and Records Administration of the United States, Washington, DC
State Department (RG59)

## Private Papers

C.S. Andrews papers, University College Dublin Archive (UCDA)
Frederick H. Boland manuscript, copy in possession of the author
Joseph Brennan papers, NLI (National Library of Ireland)
John A. Costello papers, UCDA
Eamon de Valera papers, UCDA
Seán MacEntee papers, UCDA
Patrick McGilligan papers, UCDA
William Norton papers, Irish Labour History Society (IHLS)
Pádraic O'Halpin papers, UCDA
Mackenzie King diaries: http:www.collectionscanada.gc.ca/databases/king/index-e.html

## Political Party Archives

Fianna Fáil party papers, UCDA
Fine Gael party papers, UCDA

## Official Publications

Dáil Debates
Seanad Debates
Central Bank Reports

## NEWSPAPERS AND PERIODICALS

*Bell, The*
*Christus Rex*
*Cork Examiner*
*Economist*
*Evening Herald*
*Hibernia*
*Industrial Review*
*Irish Council of the European Movement Newsletter*
*Irish Independent*
*Irish Industry*
*Irish Monthly*
*Irish Press*
*Irish Times, The*
*Irish Times Review and Annual, The*
*Leader, The*
*Round Table*
*Standard, The*
*Statist, The*
*Studies*
*Sunday Independent*


## INTERVIEWS

Sir Christopher Audland
Colm Barnes
Tom Barrington
John Carroll
Seán Cromien
Patrick Lynch
John F. McCarthy interview with Seán Lemass
Domhnall McCullough
Joseph McCullough
Charles Murray
Donal Nevin
J.C. Nagle
Tadhg Ó Cearbhaill
Aodogan O'Rahilly
Louis Smith
T.K. Whitaker


## SELECT PUBLICATIONS

Aldous, Richard and Niamh Puirséil, *We Declare: Landmark Documents in Ireland's History* (London, 2008)

Allen, Kieran, *Fianna Fáil and Irish Labour: 1926 to the Present Day* (London, 1997)

Andrews, C.S., *Man of No Property: An Autobiography* (Dublin, 1982), vol. 2

Arnold, Bruce, *Jack Lynch: Hero in Crisis* (Dublin, 2001)

Baker, Susan, 'Nationalist ideology and the industrial policy of Fianna Fáil: The evidence of the *Irish Press* (1955–72)', *Irish Political Studies*, vol. 1 (1986)

Barrington, Ruth, *Health, Medicine and Politics in Ireland, 1900–1970* (Dublin, 1987)

Barry, Frank, 'Theoretical and pragmatic elements in the civil service debates on trade liberalisation', paper to '*Economic Development* 50 Years On', a conference in honour of T.K. Whitaker

—— and Stephen Weir, 'The politics and process of trade liberalisation in three small peripheral European economies', paper presented to GlobalEuroNet workshop: 'Economic convergence of small peripheral countries in the post-Second World War. Examples of Finland, Ireland and Portugal', Department of Social Science History, University of Helsinki, Finland

Berger, Stefan and Hugh Compston, *Policy Concertation and Social Partnership in Western Europe* (Oxford, 2002)

Bew, Paul, *Ireland: The Politics of Enmity, 1789–2006* (Oxford, 2007)

—— and Henry Patterson, *Seán Lemass and the Making of Modern Ireland, 1945–66* (Dublin, 1982)

Brock, C., 'The CIO Industrial Survey', *Journal of the Statistical and Social Inquiry Society of Ireland*, vol. 21 (1963–64)

Brown, Terence, *Ireland: A Social and Cultural History, 1922 to the Present* (Ithaca, NY, 1985)

Browne, Noël, *Against the Tide* (Dublin, 1986)

Cahan, J.F., 'Ireland's role in a free trade area', *Studies*, vol. xlvii, no. 186 (summer 1958)

Carroll, Joseph T., 'General de Gaulle and Ireland's EEC application' in Pierre Joannon (ed.), *De Gaulle and Ireland* (Dublin, 1991)

Chubb, Basil (ed.), *Federation of Irish Employers 1942–1992* (Dublin, 1992)

—— 'Ireland 1957' in D.E. Butler (ed.), *Elections Abroad* (London, 1959)

—— *The Government and Politics of Ireland* (Oxford, 1971)

—— and Patrick Lynch, *Economic Development and Planning* (Dublin, 1969)

Collins, Neil, 'Still recognisably pluralist? State–farmer relations in Ireland' in Ronald Hill and Michael Marsh (eds), *Modern Irish Democracy: Essays in Honour of Basil Chubb* (Dublin, 1993)

Coogan, Tim Pat, *De Valera: Long Fellow, Tall Shadow* (Dublin, 1993)

Daly, Mary, *The Spirit of Earnest Inquiry: The Statistical and Social Inquiry Society of Ireland 1847–1997* (Dublin 1997)

—— *Social and Economic History of Ireland Since 1800* (Dublin, 1981)

—— 'An Irish Ireland for business? The Control of Manufactures Acts, 1932 and 1934', *Irish Historical Studies*, vol. xxiv, no. 94 (Nov. 1984)

—— *Industrial Development and Irish National Identity 1922–1939* (Dublin, 1992)

—— *The First Department: A History of the Department of Agriculture* (Dublin, 2002)

Davis, Troy, *Dublin's American Policy: Irish-American Diplomatic Relations, 1945–1952* (Washington DC, 1998)

Delaney, Enda, *Demography, State and Society: Irish Migration to Britain, 1921–1971* (Liverpool, 2000)

—— *Irish Emigration Since 1921* (Dublin, 2002)

—— 'The vanishing Irish? The exodus from Ireland in the 1950s' in Dermot Keogh, Finbarr O'Shea and Carmel Quinlan (eds), *The Lost Decade: Ireland in the 1950s* (Cork, 2004)

—— 'Emigration, political cultures and the evolution of post-war Irish society' in Brian Girvin and Gary Murphy (eds), *The Lemass Era: Politics and Society in the Ireland of Seán Lemass* (Dublin, 2005)

Devine, Francis, '"A dangerous agitator": John Swift, 1896–1990, socialist, trade unionist, secularist, internationalist, labour historian', *Saothar*, no. 15 (1990)

Dunphy, Richard, *The Making of Fianna Fáil Power in Ireland 1923–1948* (Oxford, 1995)

Fanning, Bryan, *The Quest for Modern Ireland: The Battle for Ideas, 1912–1986* (Dublin, 2008)

Fanning, Ronan, *The Irish Department of Finance 1922–58* (Dublin, 1978)

—— 'Economists and governments 1922–58' in Antoin Murphy (ed.), *Economists and the Irish Economy from the Eighteenth Century to the Present Day* (Dublin, 1984)

—— 'The genesis of economic development' in John F. McCarthy (ed.), *Planning Ireland's Future: The Legacy of T.K. Whitaker* (Sandycove, 1990)

—— '*Raison d'état* and the evolution of Irish foreign policy' in Michael Kennedy and Joseph Skelly (eds), *From Independence to Internationalism: Irish Foreign Policy, 1916–1966* (Dublin, 2000)

Farrell, Brian, *Chairman or Chief? The Role of Taoiseach in Irish Government* (Dublin, 1971)

—— *Seán Lemass* (Dublin, 1983)

Feeney, Tom, *Seán MacEntee: A Political Life* (Dublin, 2009)

Ferriter, Diarmaid, *The Transformation of Ireland, 1900–2000* (London, 2004)

—— *What if?: alternative views of twentieth-century Ireland* (Dublin, 2006)

—— *Judging Dev: A Reassessment of the Life and Legacy of Eamon de Valera* (Dublin, 2007)

FitzGerald, Garret, 'Ireland and the Free Trade Area', *Studies*, vol. xlvii, no. 186 (spring 1957)

—— 'Mr Whitaker and industry', *Studies*, vol. xlviii, no. 190 (summer 1959)

—— *Planning in Ireland: A P.E.P. Study* (Dublin, 1968)

—— 'Grey, white and blue: A review of three recent economic publications' in Basil Chubb and Patrick Lynch (eds), *Economic Development and Planning* (Dublin, 1969)

—— *All in a Life: An Autobiography* (Dublin, 1991)

—— 'Four decades of *Administration*' in *Administration: Cumulative Index, Volumes 1–40 (1953–1992)* (Dublin, 1994)

FitzGerald, Maurice, *Protectionism to Liberalisation: Ireland and the EEC, 1957 to 1966* (Aldershot, 2000)

—— 'Ireland's relations with the EEC: From the Treaties of Rome to membership', *Journal of European Integration History*, vol. 7, no. 1 (2001)

Foster, R.F., *Modern Ireland, 1600–1972* (London, 1988)

—— *Luck and the Irish: A Brief History of Change, 1970–2000* (London, 2007)

Gallagher, Michael, *Electoral Support for Irish Political Parties, 1927–1973* (London, 1976)

—— *The Irish Labour Party in Transition, 1957–82* (Dublin, 1982)

Garvin, Tom, 'The destiny of soldiers: tradition and modernity in the politics of de Valera's Ireland', *Political Studies*, vol. 26, no. 3 (1978)

—— *The Evolution of Irish Nationalist Politics* (Dublin, 1981)

—— *Preventing the Future: Why was Ireland so Poor for so Long?* (Dublin, 2004)

Geiger, Till, 'The enthusiastic response of a reluctant supporter: Ireland and the Committee for European Economic Co-operation in the summer of 1947' in Michael Kennedy and Joseph Morrison Skelly (eds), *Irish Foreign Policy 1919–1966: From Independence to Internationalism* (Dublin, 2000)

—— and Michael Kennedy, *Ireland, Europe and the Marshall Plan* (Dublin, 2004)

Gibbons, John P., 'The origins and influence of the Irish Farmers' Association', PhD thesis, University of Manchester, 1990

Girvin, Brian, *Between Two Worlds: Politics and Economy in Independent Ireland* (Dublin, 1989)

—— 'Trade unions and Economic Development' in Donal Nevin (ed.), *Trade Union Century* (Cork and Dublin, 1994)

—— '*Economic Development* and the politics of EC entry: Ireland 1955–63', paper presented at 'The First Attempt to Enlarge the European Community, 1961–63', conference at the European University Institute, Florence, February 1994

—— 'Irish agricultural policy, Economic Nationalism and the Possibility of Market Integration in Europe' in Brian Girvin and R. T Griffiths (eds), *The Green Pool and the Origins of the Common Agricultural Policy* (London, 1995)

—— 'Irish economic development and the politics of EEC entry' in R.T. Griffiths and S. Ward (eds), *Courting the Common Market: The First Attempt to Enlarge the European Community, 1961–63* (London, 1996)

—— 'Politics in wartime: governing, neutrality and elections' in Brian Girvin and Geoffrey Roberts (eds), *Ireland and the Second World War: Politics, Society and Remembrance* (Dublin, 2000)

—— From Union to Union: Nationalism, Religion and Democracy from the Act of Union to the European Union (Dublin, 2002)

—— 'Did Ireland benefit from the Marshall Plan? Choice, strategy and the national interest in a comparative perspective' in Till Geiger and Michael Kennedy, *Ireland, Europe and the Marshall Plan* (Dublin, 2004)

—— *The Emergency: Neutral Ireland 1939–45* (London, 2006)

—— and Gary Murphy (eds), *The Lemass Era: Politics and Society in the Ireland of Seán Lemass* (Dublin, 2005)

—— and Geoffrey Roberts (eds), *Ireland and the Second World War: Politics, Society and Remembrance* (Dublin, 2000)

Hardiman, Niamh, *Pay, Politics, and Economic Performance in Ireland 1970–1987* (Oxford, 1988)

—— 'The state and economic interests: Ireland in comparative perspective' in J.H. Goldthorpe and C.T. Whelan (eds), *The Development of Industrial Society in Ireland* (Oxford, 1992)

Hederman, Miriam, *The Road to Europe: Irish Attitudes 1948–1961* (Dublin, 1983)

Honohan, Patrick and Cormac O'Grada, 'The Irish macroeconomic crisis of 1955–56: How much was due to monetary policy', *Irish Economic and Social History*, vol. xxv (1998)

Horgan, John, *Seán Lemass: The Enigmatic Patriot* (Dublin, 1997)

—— *Noël Browne, Passionate Outsider* (Dublin, 2000)

—— *Irish Media: A Critical History Since 1922* (London, 2001)

Hutton, Seán, 'Labour in the post-independence Irish state: An overview' in Seán Hutton and Paul Stewart (eds), *Ireland's Histories: Aspects of State, Society and Ideology* (London, 1991)

IBEC Technical Services Corporation, *An Appraisal of Ireland's Industrial Potential* (Dublin and New York, 1952)

Jacobsen, John Kurt, *Chasing Progress in the Irish Republic: Ideology, Democracy and Dependent Development* (Cambridge, 1994)

Jacobson, David, 'Theorizing Irish industrialisation: The case of the motor industry', *Science and Society*, vol. 53, no. 2 (summer 1989)

Katzenstein, Peter, *Small States in World Markets* (Ithaca, NY, 1985)

Keane, Elizabeth, *Seán MacBride: A Life* (Dublin, 2007)

Keatinge, Patrick, *The Formulation of Irish Foreign Policy* (Dublin, 1973)

—— 'Ireland and the world, 1957–82' in Frank Litton (ed.), *Unequal Achievement: The Irish Experience, 1957–1982* (Dublin, 1982)

Kennedy, Kieran A., Thomas Giblin and Deirdre McHugh, *The Economic Development of Ireland in the Twentieth Century* (London, 1988)

—— and Brendan R. Dowling, *Economic Growth in Ireland: The Experience Since 1947* (Dublin, 1975)

Kennedy, Liam, *The Modern Industrialisation of Ireland, 1940–1988* (Dublin, 1989)

Kennedy, Michael, *Division and Consensus: The Politics of Cross-border Relations in Ireland, 1925–1969* (Dublin, 2000)

—— and Eunan O'Halpin, *Ireland and the Council of Europe: From Isolation Towards Integration* (Strasbourg, 2000)

—— and Joseph Skelly (eds), *From Independence to Internationalism: Irish Foreign Policy, 1916–1966* (Dublin, 2000)

Keogh, Dermot, *Ireland and Europe 1919–1989: A Diplomatic and Political History* (Cork, 1990)

—— 'The diplomacy of "dignified calm": An analysis of Ireland's application for membership of the EEC, 1961–1963', *Journal of European Integration History*, vol. 3, no. 1 (1995)

—— 'Irish neutrality and the first application for membership of the EEC' in Michael Kennedy and Joseph Skelly (eds), *From Independence to Internationalism: Irish Foreign Policy, 1916–1966* (Dublin, 2000)

—— Finbarr O'Shea and Carmel Quinlan (eds), *The Lost Decade: Ireland in the 1950s* (Cork, 2004)

—— *Jack Lynch: A Biography* (Dublin, 2008)

—— with Andrew McCarthy, *Twentieth Century Ireland: Revolution and State Building* (Dublin, 2005)

Keogh, Niall, *Con Cremin: Ireland's Wartime Diplomat* (Cork, 2006)

Keynes, John Maynard, 'National self-sufficiency', *Studies*, vol. xxii, no. 73 (June 1933)

Laffan, Brigid and Jane O'Mahony, *Ireland and the European Union* (London, 2008)

Lalor, Stephen, 'Planning and the civil service 1945–1970', *Administration*, vol. 43, no. 4 (1995–96)

Lamb, Richard, *The Macmillan Years 1957–1963: The Emerging Truth* (London, 1995)

Lee, J.J., 'Economic development in historical perspective' in John F. McCarthy (ed.), *Planning Ireland's Future: The Legacy of T.K. Whitaker* (Sandycove, 1990)

—— *Ireland 1912–1985: Politics and Society* (Cambridge, 1989)

—— (ed.), *Ireland 1945–1970* (Dublin, 1979)

—— 'Seán Lemass' in J.J. Lee (ed.), *Ireland 1945–1970* (Dublin, 1979)

—— and Gearóid Ó Tuathaigh, *The Age of de Valera* (Dublin, 1982)

Longford, Lord and Thomas P. O'Neill, *Eamon de Valera* (London, 1970)

Lynch, Patrick, 'The economist and public policy', *Studies*, vol. xlii, no. 167 (autumn 1953)

—— 'The Irish economy since the war, 1946–51' in Kevin B. Nowlan and T. Desmond Williams (eds), *Ireland in the War Years and After, 1939–51* (Dublin, 1969)

—— '1894–1994: An overview' in Donal Nevin (ed.), *Trade Union Century*

Lyons, F.S.L., *Ireland Since the Famine* (London, 1971)

McCarthy, Charles, *The Decade of Upheaval: Irish Trade Unions in the Nineteen Sixties* (Dublin, 1973)

—— *Trade Unions in Ireland* (Dublin, 1977)

McCarthy, John F., 'Ireland's turnaround: Whitaker and the 1958 plan for economic development' in John F. McCarthy (ed.), *Planning Ireland's Future: The Legacy of T.K. Whitaker* (Sandycove, 1990)

McCullagh, David, *A Makeshift Majority: The First Inter-party Government, 1948–51* (Dublin, 1998)

Maher, D.J., *The Tortuous Path: The Course of Ireland's Entry into the EEC 1948–73* (Dublin, 1986)

Manning, Maurice, *James Dillon: A Biography* (Dublin, 1999)

—— 'The Farmers' in J.J. Lee (ed.), *Ireland 1945–1970* (Dublin, 1979)

—— *The Blueshirts* (Dublin, 1986, 2nd edn)

Marsh, Arnold, *Full Employment in Ireland* (Dublin, 1945)

Marsh, Michael 'Explanations for party choice' in Michael Gallagher and Michael Marsh (eds), *How Ireland Voted 2007: The Full Story of Ireland's General Election* (Dublin, 2008)

Matthews, Alan, 'The state and Irish agriculture, 1950–1980' in P.J. Drudy (ed.), *Ireland: Land, Politics and People* (Cambridge, 1982)

Meenan, James, *The Irish Economy Since 1922* (Liverpool, 1970)

Milward, Alan, *The Reconstruction of Western Europe: 1945–1951* (London, 1984)

Mjoset, Lars, *The Irish Economy in a Comparative Institutional Perspective* (Dublin, 1992)

Morrissey, Martin, 'The politics of economic management in Ireland 1958–70', *Irish Political Studies*, vol. 1 (1986)

Moynihan, Maurice, *Currency and Central Banking in Ireland 1922–60* (Dublin, 1975)

—— (ed.), *Speeches and Statements by Eamon de Valera* (Dublin, 1980)

Murphy, Gary, 'Fostering a spurious progeny? The trade union movement and Europe, 1957–1964', *Saothar*, no. 21 (1996)

—— 'Government, interest groups and the Irish move to Europe, 1957–1963', *Irish Studies in International Affairs*, no. 8 (1997)

—— 'Towards a corporate state? Seán Lemass and the realignment of interest groups in the policy process 1948–1964', *Administration*, vol. 47, no. 1 (1999)

—— 'A wider perspective: Ireland's view of Western Europe in the 1950s' in Michael Kennedy and Joseph Skelly (eds), *From Independence to Internationalism: Irish Foreign Policy, 1916–1966* (Dublin, 2000)

—— 'The Irish Government, the National Farmers' Association and the European Economic Community, 1955–1964', *New Hibernia Review*, vol. 6, no. 4 (2002)

—— *Economic Realignment and the Politics of EEC Entry: Ireland, 1948–1973* (Bethesda, Md., 2003)

—— '"An exercise that had to be undertaken ...": The Marshall Plan and the genesis of Ireland's involvement in European Integration' in Till Geiger and Michael Kennedy (eds), *Ireland, Europe and the Marshall Plan* (Dublin, 2004)

—— 'From economic nationalism to European Union' in Brian Girvin and Gary Murphy (eds), *The Lemass Era: Politics and Society in the Ireland of Seán Lemass* (Dublin, 2005)

Murphy, Gary and John Hogan, 'Fianna Fáil, the Trade Union Movement and the Politics of Macroeconomic Crises, 1970-1982', *Irish Political Studies*, vol. 23, no. 4, 2008

Murphy, Gary and Niamh Puirséil, ' "Is it new allowance?": Irish Entry to the EEC and popular opinion', *Irish Political Studies*, vol. 23, no. 4. 2008

Murphy, John A., *Ireland in the Twentieth Century* (Dublin, 1989, 2nd edn)

Nevin, Donal, 'Industry and labour' in Kevin B. Nowlan and T. Desmond Williams (eds), *Ireland in the War Years and After, 1938–51* (Dublin, 1969)

—— (ed.), *Trade Union Century* (Cork and Dublin, 1994)

Nowlan, Kevin B. and T. Desmond Williams, *Ireland in the War Years and After, 1938–51* (Dublin, 1969)

O'Brien, Mark, *De Valera, Fianna Fáil and the Irish Press: the truth in the news?* (Dublin, 2001)

—— *The Irish Times: A History* (Dublin, 2008)

Ó Broin Leon, *Just Like Yesterday: An Autobiography* (Dublin, 1985)

O'Connor, Emmet, *A Labour History of Ireland, 1824–1960* (Dublin, 1992)

Ó Drisceoil, Donal, *Peadar O'Donnell* (Cork, 2001)

Ó Grada, Cormac, *A Rocky Road: The Irish Economy Since the 1920s* (Manchester, 1997)

—— and Brendan M. Walsh, 'The economic effects of emigration: Ireland' in Beth J. Asch (ed.), *Emigration and its Effects on the Sending Country* (Santa Monica, CA, 1994)

O'Halpin, Eunan, *Defending Ireland: The Irish State and its Enemies Since 1922* (Oxford, 1999)

O'Hearn, Denis, 'The road from import-substituting to export-led industrialisation in Ireland: Who mixed the asphalt, who drove the machinery, and who kept making them change direction', *Politics and Society*, vol. 18, no. 1 (1990)

O'Leary, Cornelius, *Irish Elections 1918–1977: Parties, Voters and Proportional Representation* (Dublin, 1979)

O'Mahony, David, 'Economic expansion in Ireland', *Studies*, vol. xlviii, no. 190 (summer 1959)

O'Mahony, David, *The Irish Economy* (Cork, 1964)

Ó Muircheartaigh, F. (ed.), *Ireland in the Coming Times: Essays to Celebrate T.K. Whitaker's 80 Years* (Dublin, 1998)

O'Sullivan, Michael, *Seán Lemass: A Biography* (Dublin, 1994)

Ó Tuathaigh, M.A.G., 'The land question, politics and Irish society, 1922–1960' in P.J. Drudy (ed.), *Ireland: Land, Politics and People*

Patterson, Henry, *Ireland Since 1939* (Oxford, 2002)

Philbin, William J., 'The Irish and the new Europe', *Studies*, vol. li, no. 201 (spring 1952)

Pratschke, John L., 'Business and labour in Irish Society, 1945–70' in J.J. Lee (ed.), *Ireland 1945–70*

Puirséil, Niamh, 'Labour and coalition: the impact of the first Inter-Party Government, 1948–51', *Saothar*, no. 27 (2002)

—— 'Political and party competition' in Brian Girvin and Gary Murphy (eds), *The Lemass Era: Politics and Society in the Ireland of Seán Lemass* (Dublin, 2005)

—— *The Irish Labour Party, 1922–73* (Dublin, 2007)

Rafter, Kevin, *The Clann: The Story of Clann na Poblachta* (Cork and Dublin, 1996)

Robins, Joseph, *Custom House People* (Dublin, 1993)

Ryan, Louden, 'Irish manufacturing industry: The future', *Studies*, vol. xliv, no. 173 (spring 1955)

Savage, Robert, *Seán Lemass* (Dundalk, 1999)

Sharp, Paul, *Irish Foreign Policy and the European Community: A Study of the Impact of Interdependence on the Foreign Policy of a Small State* (Aldershot, 1990)

Sinnott, Richard, *Irish Voters Decide: Voting Behaviour in Elections and Referendums Since 1918* (Manchester, 1995)

Skelly, Joseph Morrison, *Irish Diplomacy at the United Nations, 1945–1965: National Interests and the International Order* (Dublin, 1997)

Skinner, Frank, *Politicians by Accident* (Dublin, 1946)

Smith, Louis P.F., 'The role of farmers' organizations', *Studies*, vol. xliv, no. 173 (spring 1955)

—— and Seán Healy, *Farm Organisations in Ireland: A Century of Progress* (Dublin, 1996)

Swift, John P., *John Swift: An Irish Dissident* (Dublin, 1991)

Tobin, Fergal, *The Best of Decades: Ireland in the Nineteen Sixties* (Dublin, 1984)

Travers, Pauric, *Eamon de Valera* (Dublin, 1994)

Varley, Tony, 'Farmers against nationalists: The rise and fall of Clann na Talmhan in Galway' in Gerard Moran and Raymond Gillespie (eds), *Galway: History & Society* (Dublin, 1996)

Walsh, Brendan M., 'Economic growth and development, 1945–70' in J.J. Lee (ed.), *Ireland 1945–70* (Dublin, 1979)

Whelan, Bernadette, 'Ireland and the Marshall Plan', *Irish Economic and Social History*, no. xix (1992)

—— 'Integration or isolation? Ireland and the invitation to join the Marshall Plan' in Michael Kennedy and Joseph Skelly (eds), *From Independence to Internationalism: Irish Foreign Policy, 1916–1966* (Dublin, 2000)

—— *Ireland and the Marshall Plan, 1947–57* (Dublin, 2000)

Whitaker, T.K., 'The Finance attitude' *Administration*, vol. 2, no. 3 (1953)

—— 'Capital formation, saving and economic progress', *Administration*, vol. 4, no. 2 (1956)

—— 'The Irish economy since the Treaty', *Annual Report of the Central Bank*, 1976.

—— *Interests* (Dublin, 1983)

—— 'Economic development 1958–1985' in Kieran A. Kennedy (ed.), *Ireland in Transition: Economic and Social Change Since 1960* (Cork and Dublin, 1986)

—— *Protection or Free Trade – The Final Battle* (Dublin, 2006)

Whyte, J.H., *Church and State in Modern Ireland 1923–1979* (Dublin, 1980)

Williams, T.D., 'Irish foreign policy, 1949–69' in J.J. Lee (ed.), *Ireland 1945–1970* (Dublin, 1979)

Yeats, Michael B., *Cast a Cold Eye: Memories of a Poet's Son and Politician* (Dublin, 1998)

Walsh, John, *Patrick Hillery: The Official Biography* (Dublin 2008)

Wills, Clair, *That Neutral Island: A Cultural History of Ireland During the Second World War* (London, 2007)

# INDEX

(GATT) 19, 172, 265, 268, 282, 283
General elections 29, 43, 52, 90, 112, 157,
  162, 165, 166, 236, 243, 259, 280, 281,
  302, 306
Girvin, Brian 43, 70, 179
Glenavy, Lord 33, 34, 91
Greece 237, 254, 255, 291
Greene, Juan 206, 207, 208, 210, 211,
  213, 218, 219, 228, 229, 230
Green Party 13, 309
*Guardian*, the 287

# H

Hague, The 52
Harman, Nicholas 282
Haughey, Charles 233
Healy, Seán 206, 227
Heath, Edward 273
Herlihy, Brendan 122
*Hibernia* 121, 193, 198, 283
Hillery, Patrick 297, 304
Hoffman, Paul 59, 64
Horgan, John 26, 168
Hudson, Laurence 176

# I

Index of Economic Freedom 14
India 53, 214
Industrial Advisory Council 112
Industrial Credit Corporation 25
Industrial Development Authority (IDA)
  44, 45, 46, 47, 49, 50, 93, 100, 102,
  107, 112, 115, 120, 131, 141, 142, 148,
  254
Industrial Efficiency Bill 39, 40
Institute of Bankers 73, 74
Inter-Party Government 30, 33, 36, 40,
  42, 44, 47, 49, 51, 52, 54, 55, 63, 70,
  73, 74, 79, 80, 90, 99, 101, 104, 105,
  106, 108, 110, 112, 151, 157, 158, 161,
  165, 204, 213, 238, 305, 306
International Monetary Fund 120, 305
Irish Bakers', Confectioners' and Allied
  Workers' Amalgamated Union 177
Irish Business and Employers' Confederation (IBEC) 93, 95
Irish Congress of Trade Unions (ICTU)

119, 178, 179, 180, 181, 182, 183, 192,
  194, 195, 197, 198, 199, 200, 201, 202,
  203, 204, 222
Irish Creamery Milk Suppliers' Associa-
  tion (ICMSA) 205, 206
Irish European Movement 265
Irish Farmers' Association (IFA) 261
*Irish Independent*, the 150, 161, 228
*Irish Industry* 184
Irish National Union of Vintners', Gro-
  cers' and Allied Trades' Assistants 198
*Irish Press*, the 63, 75, 110, 162, 224, 230,
  287, 308
*Irish Times, The* 110, 149, 150, 157, 162,
  192, 208, 225, 233
Irish Trade Union Congress (ITUC) 24,
  41, 42, 76, 77, 87, 88, 99, 174, 179
Irish Transport and General Workers'
  Union (ITGWU) 41, 42, 198, 199,
  200, 202
Isolationism 18, 19, 215, 306
Italy 73, 214

# K

Kavanagh, James 287
Kavanagh, Liam 153
Kavanagh, Patrick 140
Kelly, James Plunkett 43
Keogh, Dermot 147, 271
Keynes, John Maynard/Keynesianism 25,
  34, 37, 72, 73, 74, 79, 132
Kilkenny 230, 231

# L

L'Estrange, Gerry 281
Labour Court 29, 38, 43
Labour Party 30, 40, 41, 42, 43, 80, 87,
  99, 104, 106, 107, 155, 282, 283, 284,
  296
La Fréniere, John 158, 164, 168
Larkin, James 41, 42, 87, 179
*Leader, The* 85, 89, 121, 157
Lee, Joe 29, 165
Lemass, Seán 19, 22, 24, 26, 29, 38, 39,
  40, 41, 42, 43, 44, 45, 47, 48, 49, 52,
  53, 55, 75, 76, 85, 92, 93, 96, 97, 99,
  100, 102, 103, 104, 109, 113, 114, 115,

349